The
Collective
Edge

The
Collective
Edge

Unlocking the Secret Power of Groups

Colin M. Fisher

AVERY
an imprint of Penguin Random House
New York

AVERY

an imprint of Penguin Random House LLC
1745 Broadway, New York, NY 10019
penguinrandomhouse.com

Book design by Ashley Tucker

Library of Congress Cataloging-in-Publication Data

Names: Fisher, Colin M. author
Title: The collective edge: unlocking the secret power of groups /
    Colin M. Fisher.
Description: New York: Avery, an imprint of Penguin Random House, [2025] |
    Includes index.
Identifiers: LCCN 2024062097 (print) | ISBN 9780593715345 hardcover |
    ISBN 9780593716762 ebook
Subjects: LCSH: Social groups
Classification: LCC HM716 .F57 2025 (print) | LCC HM716 (ebook) |
    DDC 305—dc23/eng/20250507
LC record available at https://lccn.loc.gov/2024062097
LC ebook record available at https://lccn.loc.gov/2024062098

ISBN (international edition): 9798217176854

Printed in the United States of America
1st Printing

The authorized representative in the EU for product safety and compliance is Penguin Random House Ireland, Morrison Chambers, 32 Nassau Street, Dublin D02 YH68, Ireland, https://eu-contact.penguin.ie.

Dedicated to the memory of Linda Fisher,
who gave me more than I can say

CONTENTS

INTRODUCTION

Ask the name of the villain in the Harry Potter saga, and almost everyone will answer Lord Voldemort. But as a social scientist who studies group dynamics, I see a far more pernicious villain: the Sorting Hat.

When placed upon the heads of aspiring eleven-year-old magic-users, the Sorting Hat assigns each student to one of four "houses." Each house has strong distinguishing traits—the brave are separated from the brainy, the loyal from the devious. Uniforms mark students' house memberships wherever they go. The houses compete against one another in almost every aspect of school life. Students root against, and often vilify, those from other houses while supporting their own. Over the course of seven thick books, no one ever leaves the house to which the Sorting Hat assigned them. Nor does anyone seek to dispose of the hat and its sinister grouping, despite the clear role it plays in drawing the dividing lines for the wars that bookend the story.

The Sorting Hat can remain a hidden villain because it seems so familiar in our world. We don't need magical headwear to sort people. Our brains do it for us. You carry an inner sorting hat with you wherever you go. Human society is built on sorting ourselves and others into groups. We sort people based on broad characteristics like nationality, politics, and gender. We also sort people into smaller, tight-knit groups, such as family, friends, a work team, a sports team, or a band.

We are collective creatures. Our memberships in ever-shifting, overlapping groups govern our experience of the world. Many of us wake up among family or roommates but then go to work and behave quite differently among our coworkers. After work, we may meet up with friends and think and act differently again. We may spontaneously stumble into a group for a few minutes, like a street performer's audience or a disgruntled group of stranded commuters waiting on a delayed subway train. In each situation, we think and behave differently because of how we believe we fit within that group.

Understanding human behavior means understanding group dynamics—the obvious and hidden ways in which our thoughts, feelings, and behaviors are shaped by groups. In nearly every moment of our lives, we feel the pull of groups whispering to us to conform to the unspoken rules of being among other humans. In the street performer's audience, we clap when others clap and feel the swell of others' enjoyment. Without even realizing it, we conform to avoid standing out, applauding along even when we're privately unimpressed. We compete for acclaim from our fellow group members at work and at home, and when outsiders threaten them, we defend our collectives as if they were part of ourselves. Taken to extremes, our inner sorting hats have guided humanity's greatest accomplishments . . . and our greatest evils.

The Emergency Rescue Committee

In 1940, American journalist Varian Fry went to Marseille, France, "with $3,000 taped to his leg, a list of 200 endangered artists and intellectuals, and instructions to help them evacuate." Fry didn't show up and rescue two hundred people on his own— he built a group. And that group, known as the Emergency Rescue Committee (ERC), helped more than two thousand refugees escape the Nazis in a little over a year.

When he went to France, Fry was equipped with a clear, important goal, but he had little guidance on how to accomplish it. He was no diplomat, no secret agent. "I had never done underground work before," Fry wrote. "And I did not know a single person on the list . . . I was at a complete loss about how to begin, and where."

Fry started with writing letters to the two hundred refugees on his list. Some, like philosopher Walter Benjamin, had already died by suicide to avoid capture. But most still needed Fry's help. Soon after he arrived, word of Fry's mission spread. The hotel where he was staying was quickly overrun with requests from thousands looking for passage out of France.

Fry couldn't do it alone. He needed a team.

He soon found one. Labor activist Frank Bohn was working to get his fellow union members out of the country and shared what he had learned with Fry. Heiress Mary Jayne Gold funded much of the ERC's work, used her social skills and connections, and later, worked with British intelligence to oppose the Nazis. Albert Hirschman, a young political activist, aspiring economist, and refugee, worked tirelessly to help other refugees find unmarked trails over the towering Pyrenees mountains while evading French and German authorities. Former police officer Daniel Bénédite helped manage operations and evade law enforcement when needed. Cartoonist Willi Spira falsified immigration documents. Administrator Lena Fishman, who was fluent in Russian, Polish, and Spanish, wrote letters and interviewed refugees. Even when their freedom and lives were threatened, each member played their part because the bonds that held them together were stronger than self-interest.

A purely self-centered, individualistic view of humanity can't explain the ERC's existence. When you ruminate on overwhelming problems, like the rise of the Nazis, it's natural to feel helpless. And when confronted with real threats, it's easy to look out for yourself—breaking bonds, rather than forming them.

Yet we can see both the good and the evil of group dynamics in the ERC's story. To the good, the ERC leveraged the social glue that group membership provides, which allows us to cooperate even in the direst of circumstances. At the extreme, some of those in the ERC suffered and died to help fellow group members.

But the ERC was necessary because the Nazis had weaponized the dark sides of our group-based thinking. They fed our inner sorting hat's ugly hungers, praising "us" and blaming "them." So many people perpetrated or tolerated unspeakable cruelty during the murder of millions of innocent people. Although Nazi Germany is one of the most potent examples of weaponizing group thinking, it isn't hard to see people still exploiting our tendencies to favor some groups and vilify others today. It happens in the schoolyard, the workplace, and at the heights of political power.

Our loyalty to our own groups and our villainy toward others permeate the stories that epitomize humanity. The wonderful and terrible aspects of human behavior can be explained, understood, and even tamed by the overlooked science of group dynamics. The research I'll share with you in this book holds the keys to understanding why humans cooperate, conform, and compete. That science also holds the secrets to what you can do about it.

Why Should I Read a Book about Group Dynamics?

Because collective living is inescapable, humans navigate its peculiarities, promises, and perils every day. From the macro to micro level—the nation-state to the work meeting, the religion we follow to the family barbecue—group dynamics are shaping our lives. Our ability to cooperate is the foundation of human accomplishment. Nearly every scientific discovery, world-changing business, desert island musical album, and legendary sports team has a great group at its core. But we spend surprisingly little time thinking about what groups really are, how they work, and how to get the best out of them.

What most people do know about group dynamics isn't good. Groups pique our interest for all the wrong reasons: conformity, polarization, prejudice, conflict, and general mass stupidity. Politicians prey on the dark side of our inner sorting hat, prompting us to blame, dehumanize, and mistreat anyone who isn't part of our group. Social media isolates us from the communities we live in while strengthening intergroup hate and intolerance. Our tendency to sort ourselves and others into groups underlies political conflict, war, and atrocity.

We need better groups—groups that are solutions, not problems. It's time to break out of individualistic mindsets that see groups as necessary evils. It's time to tell a different story about the amazing, but overlooked, power of groups to achieve great things—under the right conditions. Whether you want to change yourself, your work group, or the world, you need to work *with* the invisible forces of group dynamics instead of being mindlessly pushed around by them.

In this book, you'll discover *how to use the science of group dynamics to live and work together better.* The secrets to getting the best from our groups—and from ourselves—are embedded within six conditions you can use to promote effective cooperation: composition, goals, tasks, norms, psychological safety, and coaching. Shaping these conditions allows you to unlock the power hidden in the overlooked science of group dynamics. Understanding them is the key to building effective, deeply rewarding groups.

This book isn't just for traditional team leaders; it's for everyone who wants to understand human behavior and the world around them. Good group thinking can improve your relationships at home, at work, or at school. It can help you make better decisions, be more creative, and feel like you truly belong.

Pieces of the group dynamics puzzle are scattered across social sciences, including social psychology, sociology, economics, anthropology, political science, neuroscience, and management. Bringing together the latest research that helps explain everything from billionaire yacht-collecting habits to the discovery of DNA's secrets to *Star Trek* villains, my goal in this book is to provide you with a deep yet accessible overview of what science has taught us (and what it hasn't) about groups and explore how we can use scientific research on group dynamics to change and better understand ourselves.

I was a part of dozens—maybe hundreds—of groups in my first career as a professional jazz trumpet player. I played with groups that lasted for decades (like the Either/Orchestra) and others for minutes (like in jam sessions). I've always been fascinated by how strangers can spontaneously become more than the sum of their parts. Somehow, I managed to convince Harvard University to give me a PhD as I searched for the answers. Today, as an organizational scientist and professor at University College London, I teach students, executives, and government leaders how to lead, help, and coach teams and organizations to live up to their potential.

Throughout the book, I'll share stories from both my own and others' experiences so you can picture what the insights gained from rigorous social science research really feel like—and hopefully apply them in your own life. These stories are like handles that allow you to grasp the scientific research that brings together hundreds of thousands of people's experiences. That should be more reliable than the anecdotal lessons from any single person—me, you, a famous athlete, a celebrity, or a business executive—which are too often how people learn about group dynamics and leadership.

This book is divided into four main sections, each composed of three or four chapters. Section I: Cooperation will explain what groups are and how we derive the major benefit of collective living—striving toward common goals to achieve more than we could alone. Next, we focus on two other important consequences of our collective tendencies: conformity in Section II and competition in Section III, both of which have well-documented dangers—and surprising benefits. I'll explain how science teaches us to manage these paradoxes of group life so you can have a truly effective collective. Finally, in Section IV: Leading Groups, we'll reimagine leadership not as the province of individual heroes and villains, but as a team sport in which we all do our part to improve and maintain our groups' fundamental structure. Along the way, I'll offer "Group Thoughts"—practical applications of the principles covered in that section, which I hope will allow you to use the insights more easily.

This book has a lot of terrain to explore, bringing together hundreds of studies conducted over several decades. As such, we'll take a high-level view of group dynamics that provides a new perspective on our social world. I think of such perspectives as lenses, like infrared goggles that reveal patterns we normally can't see.

Seeing the world from a **collective perspective** is transformative. Adopting a group lens for understanding human behavior illuminates new facets of common and extraordinary moments, allowing us to see the invisible forces at play in shaping our day-to-day lives. At work and in life, you'll rethink everything when you observe the social world at the group level, rather than in terms of individuals. It will give you a collective edge.

Let's find out how.

The

Collective
Edge

Cooperation

Although we live and work in groups, our minds have a bias toward individualistic explanations for both our own and others' behavior. This leads us to overlook the role of groups and group dynamics in shaping the world (Chapter 1). But group dynamics are the key to cooperation—the superpower that has enabled us to take over the planet. The apex of cooperation is group synergy—when collections of individuals are literally more than the sum of their parts (Chapter 2). Alas, synergy is rare, and groups are usually less than the sum of their parts because of predictable (and often avoidable) process losses in effort and coordination. To maximize our chances of synergy, we have three main tools that provide structure for groups: task design, group composition, and goals (Chapter 3). Whether you are a group leader or the newest member of a team, you should use these tools at a crucial time in group development: launch (Chapter 4).

CHAPTER 1

The Myth of the Lone Genius

The Allure of Individualism in a Group-Based World

Geneticist James Watson received perhaps the highest honor a scientist can get in today's society: In the BBC biopic about his life, *The Race for the Double Helix,* he was portrayed by Jeff Goldblum (you know, the actor who played the scientist in *Jurassic Park* and *The Fly*). Oh, and Watson also won the Nobel Prize.

The Race for the Double Helix (known as *Life Story* in the UK) dramatizes the duel between two teams to discover the structure of DNA. On one side was the dynamic duo of Watson, the brash American Batman, and his reserved British Robin, biophysicist Francis Crick. On the other side were boring, methodical,

British stick-in-the-mud scientists Maurice Wilkins and Rosalind Franklin.

According to Watson's memoir, *The Double Helix*, on which the film is based, Wilkins and Franklin were sitting on the data needed to crack the case. But they lacked the imagination to see it. The critical data were contained in Franklin's new X-ray image of DNA, known as "Photograph 51." Watson tells us that he secretly gained access to Photograph 51 and the accompanying data files over the objections of Franklin, Wilkins's surly subordinate. "Clearly Rosy had to go or be put in her place," Watson wrote, disregarding that no one called her "Rosy," and she wasn't Wilkins's subordinate. "There was no denying she had a good brain. If only she could keep her emotions under control." Watson told the world he had his eureka moment after one look at the ill-gotten image, seeing what Franklin and Wilkins could not— the "secret to life."

There's only one problem with all this: It isn't true. (Okay, there are other problems, like the toxic sexism.) There was no race between the two teams—Franklin shared the data willingly, viewing it as a collaboration between her team and Watson and Crick's. Watson and Crick biographers Matthew Cobb and Nathaniel Comfort recently found new evidence clarifying Franklin's role in the Nobel-winning discovery. As they told *Science News*:

> We found a program of a Royal Society exhibition . . . [that includes] a brief summary of the structure of DNA signed by everybody, presented by Franklin. It was like a school science fair. She's standing there in front of a model explaining it to everybody, and all their

names are on it [Franklin, Wilkins, Watson, and Crick]. So this isn't a race that's been won by Watson and Crick. I mean, they did get there first, don't get us wrong. But it wasn't seen that way at the time. They could not have done it without the data from Franklin and Wilkins. And everybody—at least at this stage in 1953—is accepting that and seems okay with it . . . We're moving away from the Hollywood thriller that Watson wrote, where [Watson's] sneaked some data. That version is really exciting. It's just not true. [We're moving] to something that's much more collaborative.

That's right, the discovery of the secret to life wasn't Watson's heroic genius, as implied in the book. Nor was it the duo of Watson and Crick from the movie. This discovery required a collective.

Why did we need a group to crack the structure of DNA? Like a lot of science, you need deep expertise to even understand what questions to ask and how to answer them. Neither Watson nor Crick could have produced Photograph 51 or collected the data about what it depicted. Franklin and Wilkins, however, were world leaders in X-ray crystallography and its application to DNA.

But Franklin and Wilkins were missing two things Watson and Crick brought—Crick's expertise in wet, living structures and Watson's talent for creating theoretical models without data. DNA looks quite different when wet, which is when it is in its active, double-helix form. Wilkins, who had the idea to use X-ray crystallography on DNA and hired Franklin, knew that Franklin's expertise was in interpreting the dry form. And Franklin herself didn't think much of theoretical modeling, preferring to wait for data. The DNA structure problem was too complicated for any one person to deal with. You couldn't just add up their expertise; you needed to multiply contributions from all four people.

Why, then, don't quizmasters credit the whole super-team of Franklin, Wilkins, Watson, and Crick? Partially because Watson was a bit of an attention-hogging asshole. Even Crick and Wilkins (who shared the 1962 Nobel with Watson) protested Watson's based-on-a-true-story book, leading Harvard University Press to cut ties with him. In his later life, Watson made a hobby of advancing racist, sexist, and anti-Semitic theories. As late as 2018, he continued to insist on genetic race- and sex-based differences in intelligence with no evidence. The scientific community ostracized him; biologist Edward O. Wilson called him "the most unpleasant human being I had ever met." Even the lab he directed stripped him of his titles because he wouldn't stop spewing hatred.

Of course, it wasn't just Watson's fault that Franklin didn't get the credit she deserved. Because they shared Watson's sexism, many people were unwilling to recognize her contribution to the discovery. Rosalind Franklin died of ovarian cancer in 1958, before Watson's book and the Nobel Prize committee overlooked her; she didn't get a chance to tell her own version of the story. It has long been public knowledge that Watson's account glorified himself and demeaned Franklin's contribution in overtly sexist ways. Yet in 2012, the US Library of Congress named *The Double Helix* one of eighty-eight "Books That Shaped America." Among science enthusiasts, Watson and Crick are household names; Wilkins, Franklin, and others involved in the discovery still don't get their due.

We're suckers for stories of individual greatness—"Great Man" theories of genius and innovation. History books attribute almost every human accomplishment to an individual (usually a man) like Watson. But like *The Double Helix*, these stories only scratch the surface. If we dig, we usually find a group doing the actual work. The lone genius is more myth than reality. Groups make the world go round.

In one of my favorite studies, titled "The Increasing Dominance of Teams in Production of Knowledge," Northwestern University researchers Stefan Wuchty, Benjamin F. Jones, and Brian Uzzi investigated whether groups produce more knowledge than individuals. They looked at all the discoveries from 1955 to 2000 that they could get their hands on—19.8 million research articles and 2.1 million patents. The share of team (relative to individual) discoveries grew in every STEM (science, technology, engineering, and mathematics) field. And the teams themselves also grew. "In the sciences," the authors wrote, "team size has grown steadily each year and nearly doubled from 1.9 to 3.5 authors per paper over 45 years." Team discoveries were far more likely to be influential breakthroughs that future scientists, inventors, and entrepreneurs built upon. "For example, a team-authored paper in science and engineering is currently 6.3 times more likely than a solo-authored paper to receive at least 1,000 citations," they added. That's the academic equivalent of a blockbuster; most papers receive fewer than ten.

It wasn't always like this. In the 1950s, solo scientists and inventors were more likely to fail but also more likely to make breakthrough discoveries. But the odds that working alone is a winning strategy have gotten worse as the years have passed.

We can only speculate why teams appear to have gotten better—or individuals have gotten worse—at discovery and invention. Many scientists believe that the world is simply more complicated than it used to be. The discoveries you can make alone by getting into the bathtub or sitting under an apple tree are long since made. It takes a lifetime just to master one tiny, specialized slice of the universe. There's also evidence that this is right—science, education, and work are all getting more specialized. You can be an expert in mitochondrial phylogenetics, but not all of biology. And the problems that need solving demand expertise from multiple domains, which now means you have to work with a team. The days of Renaissance polymaths like Leonardo da Vinci and Maria Sibylla Merian, a German illustrator and entomologist who taught the world about metamorphosis, might be over.

But to explain the increasing advantage of teams in producing knowledge, I think two other factors are more important than a specialized, complex world. First, humans have simply gotten better at collaboration—we are constantly improving our ability to communicate and collaborate across time and space. (Although it may not seem like it if you are stuck in a pointless work meeting.) Second, individuals may not have been doing much of the science and inventing in the first place. Like Watson, some individuals were just better at taking the credit for themselves. For instance, who invented the light bulb? If you said Thomas Edison, you'd be wrong. Incandescent light bulbs were invented before Edison was born. Edison was building on the work of many others when he filed his patent for a commercially viable, mass-market light bulb. But even that version of the light bulb was a group effort: He worked with his group of "Muckers," whose names are mostly forgotten, to create it. But Edison put his name on the patent and took the credit, and the rest is history.

We are accustomed to heroic stories from the history of human accomplishment—some brilliant, underappreciated genius toiling alone, overcoming rejection and failure. A general with a clever plan, leading the troops to an unlikely victory. We remember the individual but forget the group.

Our struggle to discern the role of groups in our lives is part of one of the most important discoveries of social psychology: the "fundamental attribution error." *Attribution* refers to explaining why a person has behaved as they have. Why was Mike late for that meeting? And the *error* is too much individualism—we default to personality as our core explanation. In our heads, we think Mike was late because he's flaky. We don't consider that, as he was about to leave for the meeting, his ailing mother might have called him for help.

The same is true on the positive side of the coin. When someone founds a billion-dollar business, it's because they're a genius. We don't consider the advantages they may have had in their lives. When trying to understand others' behavior, we don't give enough credence to the groups and situations that helped or hurt them along the way.

We have similar problems when thinking about how we contribute to groups. You (yes, you, too) are prone to "egocentric biases"—our brain's tendency to artificially inflate our own importance and contributions. A famous example is The Lake Wobegon Effect, named for the fictional town in *A Prairie Home Companion* where "all the children are above average." A 2018 study, for instance, found that 65 percent of Americans believe they have above-average intelligence. Average should be exactly 50 percent, so at least 15 percent of us are overestimating ourselves.

These individualistic fallacies get concentrated in groups, such that everyone becomes a bit James Watson-y and overclaims credit for the groups' accomplishments. One representative study asked members to estimate their percent contribution to their groups' performance. If everyone was perfectly accurate, the sum would be 100 percent. But because most people overestimated their value to the group, the total was much, much more than that. In one experiment, members' estimates added up to 235 percent!

Together, egocentrism and individualism lead us to misunderstand both success and failure—we overestimate our own role in success, overlooking the groups that helped us get there. And whether a group succeeds or fails, we look for the one person who should get all the praise or blame.

In other words, taking a collective perspective is hard. Our brains struggle to "see" the influence of groups that are all around us. We prefer individualistic explanations to collective ones, especially when things go wrong.

Even understanding what a group is can be tricky. After all, we can't credit or blame groups appropriately if we don't understand what they are. So to get it right, we first need to understand: What is a group anyway?

Scenes from a Jam Session

On Thursday evenings, I sling my trumpet case over my shoulder and head out to a club in East London called Grow. When I arrive, the house band, Stratos, is already going strong. The band is playing a kind of modern jazz that evokes the 1960s music of saxophonists Wayne Shorter and Joe Henderson. Stratos is a quartet, led by bassist Rio and tenor saxophonist Dom and flanked by a drummer and guitarist. Standing in a pack of around forty twenty- and thirtysomethings, with a drink in hand, I take in the music. The musicians are rising stars of the London scene; playing at Grow is an opportunity for them to stretch themselves without the constraints of a "function gig" like a wedding reception, fancy office party, or jazz brunch.

In the second song of the second set, Rio calls me to the stage and asks what I want to play. The first song was up-tempo, so I call for the more spacey and relaxed "Beatrice" by Sam Rivers. Jam sessions like this one allow attending musicians to jump in and out of performing on stage. After that song, other musicians come up and join us. Dom goes to have a drink, leaving me as the only horn player on stage, so I front the band for the rest of the evening (although he returns for the last song of the night).

After the set, a few people crowd around the stage, asking questions. "How did you become part of the band?" "Where are you all playing next?" "How did you all meet?"

I'm not a member of the group, I explain.

The question is: Why am I not part of the group? Outside observers clearly perceived me to be. Objectively, I played just as much, or perhaps more, of the second set than some of the musicians who were paid to be there. Yet neither I nor the other musicians believe I'm part of Stratos. In fact, we know I'm not part of the group—I'm just sitting in.

So how do we know who is part of a group, if not by their objective behavior or others' perceptions? Well, it comes down to the fact that Stratos and I all agree that I'm not in the group—that the group has clear boundaries.

The dividing lines between groups aren't always so clear-cut, however. *Group* can refer to a spectrum of collections of individuals, from broad social categories to small teams. What Liverpudlians, spelunkers, and the cast of *Friends* have in common is (a) they are composed of multiple individuals (most studies suggest you need at least three people to be considered a group) and (b) it's possible to distinguish who's included from who isn't. But groups vary widely in size, function, and how long they stay together—as well as how clear it is who is a member and who is not. Can we really think of a group like The Beatles in the same way we think of a broad social category like Americans? Well, sort of . . .

Our inner sorting hats are laser-focused on finding potential patterns in collections of people. Unfortunately, this phenomenon of group perception has perhaps the worst name in all social science: "group entitativity." (Try saying it out loud . . .) Although unpleasant to write, read, and say, group entitativity has a potentially transformational idea within it: No collection of humans can be perceived without our inner sorting hat inferring their group memberships, especially their relationships to one another. In other words, for any collection of people, there's always a bit of what we'll call "groupiness."

I understand why people watching the Grow jam session thought I was part of the band, because the main four signs of groupiness were all present. We were standing on stage together (proximity). We are all jazz musicians who clearly know some of the same music (similarity). And there's a clear pattern to our interaction—we play a melody, then take turns improvising solos, then return to the melody (recognizable interaction patterns). And if things go well, we're all up there on stage to receive the applause or, if they don't go so well, dodge the overripe produce (members share a common fate).

It's pretty logical that these four clues—proximity, similarity, recognizable interaction patterns, and common fate—signal groupiness. If people are in the same place at the same time, they probably have some similarity. And further signals of similarity— like uniforms, a family resemblance, or showing common interests like jazz, juggling, or jousting—make a collection of individuals seem even groupier. If there's a recognizable pattern to individuals' interactions, it signals familiarity. And when people share a common fate in addition to these other cues, that's the groupiest!

Because talking about high and low levels of groupiness is inconvenient, many people find it helpful to label different kinds of groups. At the lowest levels of groupiness are social categories: labels for shared attributes like introverts, foodies, or spelunkers. Or more commonly, race, gender, and age group (e.g., babies, teens, millennials, Gen X, etc.). Although social categories denote similarity, members of a social category often lack proximity, interaction patterns, and a common fate. They aren't very groupy.

Crowds like the audience at Grow are groupier than social categories. The proximity of crowds can imply similarity (what kind of person comes to Grow late on a Thursday night?) and shared purpose (hanging out, listening to music, drinking) and raises the potential for a common fate (the audience listens to the same music; if the roof caves in, they experience it together). There might even be patterns of interaction, like clapping, getting quiet, or waiting in line at the bar.

A little groupier are coacting groups, like people who work in a customer-service call center. You all work in the same place for the same organization and are doing the same basic work. But for coacting groups, most of the work is independent, and common fate is weaker than the groupiest of groups: teams.

The classic definition of *team* was coined by my mentor and collaborator, the late J. Richard Hackman, whose research inspired much of what you'll read here. Richard was a literal and figurative giant in group dynamics: a burly six feet, six inches tall, with a tremendous basso profundo voice. He loved junk food—so much so that, when I was in grad school, I kept popcorn and candy near my desk to lure him there. And he defined what it means to be a *real team*: a bounded collection of individuals that works interdependently toward a common purpose. Real teams are the easiest groups to identify—sports teams, jazz combos, or work teams—because they have all four groupiness triggers: proximity, similarity, recognizable interaction patterns, and a common fate.

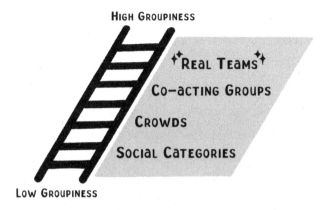

Real teams are humanity's best tool for solving problems. Collaboration works when we know who we're working with and learn each other's strengths and idiosyncrasies, like who needs a text reminder for the meeting or a Diet Coke to really think clearly. The new businesses, bands, sports dynasties, and political activists who change the world for the better have historically been real teams, like the ERC.

But real teams are becoming an endangered species. The COVID pandemic and remote work accelerated an un-teaming trend that was already occurring. Old conceptions of teams are weakening at work. Flexible work arrangements like working from home are flummoxing managers who used to relying on proximity to determine patterns of interaction. In many of the organizations I work with, teams last a few weeks at most; they work together on a single project and then move on. And many never meet face-to-face. Groupiness at work is weaker than ever.

Our collective tendencies aren't just weaker in our work lives; we're living in an age of unprecedented individualism. The decline of collectivism—the belief that we are all part of a larger whole—has rendered the world nearly unrecognizable to our ancestors from a century ago. From 1900 to 2000, individualistic values have increased and collectivist values have declined all over the world. More people live alone than ever before. Families are smaller. We spend less time hanging out with our friends and neighbors. We even speak with more individualistic language, using words like *unique, personal,* and *independent* at higher than ever rates. More than ever before, we are taught to think of ourselves as islands isolated from the many collectives of which we are a part.

It's no wonder that we look to individuals as the cause of good and ill: stars and bad apples, celebrities and outcasts, heroes and villains. We glorify the individual, attributing people's accomplishments to their individual traits. Their moxie, talent, and humility explain their success. Their indolence, softness, and entitlement explain their failures.

If you picked up this book in a bookstore, you may have seen it beside biographies of celebrities or books full of tips and tricks to keep the island of "you" healthy and happy in a turbulent world. For too many people, the individual is the most interesting and important topic—and the locus of change in the world. Solutions are tailored to our individualistic mindsets, where improvements start and end between our ears, not among each other.

But this focus on the individual doesn't seem to be improving the world. People feel lonelier and more isolated than ever before. Our mental health has been declining, and we have become a society teeming with stress, anxiety, and depression. As sociologist Robert Putnam observed decades ago, the threads that connect our communities—our neighborhoods, schools, and families—have frayed. It's harder than ever to get us to make common cause with one another.

If you learn to live and work collectively and effectively, you can help reverse these trends. You can strike a balance that honors each individual in a way that strengthens the collective, rather than weakening it. You can find your equivalent of jam sessions, where you connect with others. You can bring together your family, friends, neighbors, and coworkers to cooperate. Groups offer a vehicle to accomplish what you can't do alone and provide a sense of belonging. The antidote to many ills is embedded within group dynamics. Good group thinking can strengthen relationships, helping us stick together and, like the ERC, make "we" more important than "me."

The takeaway is to put on your group glasses when you want to understand or change the world. To go beyond the individualistic explanations for your own behavior and for that of others. A collective perspective offers new avenues to improve your life and the lives of others. And if you play your cards right, your group can become more than the sum of its parts and find a near-mythical collective state: synergy.

CHAPTER 2

The Alchemy of Synergy

When Groups Are More (or Less)
than the Sum of Their Parts

I fell in love with jazz when I was thirteen years old. Even though my trumpet playing sounded like a whiny baby elephant (my braces didn't help much), I wanted to try out for my junior high school jazz band. So, to inspire me, my mom signed me up to get the introductory jazz kit from Columbia House's CD club. The kit contained three albums: Louis Armstrong's *Hot Fives and Hot Sevens*, Duke Ellington's *Ellington at Newport*, and Miles Davis's *Kind of Blue*. It was *Kind of Blue* that changed my life.

Stand next to any jazz aficionado for too long and you risk hearing about *Kind of Blue*. It's the bestselling jazz album of all time, with nearly five million copies sold. It's an undisputed classic, beloved by everyone from Pink Floyd's Richard Wright to The Roots' Questlove to British actress Dame Judi Dench, and has influenced countless musicians and artists since its release in 1959. Infatuation with *Kind of Blue* is so cliché that, among jazz musicians, it's almost uncool to claim it as your favorite album. Almost.

Explanations for *Kind of Blue*'s success often contrast its exploratory, melody-driven, modal compositions and improvisations with its driving, harmony-led bebop predecessors. And of course, the band members were all masters. Pianist Bill Evans and saxophonists John Coltrane and Cannonball Adderley went on to lead their own historically great ensembles. Bassist Paul Chambers, pianist Wynton Kelly, and drummer Jimmy Cobb are jazz legends in their own rights.

But what makes *Kind of Blue* so special is that the combination of these particular musicians on this particular album led to something greater than the sum of its parts.

I'm loath to reduce the music to words. As comedian Martin Mull quipped, "Writing about music is like dancing about architecture." So go listen to the album if you haven't. I'll wait.

Perhaps you noticed that each musician's approach to improvising was a study in contrasts. Davis's solos were sparse and fragile. Coltrane's were muscular and notey, presaging the "sheets of sound" of his later music. Adderley's and Kelly's were bluesy takes on bebop. Evans's were lush and meditative. Each musician's idiosyncratic approach accentuated the beauty of the others, making the whole shimmer and giving the album its unparalleled character in bringing together various kinds of . . . blue.

There are rare moments, like in making *Kind of Blue*, when groups are more than the sum of their parts. Those moments are honest-to-goodness *synergy*, that often-ridiculed business buzzword. Synergy is when the collective outcome is greater than what you would predict from adding up individual capabilities. When you're part of a great group, you're inspired to work harder than you knew you could. You wordlessly coordinate, anticipating other members' every move, like a no-look pass in basketball. Your skills complement one another's. And you make each other better, while your inner sorting hat snoozes quietly in the corner.

Proving the existence of synergy, however, has been complicated. It requires difficult—sometimes impossible—comparisons. Can we prove that a group product like *Kind of Blue* is truly more than the sum of its parts when there isn't any way for individuals working alone to create it? To study synergy, social scientists have to engineer ways to compare individual and group performance. Like the study of patents and innovations from Chapter 1, we can compare the performance of individuals working solo to groups working collaboratively. Or we can ask whether the same person performs better working alone or in a group. Or we can compare the output of a coacting group, made of individuals who work independently but are put in a single category, to a real team of the same size. It's not easy!

Over the decades, the search for synergy has taken a lot of twists and turns. So bear with me as I take you through studies of the pulling power of oxen, people screaming alone in laboratories, and funky room-assignment puzzles, or skip to the end of the chapter and I'll summarize the takeaways (but you'd be missing out on oxen jokes).

The Search for Synergy Keeps Finding Process Losses

The search for synergy began with perhaps the first-ever psychology experiment. Ironically, that experiment wasn't conducted by a psychologist. And double ironically, the experiment showed that groups were significantly *less* than the sum of their parts.

Back in 1882, a French agricultural engineer named Maximilien Ringelmann was obsessed with trying to figure out the optimal number of oxen to pull a cart. For instance, let's say you're a nineteenth-century French farmer. You have six oxen who pull carts to move stuff around the farm, plow the fields, and such. And—bonus—you have carts of various sizes. How should you assign oxen to carts? Do you want all six oxen to each pull their own small carts? Would you be better off with three larger carts, pulled by two oxen each? Or one enormous cart pulled by all six oxen?! Sacrebleu!

Now, you sometimes need a group of oxen (known as a yoke) to pull really heavy stuff. And remember, the yoke also has to pull the weight of the person driving the cart and the cart itself. So fewer carts means greater efficiency because there's less weight to pull (fewer people, fewer wheels, etc.). But as any nineteenth-century farmer would tell you, oxen have problems working together. They walk at slightly different paces. They occasionally get distracted by grass. And they sometimes like to headbutt one another.

What Ringelmann wanted to know was: Does the additional

pulling power from a yoke of oxen offset their coordination problems? Ringelmann set up an experiment to find out how much power was lost with yokes of various sizes. However, the oxen were more interested in chewing on Ringelmann's rope than in participating in his studies. So he decided to experiment with humans instead.

Ringelmann figured that people had some of the same coordination challenges as oxen, although with less headbutting. But he was startled by the extent of these problems. On average, each man in his study (they were all men) could pull about 188 pounds (85kg) when working alone. But when working in groups of seven, the men pulled a mere 143 pounds each (65kg). That's only 76 percent of the sum of the parts—a decline of 24 percent!

Like a lot of group dynamics research, Ringelmann's findings were ignored for years. In fact, Ringelmann himself ignored them, waiting more than thirty years to publish. But this insight, known as the Ringelmann Effect, proved to be his enduring contribution to science: As groups get larger, each individual contribution gets smaller. The effect is most pronounced in smaller groups, where adding, say, the fourth person to a three-person group leads to a big decrease in individual production. But adding the twenty-fifth person to a twenty-four-person group has a much smaller effect.

The question, though, is why? Is this all about oxlike coordination problems? Or are people actually putting in less effort when working in groups?

In the 1970s, social psychologist Bibb Latané and his colleagues conducted a clever experiment to untangle the two pillars of **group process**: **coordination** and **effort**.

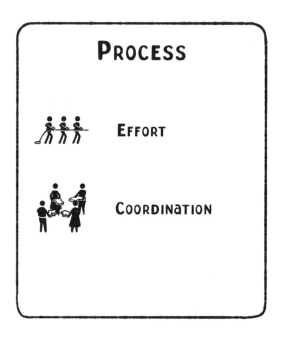

To prove that coordination wasn't the only problem in group tasks, they used a task that required no coordination—cheering. Participants were told that they were part of a study on acoustics. They were shut in a soundproofed room and asked to put on cool 1970s headphones. Researchers then told the participants that they were either cheering alone, with one other person, or with five other people.

Now, as you might suspect, this was a ruse. They weren't part of real groups. The experiment was to see whether, when you believe you are part of a group, you exert less effort. And that's indeed what they found. In pseudogroups of two, people cheered only 82 percent as loudly as when they believed they were shouting alone. And when they believed they were in groups of six, they hollered even less vigorously—only 74 percent as loudly as they did alone. That's pretty close to the same results Ringelmann had obtained nearly a century earlier.

The researchers also compared pseudogroups to real interacting groups. Because of coordination problems, interacting groups performed even worse than pseudogroups. Groups of two performed at 71 percent of their individual capacities, and groups of six at only 40 percent! As the researchers put it, that gives a new perspective on an old cliché: "As in pulling ropes, it appears that when it comes to clapping and shouting out loud, many hands do, in fact, make light the work."

The funny thing is, many people don't realize that they aren't trying as hard as they can in groups, which Latané and colleagues named "social loafing." When researchers ask, many people swear that they're trying just as hard as they do when they're completing the task on their own. It seems that they're unaware of their reduction in effort. Social loafing can be unconscious; our prehistoric brains goad us into conserving energy to search for food, drink, or sex later. (Our primitive brains are quite the hedonists.) So even when we think we're giving it our all in a group, we might not be.

Although early research was suggestive, we should have healthy skepticism about any individual study—especially old psychology studies. We want to see consistent replication—that researchers can obtain the same effect over and over again. And that's what "meta-analysis"—a study of other research studies—can help us understand. Meta-analyses aggregate many studies to assess how large and reliable an effect is.

It turns out, social loafing is really large and reliable. A meta-analysis of seventy-eight studies has confirmed that people try less hard in groups. The bigger the group, the less hard they try.

Social loafing occurs in physical tasks like rope-pulling, shouting, and rowing. It also occurs in mental tasks, like brainstorming ideas and rating job candidate résumés. It happens in all kinds of groups, regardless of culture and demographics. (Although it's a little less bad in collectivist cultures than in individualistic ones.)

The first century of group dynamics research painted an unflattering picture of groups. The two main components of group process—coordination and collective effort—seemed to harm individual performance. Groups create coordination challenges, and they lead to social loafing. Thus, many researchers began to believe that group synergy was a hoax. In 1924, Floyd Allport, a pioneer in experimental social psychology, wrote, "The actions of all are nothing more than the sum of actions of each taken separately." And Allport's view caught on after oodles of post–World War II research showed how conformist, irrational, and downright evil groups could make otherwise good, rational people. The search for synergy was called off, and group research fell out of fashion in social science. Psychologists turned inward to understand individual subjective experiences and the workings of the brain. Sociologists and economists examined cultures and nations, zooming farther and farther out from group life. The quest to discover the secrets of synergy had stalled.

In the 1970s, social psychologist Ivan Steiner formally proposed that synergy was a myth—and in doing so, restarted the search for it. Steiner took the logical, but extreme, position that groups are always less than the sum of their parts; the question is just how much less. He distilled his theory of cooperation to the equation: $AP = PP - PL$. In English, this means the actual productivity of a group (AP) is equal to the potential productivity of members added together (PP) minus "process losses" (PL)—the lost productivity due to social loafing and coordination problems.

One day at the University of Illinois, Steiner was giving a lecture, explaining his AP = PP – PL theory. In the audience was young PhD student Richard Hackman. "Where is PG?" Hackman asked, presaging his lifelong love of ambiguous acronyms. "Where are the process gains?" Steiner gave him a hard look and said, "I'll put them in the equation when someone proves they exist."

Process gains were the holy grail of early research on groups—elusive evidence that synergy was more than a myth. In fact, process gains are just another (less catchy) way of saying "synergy." They are times that groups would hypothetically improve upon what individuals would or could do alone.

Richard and his collaborators (like me!) spent the intervening decades studying how to help groups minimize process losses and foster process gains. Process gains—that alchemical synergy—do exist. Groups can be more than the sum of their parts. The Beatles' various solo ventures aren't held in as high esteem as their work together. Almost every organization depends on teams to solve problems no individual can—Apple, Pfizer, NASA, you name it. Even fictional teams do better—team-ups like The Avengers outperform solo missions almost every time. You can't defeat Thanos until you all work together.

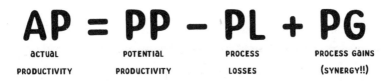

$$AP = PP - PL + PG$$

| **ACTUAL** | **POTENTIAL** | **PROCESS** | **PROCESS GAINS** |
| **PRODUCTIVITY** | **PRODUCTIVITY** | **LOSSES** | **(SYNERGY!!)** |

Steiner's group productivity formula (with Hackman's addendum).

Unfortunately for me, Marvel movie characters don't count as scientific evidence. (If they did, it would make my job much easier.) Luckily, research on synergy has come a long way since Hackman suggested adding process gains to Steiner's equation.

The Potential for Process Losses and Gains Depends on the Task

One of the most important catalysts for synergy doesn't have anything to do with the members' characteristics or how the group interacts. It's the work a group is trying to get done—the task. The tasks where we see evidence of social loafing are quite different than the tasks where groups consistently outperform individuals. Social loafing is most common in simple tasks—pulling a rope, shouting and clapping, or even brainstorming ideas. Yet evidence for superior group performance emerges in complex, knowledge-intensive tasks like innovation, invention, and research.

But the observation that group synergy is most likely in complex tasks still needed to be tested. To fix this, MIT Professor Abdullah Almaatouq teamed up with fellow groups researchers Mohammed Alsobay, Ming Yin, and Duncan Watts. The researchers created puzzles of varying complexity that could be solved by either individuals or groups of three. The tasks were logic puzzles with multiple solutions, like assigning students to dorm rooms with rules about who could room together or be neighbors. Simple puzzles had only a few rooms and rules, while complex puzzles had many.

This approach allowed the researchers to make a lot of different comparisons. Who solved the problem best (that is, followed the rules and made the fewest mistakes)? The group? The average individual? The best individual in the group? And importantly, who was most efficient—how long did it take groups and individuals to perform well? Although groups might get better answers, they might be so slow that they aren't efficient enough to bother with. After all, if groups are as slow and lazy as Steiner thought, maybe we'd get more scientific discoveries if everyone worked on their own—even if groups eventually come up with marginally better ideas.

Well, I probably wouldn't have written this book if groups weren't good for something. The researchers found that synergy is indeed most likely in complex tasks. In complex tasks, groups were more efficient than the average—or even the best—individual. But the reverse was true in simple tasks, where groups were less efficient than individuals working alone. Although the best individual still often got slightly better answers than the group in complex tasks, it took individuals almost 50 percent longer.

These findings help resolve the seeming paradox between research showing a collective edge in complex tasks like invention and discovery but an individual advantage in simple tasks like rope-pulling. If you're doing something relatively simple, coacting groups, like call centers, work well. But for complex tasks, you need more than one mind working toward a solution.

Obviously, giving a group a complex task isn't enough to get synergy. Many groups doing essential, complex work still have process losses, not synergy. So when is synergy most likely? That's what we're going to talk about throughout this book.

For soulless corporate jargon, *synergy* is surprisingly apt when you think about it—its Greek derivatives literally mean "together-work." But synergy isn't any old kind of together-work. It represents the process gains Richard Hackman asked about—when the whole is more than the sum of its parts. Davis, Coltrane, Adderley, Evans, Kelly, Chambers, and Cobb melding their disparate styles into a cohesive whole. Crick, Franklin, Watson, and Wilkins combining their knowledge and skills to discover something no human had known before.

When we deconstruct the cooperation process, synergy hopefully won't seem so mysterious.

But Steiner's maxim is what keeps me in business—process losses are everywhere, while synergy remains elusive. Synergy is elusive because groups are open social systems, where members affect one another but the outside world still gets in. For better or worse, open systems don't lend themselves to rigid, top-down control. Instead, we need to think in terms of what Hackman called "conditions, rather than causes." Trying to produce synergy is like gardening. You have some control over the soil and location. You can water and feed your plants. But you can't *cause* them to grow. You don't control the weather. You don't control pests or disease. You can only do your best to put in place the *conditions* for them to grow. How do you do that?

CHAPTER 3

More than a One-Hit Wonder

How Groups Cooperate Effectively

If you've seen any episodes of VH1's *Behind the Music,* you know that bands rarely stay together for long—or even stay on speaking terms. The Beatles burned brightly for seven or eight years, but by the end, John, Paul, George, and Ringo avoided even being in the same room together. Most groups don't make it nearly that long. There are countless examples of one-hit wonders that climb to the top of the charts but burn themselves out on the way. The Knack had a number-one hit in 1979 with "My Sharona" but disbanded a short time later because of "internal dissent." British rock band Mungo Jerry sold thirty million copies of their

1970 hit, "In the Summertime." After that, an internal power struggle split the band in half. Playing together and staying together is tough.

But one band survived and thrived in the rough world of rock and roll longer than almost any other. The Rolling Stones have been together for more than sixty years. They released their first album in 1964, and their most recent is *Hackney Diamonds*, released in 2023 at an event not too far from my Hackney home. For a group of sixty- to eighty-somethings, it's pretty impressive to release a new rock album to critical acclaim. *The Times* raved that it's "the best Rolling Stones album since 1978." They've still got it after all these years.

Comparing The Rolling Stones to The Knack or Mungo Jerry highlights something important about the meaning of *effective* cooperation. **Effective cooperation** has two dimensions. First, to consider any cooperative endeavor effective, we need to factor in **task performance**—the extent to which the group accomplished the function or task it was composed for. The Rolling Stones, The Knack, Stratos, and The Beatles were supposed to make good music—and hopefully sell some records and concert tickets along the way. The ERC succeeded in helping not only its original list of two hundred but also so many others escape the encroaching Nazis. The extent to which groups achieved their goals is an essential part of effective cooperation.

But task performance is only half of the equation. We also need to consider how group cooperation affects the humans involved. Specifically, how does cooperation shape group members' well-being and willingness to work together again, which we'll call **member satisfaction**? Do we really want to label

Mungo Jerry as an effective group if the members hate one another and never want to work together again? Do we want to
claim group cooperation is "effective" if the team wins the game
but can't compete in the next one? If you were the CEO of a company like that, you'd be out of a job fast! Because we're embedded
within social networks and organizations, we tend to cooperate
with the same people repeatedly. Ideally, a group doesn't just persist but gets better and better at cooperating over time.

If cooperating with you is painful, people might refuse to work
with you again. That's why you and other members of your group
need to be satisfied with your group memberships. Some groups
don't even have a purpose beyond supporting the enjoyment and
well-being of their members. Your book club's effectiveness depends on more than your insightful discussions of today's literature; its continued existence hinges on whether members are
satisfied with giving up one night a month to be part of it. And
that's true of all groups. People will disengage from the group if
it isn't satisfying some need or want. As Keith Richards put it in
1974, "Up until now [playing with The Rolling Stones] has always been enjoyable. None of the members have ever got to the
point where they don't want to be involved in it." That's a bar
that too many groups don't clear—work teams, social groups,
and families alike.

Our evaluations of the social world always have an instrumental dimension that examines goal attainment and an emotional,
relational dimension focused on liking, belonging, and pleasant-
ness. Groups need to excel at their tasks and foster member satisfaction to call them "effective." A team that gets the job done but
everyone involved hated it and refuses to work together again?

Not effective. A team that has a great time but does a mediocre job? Not effective.

Effectiveness and synergy are related but not identical. A group can be effective without synergy, for example, by making a good choice by majority vote. A brainstorming group can choose a good idea that a single member came up with. A group of parents can plan and clean up after their kids' prom, with each member going slower than they might on their own but still have a lot of fun. These are groups that succeed in accomplishing their tasks with a few process losses here and there. And everyone might be perfectly happy with it! Task-based synergy can happen even in groups where some members are dissatisfied, like the double-helix discoverers. In sum, team effectiveness is a joint function of what the clients of the groups' work think (that is, whoever receives and evaluates the group output) and what the members themselves think.

Although a group like Mungo Jerry can be fleetingly effective, synergy is most likely in teams that stick together. Conventional wisdom is that groups can get stale after a while. But that's not what research shows. A meta-analysis of 169 different research studies, including more than eleven thousand teams, demonstrated that staying together leads to better task performance. Teams composed of people who have worked in the same group for long periods of time develop shared ways of thinking about their work. They work harder for one another. And they figure out how to coordinate smoothly, helping them avoid conflict.

Task performance and member satisfaction, therefore, go hand in hand. You accomplish what you set out to do. That feels good. So you stick together. And maybe you learn a little something about working together in the process. And like The Rolling Stones, you can become a real team that finds synergy over and over again because you not only avoid process losses, you also coordinate in ways that bring out the best in one another and exert extraordinary effort on behalf of the group.

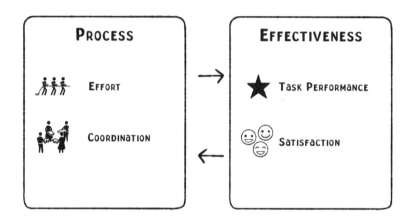

But do you have to just wander into the right train station at the right time, as the Stones' founders Mick Jagger and Keith Richards did? Or can you set yourself up to build real teams predictably?

Real Teams at IDEO

Much of the Silicon Valley cliché of a cool, creative company was birthed at IDEO—the OG of design consultancies. It's a company that I, along with Harvard professor Teresa Amabile and New York University professor Julianna Pillemer, have studied for many years. According to *MIT Technology Review*, IDEO was instrumental in "spreading the word about the value of collaboration in business." But it doesn't look much like a business. IDEO's Palo Alto office looks like a start-up mated with a playground. On an Astroturf carpet, there's a vintage Volkswagen van converted into a meeting room populated with toy Smurfs. There's a literal "Toy Lab," where designers can go to build toys for fun—and occasionally profit when toy companies come to purchase promising designs. And of course, there's everything we now expect from a Silicon Valley company—foosball tables, beer taps, and snacks everywhere. It's a wonder that anyone gets any work done!

Although IDEO's offices feel young and vibrant, the firm is middle-aged. Now a global company more than forty years old, IDEO is the old guard of Silicon Valley. Back in 1999, they were on the oldest of old-school TV shows, *Nightline*, redesigning a shopping cart and popularizing "Design Thinking" concepts now taught in nearly every business school. Shopping Cart Project team leader Peter Skillman summarized IDEO's ethos as, "Enlightened trial and error succeeds over the planning of the lone genius."

IDEO is also old-school in how it collaborates: It still works in those real teams that Hackman declared the gold standard— bounded, stable groups of two to six designers focused on a single project. Many forward-looking organizations now talk about collaboration in terms of "multi-team systems" (that is, networks of teams), "cabals," or "teaming"—ways of describing collaboration with looser boundaries and less formality. But IDEO teams still do it the old-fashioned way.

Groups cooperate best when they're more like real teams, which have two key advantages over groups with looser connections.

First, real teams have bounded, stable membership. It may sound basic, but a common problem work teams face is not knowing who to collaborate with—even when the stakes are highest. In one study, for instance, organizational psychologist Ruth Wageman and her colleagues asked 111 top management teams (as identified by the CEO) a simple question: How many members are there in your team? Stunningly, a full 93 percent of top management teams disagreed on how many people were even on the team. As Arturo Barahona, CEO of Aeromexico, exclaimed when told of his leadership team members' estimates, "My God! If we can't get this right, how can we lead the whole business?" It's hard to work together if you don't know who you're supposed to work with!

Second, real teams can have complex interdependence. Like all groupy groups, they have a common goal and a common fate. But because they're small and have clear boundaries, members can monitor one another's activities and tailor responses to that person at that moment. They can adjust how they cooperate on the fly. They don't have to operate like assembly lines but can have complex and varied ways of coordinating.

Real teams work because they satisfy all three of our core motivational drives: autonomy, belonging, and competence. Competence is our drive to get things done. It includes important needs like keeping a roof over your head and keeping you and your loved ones safe. Or less important ones like beating your personal best in a run in the park or catching a Snorlax in *Pokémon GO*. And real teams help us feel competent because they allow us to accomplish things we couldn't do alone, like making classic jazz albums, designing new shopping carts, or rescuing thousands of refugees.

Real teams also help satisfy our need for belonging—our feelings of connection to other humans. The absence of belonging is loneliness, a social pain that can be as toxic for our health as smoking or radiation. Being a member of a small, bounded group of individuals gives us something to belong to. The friendship groups, work teams, book clubs, sports teams, or bands in your life provide a sense of identity that can motivate people to act for "we," rather than just "me."

Real teams can give us a chance to satisfy our needs for competence and belonging while maintaining our third great motivational drive: autonomy. Autonomy is our sense of self-determination, that we are the masters of our own fate. And it is often in conflict with the other two drives. You sometimes need to give up some of your autonomy to accomplish a goal—which is most people's experience of work. You get money in exchange for working on other people's goals. And in doing so, you give up some freedom in how to use your time and effort. The same can be true of belonging. Identifying with large groups, like religions or nations, means following their rules—even if you don't like them. But real teams, at their best, are small enough so that we can maintain the feeling of control while still getting our other needs met.

The trick is to create the conditions where real teams can keep all three of these core drives in balance with one another. The trick is to structure for synergy.

Structuring for Synergy

IDEO does more to promote synergy than just having people work in real teams. It also gives people work they find meaningful and interesting, which keeps them motivated. IDEO employees can choose how to structure interdependence, sometimes dividing and conquering and other times improvising designs in real time.

Prior to the 1970s, most people thought that motivation was mostly a function of individual traits—some people were simply more motivated and hardworking than others. But Richard Hackman and Greg Oldham thought that characteristics of the **task** itself might be just as important as, if not more than, personality or genetics for explaining work motivation.

Hackman and Oldham set off a revolution in research: Task characteristics explained what individualistic research on worker dispositions could not. A meta-analysis covering 259 different studies including 219,625 actual human beings found that Hackman and Oldham were right: Task characteristics are extremely powerful—they explain 34 percent of the variance in job performance and 55 percent of the variance in job satisfaction. Those are ginormous effect sizes. Many well-known scientific articles feature effect sizes of 1 or 2 percent. Task characteristics have a stronger effect on collective effectiveness than smoking has on cancer risk, and about the same as the influence of exercise on cardiovascular health.

What are these fabled task characteristics? There are five of them: task variety, task identity, task significance, feedback, and autonomy.

First is task variety. You know what's boring and unmotivating? Doing the same task over and over again, like on an assembly line. People get less and less motivated to do repetitive work and yet many jobs require people to do the same tasks again and again. At IDEO, however, employees switch projects every few months. And within each project, there are lots of different things to do—interviewing and observing experts, brainstorming ideas, building and testing prototypes, or presenting to clients. Although repetition should be helpful in developing expertise and efficiency, it's very difficult to keep people caring about monotonous, repetitive work.

Second is task identity. Henry Ford's success was built on more than designing the Model T; it was built on developing assembly lines. Like most assembly lines, workers at Henry Ford's factories worked on only one part of the car. Many saw only one part of the engine all day, every day, and they certainly couldn't say which cars were the ones they worked on. But we've since discovered that's demotivating—not being able to point to a result of the work you've done. IDEO constantly refers to projects out in the world that they can see people using. Employees have portfolios featuring the work they're proud of. That is motivating.

Third is task significance—the extent to which work affects others' lives or is personally meaningful. And as research by organizational psychologist Adam Grant has shown, one of the most meaningful experiences is seeing your work help others. That can be as simple as seeing someone drive the car or use the shopping cart. It also can be more personal, like learning a musical instrument or getting to the next level of a video game. Each person gets to determine what's "significant" to them.

Fourth is feedback from the work itself, which is about being able to monitor your progress. For instance, imagine studying for a test. You read books; you review your notes. Although you're (probably) making progress, you can't see it. But on educational apps like Khan Academy or Duolingo, you see progress as you go. These apps use a strategy called "gamification," which works because it provides clear, measurable goals and real-time feedback on your progress. Simple games like *PAC-MAN* illustrate this nicely. The game begins in a maze full of dots, and you finish a level when all the dots are gone. It's very easy to see your progress as you play—the dots disappear as you eat them. The most motivating tasks have that same quality: the new video game levels getting unlocked, the IDEO prototype being built, or the people being rescued by the ERC.

And finally, we have autonomy. This is one of the core psychological needs, so its relationship to motivation is clear. People don't like feeling controlled. They will be unmotivated and unhappy when they don't feel in control of their own fate.

Extreme autonomy bordered on a management fad for a while. Valve, the video game company and maker of the Steam gaming platform, famously "leaked" an employee handbook detailing their flat, anti-autocratic organization. No one tells anyone what to do. Unlimited vacation days. You need to build "cabals" to get projects done but can decide whether to join one on your own. Medium, the blogging platform, tried but abandoned a similar management model. Google had "20 percent time," during which employees could do whatever they wanted.

Unfortunately, many of these attempts at extreme autonomy failed. Humans are motivated by autonomy—they got that right. But what programs like these often get wrong is that humans thrive on autonomy for *how* to achieve their goals, but cooperation requires agreement on *what* goals to achieve. For a chance at synergy, we need the ends of our cooperation to be clearly defined—what mountain to climb, what shopping cart to build, or what book to read. We certainly can develop these goals collectively, but that's hard. Often, the most effective group leaders are directive about what the goal is but then provide autonomy on how to achieve that goal. Famed US Army General George Patton had it right when he said, "Never tell people how to do things. Tell them what to do and they will surprise you with their ingenuity."

This gets back to the problem with an assembly-line approach to collaboration. When you dictate the process in a lot of detail, who has responsibility for when things go wrong? Whoever designed the process! The more you dictate to others how to do the work, the more you take away their sense of responsibility. That's bad for motivation.

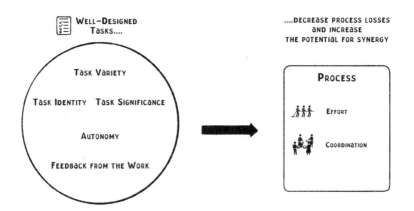

Perhaps the most important lesson of Hackman and Oldham's Task Characteristics Theory is that looking for what causes effective cooperation is hopeless. Cooperation emerges from open social systems that are in perpetual flux; people come and go, and situations change. There is no "one weird trick" that will allow us to reliably cooperate within or between groups.

Instead of looking for a single cause, we should think about the conditions under which effective collaboration emerges. That's where we'll find conditions that allow us to get that collective edge. And task design is perhaps the most important—and most overlooked—condition for promoting synergy. If you want to explain a group's performance, look first to their tasks. What is the nature of the work your group is doing? Are members working on rich, motivating tasks? Or poor, demotivating ones?

Examining task characteristics can help us break out of our individualistic mindsets. Too often, we pretend that we are islands. Our tendency to cast ourselves as the main character leads us to overlook how interdependent we truly are with our families, friends, neighbors, and coworkers. And in failing to recognize our interconnectedness, we fail to invest in the conditions for effective collaboration.

The question we really want to ponder is this: What other conditions will help us minimize process losses and maximize process gains?

CHAPTER 4

From Scream Team to Redeem Team

Launching Collaborations Beyond Team Building

USA Men's Basketball has dominated the Olympics, winning every gold medal from 1992 until 2024. Except for 2004.

The 1992 team was packed with stars. Ten of the twelve players, including Michael Jordan, Magic Johnson, and Larry Bird, were on the National Basketball Association's (NBA) official list of "50 Greatest Players in NBA History." Team members were named to the NBA All-Star team a combined sixty-eight times, earning them the moniker of the "Dream Team." The Dream Team lived up to its name, going undefeated on their way to gold, and demolishing opponents by an average of forty-four points. In the next two Olympic Games, the Dream Team's successors continued to steamroll the rest of the world, winning twenty-four consecutive games and taking home three gold medals.

The 2004 team came to Athens led by all-time NBA greats Tim Duncan and Allen Iverson and rising young stars LeBron James, Dwyane Wade, and Carmelo Anthony. Although it was short of the original Dream Team's star power, observers agreed that Team USA was still by far the most talented in the tournament.

But things quickly went wrong. They lost the opening game by a whopping nineteen points—to Puerto Rico, whose team featured one former NBA player, with no all-star games to their credit. They ended up losing not one, but three games (which is the same as the oft-overlooked USA Women's Basketball team has ever lost in Olympic competition). The 2004 Men's team later lost to Lithuania in group stage and to Argentina in the semifinal. Although they came home with a bronze medal, their performance was seen as a colossal failure. Half of the six losses the USA Men's Basketball team has ever endured came during the disastrous 2004 Athens Olympics.

How could the most talented team in the tournament perform so poorly? Bad chemistry, many suggested. Early in the tournament, their demanding head coach, Larry Brown, publicly criticized the team. "I'm angry because the mentality of this team has been like this from Day One," Brown told the media after their early struggles. "Now, we've got to coach them better and find out if we're truly ready to become a team."

But they never became the team that Brown hoped for. Guard Stephon Marbury called the 2004 Olympics "the worst 38 days of my life," laying most of the blame at Brown's feet for his unrelenting criticism.

The 2004 team was more nightmare than dream—"the Scream Team," as one ESPN headline put it. Was bad chemistry—the anti-synergy that made the whole less than the sum of its parts—truly to blame? Let's break it down.

Building a Team or Team Building?

One popular explanation for the 2004 Scream Team's struggles was a lack of collective experience. The team members were young, with an average age of about twenty-three years old. More importantly, the competition had trained and competed together for years, but Team USA had almost no experience playing as a team. Journalist Alvin Chang described how USA Men's Basketball still struggles with frequent player turnover and working around the NBA season: "It's hard for Team USA to send a consistent core group of players who have built up chemistry with each other," Chang wrote. "It's nothing compared to teams like Argentina, Spain, and even Serbia, where players have spent dozens of years learning each other's playing styles, starting as early as their teenage years."

But Team USA did what many consider the next best thing—an off-site retreat! Team USA didn't just practice together. Rather than living in the distracting media hub of the Olympic Village, where they were sought-after celebrities, they stayed off-site on a super yacht called the *Queen Mary 2*, which Carmelo Anthony nicknamed *Deuce*. *Deuce* had everything Team USA needed, including a basketball court available at all hours. Living together was like summer camp, allowing Team USA to bond, get to know one another, and build trust. They played poker and had dance parties. Allen Iverson, one of the veteran leaders, was a prolific practical joker. As teammate Dwyane Wade recounted, "Iverson was always playing around. Like in your sleep, he's going to put something in your ear. You'll be listening to your headphones, and he'll take the headphone thing out when you ain't looking, and you're like, 'What happened?' He's so quick." They learned that forward Lamar Odom was an amateur DJ and LeBron James a bookworm. In short, they did much of what team-building proponents advise to build social cohesion. So what went wrong?

Many, many people associate improving team chemistry with team building. Managers, consultants, and coaches around the world prescribe it for all manner of social ills. But what is team building? Well, a good explanation comes from those paragons of accuracy: TV ads. In the late 2000s, American Airlines launched an advertising campaign with the tagline "Make your escape." One situation they thought people would want to escape from was a team-building workshop. The ad opens on a failed trust fall. (Facilitator: "Okay, what did we learn there?") There was chess with human pieces. (Facilitator: "That's a power move because she thought diagonally!") There was talk about feelings while wearing a stovepipe hat inscribed with the word *honesty*.

I'd also be on the first plane to escape this kind of team building because it's based on a flawed premise, which assumes that trust and social cohesion must precede effective teamwork. I blame educational psychologist Bruce Tuckman for this. In the 1960s, Tuckman came up with a model of group development that made sense at the time, but subsequent research has found misleading. It owes some of its notoriety to Tuckman's poetic prowess in naming the stages of group development: forming, storming, norming, performing, and adjourning.

Tuckman came up with this "-orming" model by reviewing group-development studies, which, at the time, were chock-full of research on post–World War II group training sessions for community leaders, known as T-groups. And to be fair, the Tuckman -orming model does a pretty good job of describing training groups, social clubs, and other groups that exist only for the benefit of their members.

But using this model on real teams causes all sorts of problems. And one study highlights these flaws well.

Imagine you're a business school student. You and two of your classmates are assigned to solve a "financial puzzle" as a group. You have to estimate next year's stock price of a company from the prior five years of financial data. You discuss it with your fellow group members, but the numbers don't show much of a trend—forty-five dollars per share one year but then forty, forty-eight, fifty, and forty-two dollars in the subsequent years. Your discussion with other members is quick—you do a few rough calculations and agree on a number that seems reasonable (basically taking the average). After all, you're almost guessing.

As always, there's a trick. The instructor knows the correct answer because this is real data from a real company. Amazingly, the instructor tells you your group has done quite well—you were in the top 20 percent of the class! You then fill out a brief survey about what it was like to work in your group. How cohesive were you? Did you communicate well? How satisfied were you while working with your group?

This imaginary exercise is like a study by University of California organizational psychologist Barry Staw about how people appraise group dynamics, which has been replicated many times. In this study, there was yet another trick—the performance feedback was random. Groups were arbitrarily told that they had either done well (top 20 percent) or poorly (bottom 20 percent), regardless of their actual estimates. And the results showed that people's reports of their group dynamics were far more influenced by how well they thought they did than by their actual group dynamics. Groups that were randomly told they performed well reported being more cohesive, felt they communicated better, and were more open to change than groups that were randomly told they performed poorly.

The lesson of Staw's study is that our perceptions of task performance retroactively change how we think our group collaborated. Of course, we know when things are amazing or miserable, but most group experiences are in the middle. In those average situations, we reason backward about what's going on inside our groups—we take indications of performance and then infer the ephemeral aspects of group life that we *believe* caused it. In other words, most people have informal theories that groups perform well when they are cohesive, motivated, and communicate well.

Therefore, our brain reasons, because we got a good outcome, we must have had good group dynamics!

Contrary to Staw's study, Tuckman's -orming model posits that groups need to build trust and develop norms before they can perform a task (forming-storming-norming-performing). You can't just get to work if you don't do the trust falls! But that's the team-building myth. It doesn't match reality: Social cohesion is as much of a result of effective cooperation as it is a cause.

Although it helps to have good relationships before cooperating, the best way to develop good relationships is to cooperate effectively! You can start out indifferent to your teammates, but you'll probably like and understand them better after you accomplish something—win the game, get an A on a group project, or run a successful bake sale. I bet the Scream Team's chemistry problems wouldn't seem so important if they had won all their games by forty points and took home gold. They might not even remember whatever disagreements they had. The issues they were having were magnified by their failure. Winning cures many ills. And losing creates them—groups tend to blame one another and argue when things go wrong.

The causal arrows between group dynamics and effective cooperation go in both directions. When we cooperate well, it strengthens our relationships. When we cooperate poorly, it weakens them. That may seem obvious, but it's the opposite of the Tuckman/team-building logic. For real teams like the Scream Team, good group dynamics aren't an end in themselves—they are an outgrowth of healthy cooperation. Too often, people try to build relationships first and cooperate second. But relationships and cooperation are a never-ending circle, an Ouroboros—you need trust to cooperate, but you need to cooperate to develop trust.

The best way to start the cycle is a strong, quick launch and then getting to work. As team training expert Eduardo Salas and his colleagues have found across many studies, training intact groups in task-like environments is an effective way to build a team. But team building by having people focus on trust and social cohesion through faux-fun activities? The evidence is not great. So maybe if Team USA had started practicing much earlier rather than relying on bonding on a boat, the Scream Team would have felt more like a real team.

Group Composition: What's Your Group Made Of?

There's a simpler explanation than team chemistry for the Scream Team's underperformance: its **composition**. At the time, members of the 2004 team were the least accomplished since 1992. Tim Duncan and Allen Iverson were the only NBA All-Stars, accounting for all the teams' thirteen All-Star appearances (far short of the original Dream Team's sixty-eight). Future stars LeBron James, Carmelo Anthony, and Dwyane Wade were just out of their teens at the time, well before their prime playing years. Top players like Kobe Bryant, Kevin Garnett, and Tracy McGrady turned down invitations to join. As journalist Alvin Chang observed, "The US continued to believe they could send their B-team and still win gold."

The Scream Team didn't just lack the star power of its predecessors. It also lacked important skills. Team USA was stocked
with small forwards whose slashing style worked well in the NBA
but was ill-suited to attack the physical zone defenses that were
permitted in the Olympics. They also lacked long-distance shooting skill that was critical in international competition; the Scream
Team ranked last in the twelve-team field in three-pointers made
per game and next to last in percentage made (31.4 percent).

As Team USA found, throwing the biggest names together
isn't always a recipe for success. Research backs up the idea that
teams can struggle when they have too much star power. But a
super-duper team is a rare problem that you seldom need to worry
about—the original Dream Team and Miles Davis's all-star band
did just fine! Team USA was plagued with a more common
problem—the team was selected based on fame and prestige, with
little thought for what the task demanded.

Compose Teams for Deep Diversity

Synergy requires diverse knowledge, skills, and perspectives. *Kind
of Blue* levitated because of the contrast and complementarity
among musicians. Watson and Crick couldn't have produced or
understood Photograph 51, while Wilkins and Franklin wouldn't
have been able to model the wet form of DNA on their own. The
most famous real teams are characterized by diverse, complementary talents. Bands with all guitarists or all drummers rarely
succeed. Neither does a basketball team with all guards or all
centers. The same is true for work teams, social clubs, and politi-

cal parties—the chances of synergy go up when you have diverse skills and perspectives to offer.

Group researchers differentiate between two kinds of diversity. First, there's surface-level diversity: easy-to-observe differences in social categories like race, gender, age, and nationality. These are the kinds of diversity that get the most attention—for good reason: There's a lot of prejudice and discrimination based on these characteristics. That's a big problem. We should work tirelessly to solve it.

But from a synergy perspective, composing a group for surface-level diversity is a means to get to the second type: deep-level diversity. Deep-level diversity is about the actual differences in what people know, think, and do. Demographic differences are often proxies for different knowledge, skills, and perspectives but are no guarantee. And if it is effective cooperation that we care about, then what we want is deep-level diversity.

Theoretically, diversity should have a Goldilocks effect on team effectiveness (too hot, too cold, just right), because both too little diversity and too much diversity can harm cooperation. With too little diversity, we get conformity. That's such a common problem that we'll devote all of Section II to it. People identify with and seek out people they see as similar to themselves, an effect known as "homophily." Because of homophily, groups often end up with members who all think too similarly and have redundant knowledge and skills. A meta-analysis of 146 studies of the diversity-performance relationship showed that more diversity in expertise improves team performance, especially in complex tasks. More often than not, groups are composed of members who think too similarly. So adding deep-level diversity is what I usually prescribe.

But in theory, there's a point at which people simply think or behave too differently to cooperate effectively. Imagine a group in which each member speaks a different language—if there's no common language, the group will struggle to cooperate because members literally won't understand one another. Even if members can communicate, deep-level diversity raises the chances of conflict that can derail cooperation (more on this in Section III): When members have different perspectives, the chances they'll disagree goes up. Logically, it should be harder to get on the same page.

Moreover, any kind of diversity can evoke "us" and "them" problems. These problems are relics from ancient times, poorly adjusted to the modern world. As famed biologist Edward O. Wilson put it, "The real problem of humanity is the following: We have Paleolithic emotions, medieval institutions, and godlike technology. And it is terrifically dangerous, and is now approaching a point of crisis overall." Our personal sorting hats are part of a Paleolithic brain, trying to keep us safe and cooperating with one another. But this prehistoric thinking can be bad for cooperation.

The warped view that "us" and "them" gives us—known as "in-group/out-group biases"—impedes groups' ability to identify and discuss helpful differences. People are afraid to speak up. Differences in opinion are interpreted as threats to the groups' cohesion. For decades, researchers thought that surface-level, demographic diversity would elicit more bias than deep-level diversity. And it is true that demographically diverse groups initially tend to sort each other into "us" and "them." But does that actually harm their performance? Or do demographically diverse groups figure things out after working together for a while?

It seems like demographically diverse groups perform just fine—as long as outsiders aren't judging their performance. Organizational psychologists Hans van Dijk, Marloes van Engen, and Daan van Knippenberg found that the purported negative effects of surface-level diversity only emerged when group performance was judged subjectively by outsiders, like managers who had little contact with the team. When group performance was objective—like financial performance or tasks with correct answers—surface-level diversity had no effect on performance.

These findings have profound implications. The worry that increasingly diverse groups will struggle to collaborate seems to be mostly in our heads. Demographically diverse teams sometimes appear to struggle more because of outsiders' bias and prejudice, not because diversity is inherently bad for cooperation. Although there's clearly a limit to how differently people can view the world and collaborate, we are currently nowhere near that limit. If we want to solve big problems, we need to find ways to overcome biases and prejudice that come from our Paleolithic tendency to sort one another. And that starts with real experience cooperating with people with different perspectives.

Reading the Mind in the Eyes

Diverse and complementary skills and perspectives matter a lot. What about diverse personalities? A common misconception is that "bad chemistry" is a clash of diverse personalities and work styles. When groups go sideways, people tend to blame the vagaries of who they worked with. Student project teams, PTA bake sales, and work task forces are undermined by the difficulties of working with others who are different. Many organizations try to head off problems and compose teams with compatible personalities and work styles.

But research doesn't support any one approach to composing teams based on personality or work style. University of Connecticut professor John Mathieu, one of the leading experts on teamwork, reviewed (along with his colleagues) hundreds of studies that linked group composition to effectiveness. But they struggled to come up with a clear prescription, writing that the research literature "leads one to the inescapable conclusion that no combination of members is likely to be ideal. Inevitably, there will need to be trade-offs." In other words, guidance on how many introverts and extroverts to put together probably won't help you. (Also, commonly used tools like the Myers-Briggs Type Indicator are unhelpful pseudoscience. Don't use them for any serious purpose.)

There is one exception. Organizational scientists Anita Woolley, Christoph Riedl, and Thomas Malone led a research team that surprisingly found that the average level or maximum level of intelligence doesn't do much to predict group effectiveness. Woolley and her coauthors tried every trait they could measure to predict team success and every way to combine them: average, minimums, maximums, and variation. And of all these traits, only one emerged as a predictor of group effectiveness: social sensitivity.

Social sensitivity is the ability to detect others' emotions through nonverbal cues. In other words, if you are good at reading others' emotions intuitively, you are probably very socially sensitive. As far as we can tell, social sensitivity doesn't have much to do with individual intelligence. But it is the key to *collective* intelligence—a group's ability to perform effectively across a variety of tasks.

The test we use to measure social sensitivity is fun. It's called the "Reading the Mind in the Eyes Test." In it, you see a bunch of rectangular cutouts of eyes and eyebrows. Then you are offered four options for the emotion that person reported feeling when the photo was taken. For instance, was that person feeling jealous, panicked, arrogant, or hateful? You get a point for each one you get correct.

The average score of all group members on this test is the best tool we have to predict effective cooperation across a wide variety of tasks—besides their actual task-relevant knowledge and skills.

On average, women perform better than men on this test. Thus, groups with more women tend to have more collective intelligence and cooperate more effectively. It is important to note, though, that gender doesn't cause collective intelligence; social sensitivity is what's important.

Why does social sensitivity affect collective intelligence? Socially sensitive people can adjust their own behavior to accommodate their fellow group members' feelings. Someone is overwhelmed? You can see if they need help. Someone is really enthusiastic? You can follow their lead. Although there are other ways to be a stellar teammate, social sensitivity is the trait scientists have figured out how to measure that best predicts group effectiveness across a wide variety of tasks.

Size Matters

I've left the most important question about group composition for last: How big should your group be? With groups, the bigger, the better, right? "Many hands make light the work" and all that. That's all well and good if we have a coacting group like a call center. But real teams need everyone to coordinate. And like a yoke of oxen, the bigger the team gets, the harder coordination gets. So how big is too big, and how small is too small?

Luckily, this is the kind of question research can answer: Real teams should have between three and seven members. On average, groups with three to seven members perform best (although it of course depends on the task). And team members' satisfaction peaks between four and five members. So balancing members' satisfaction and task performance, we get three to seven members.

The reasoning is simple math: In a group, the number of dyadic relationships (that is, the links between pairs of members) goes up exponentially with the introduction of each member because each additional member has relationships with every other member. And every relationship is an opportunity for unshared perspectives, misunderstandings, and conflict. A group of two only needs to manage one relationship. A group of five, however, needs to cope with ten dyadic relationships. A group of ten needs to manage forty-five. And a group of twenty has one hundred ninety dyadic relationships! In a group of twenty, there are probably pairs that barely know one another. The chances for synergy are low, and process losses are almost guaranteed.

When I tell managers this, they understand. But they hate it because they have much bigger teams, often with ten to thirty members. So if you have a bigger "team," you probably need to split them up for different tasks, like having a task force, project group, or committee. And those task-performing groups should each have three to seven members. There's nothing worse than a meeting with twenty people trying to have a meaningful discussion and make a decision—except a meeting with twenty-five people! Don't do this. It's what gives group meetings a bad name. If your group has twenty-five members, you have a small organization, not a real team. Subdivide the work and the group, so you don't set the team up for misery. Bigger groups can vote on proposals, provide comments or questions, or split up the work. But big groups inherently lack the flexibility of smaller groups. So remember: For groups, size matters. But bigger isn't better.

One final note on group size: Groups that are too big are common because many groups try to solve problems by adding more members. Missing a particular skill or expert? Project running behind? Let's add someone! Groups of all stripes—from top management teams to PTAs, from boards of directors to book clubs—almost always grow in number over time because asking people to leave is uncomfortable but asking them to join is easy. Businesses, in particular, often feel like they need to grow to show they are successful.

But growing your group isn't necessarily a path to success if you need to get work done. Droll IBM computer architect Fred Brooks coined his famous Brooks's Law: "Adding manpower to a late software project makes it later." Although this is an exaggeration, there's a kernel of truth in there. When there are too many people, we don't work as hard as we could (social loafing), coordination becomes more difficult, and process losses swamp the potential for synergy. So the right amount of any resource—including people—is "just enough, but not too much." (Caveat: If a group is working hard and finds themselves under-resourced, managers should be willing to give them more. But it's better to start with too little and ask for more than to start with too much.)

So, in summary, real teams—those seeking synergy—should contain around three to seven members. Leaders should select for social sensitivity and task-appropriate yet diverse skills and perspectives. And those teams should train together and cooperate as soon as possible. You can skip the Tuckmanian team building.

Setting Your Sights: The Attributes of Good Cooperative Goals

After the 2004 Olympics, USA Men's Basketball selected a better mix of players with skills suited to international competition, not just the biggest stars. Some of the 2004 team's failures, however, were about the context in which it was operating.

Unlike in 2004, playing in the 1992 Olympics seemed like an important duty for an American basketball player. The top NBA players were anxious to avenge Team USA losses to the USSR in 1976 and 1988, fighting their own proxy Cold War. But by 2004, the Cold War was over and those losses were long since avenged. The main rival teams were now Argentina, Italy, Lithuania, and

France—not the USSR's "evil empire" that had loomed large in American consciousness. Signing up for the Olympics no longer seemed so important for players who needed to rest their bodies after the rigors of the NBA season. As Scream Team assistant coach Gregg Popovich noted, "You can't blame the US players who came here. You can't blame them for wanting to sightsee and go to dinner. This isn't their end-all. This was a summer basketball trip."

In 2005, famed Duke University coach Mike Krzyzewski, known as Coach K, took over as the head coach of the USA Men's National Team. The media christened the team that competed in the 2008 Olympics the "Redeem Team," which would atone for the failures of 2004. Coach K was a career college coach with little NBA experience. To recruit top NBA players like those who had stayed home in 2004, he believed the summer-trip mentality needed to change.

Luckily for Coach K, recruiting top players wasn't a problem. The young, inexperienced core from the 2004 team—LeBron James, Dwyane Wade, and Carmelo Anthony—weren't so young and inexperienced by 2008. They were entering the primes of their careers, had played together, and had improved their outside shooting. James was drawing comparisons to the best players in history. James, Wade, and Anthony were angry and motivated to change the narrative from 2004. And Kobe Bryant, probably the most prominent player to sit out in 2004, brought the team his single-minded focus on winning at all costs. Other top NBA players followed their lead and signed on. Composing an accomplished team with the right mix of skills was a lot easier this time.

Coach K and USA Basketball director Jerry Colangelo took

the opportunity to strengthen the foundations of the team. To join, players now had to make a three-year commitment to stay and train with Team USA. Team USA was finally following the example of other successful teams—and the prescriptions of research. Teams that train together and stick together get better over time.

Coach K gave a soft-spoken opening speech to a later iteration of Team USA at the beginning of training camp. "We all could be doing a whole bunch of things now," he began, addressing the room of world-famous multimillionaires. "This is the most important thing that you could do, and it's an incredible experience because you get to play for your country. But you will all get better. Even in these four days [of camp] that we are together, you'll get better. You'll get better because you make each other better. All of you are outstanding players and playing against another outstanding player or with outstanding players makes you better.

"You will never be judged by if you start on a US team or if you are the leading scorer, leading rebounder," Coach K continued. "There's only one question someone will ask: 'Did you win?' And it's our responsibility that every US player only ever gives one answer: 'Yes.'"

In this opening, Coach K checks the most important boxes to launch a team. First, he articulates a clear goal (winning the gold medal). But he also explains why it's *important* to achieve that goal. It is important, not for individual glory as starter or leader in scoring or rebounding, but for their shared identity of "your country." And he also addresses why it is worth it to make the trade-off between individual and collective needs. In this case, each player benefits as an individual by becoming a better basketball player—literal process gains by participating in the group. Whether the team wins or loses won't affect much about each individual's wealth and fame; they've already made it to near the top of their profession. They'll be asked only one question about this experience—and they've seen what happens with either answer.

I hope it's not too surprising that **clear, important goals** are essential to launching an effective collaboration. Specific, meaningful goals and effective cooperation go hand in hand. Groups need people to want to join and to give their best when they do. The 1992 and 2008 USA Men's Basketball teams were animated by a purpose that tapped into deeply held identities as Americans and great basketball players. Seeing Team USA lose in 1988 and 2004 threatened the idea that American basketball was the pinnacle of achievement. It rallied more people to the group's cause.

And once the group is formed, having a clear goal orients members' attention to the same destination. If we are trying to go to two different places, it's inevitable that we'll come apart. Clear goals are both Self-Help and Management 101. Clarity represents the "specific, measurable" components of SMART (Specific, Measurable, Achievable, Relevant, Time-bound) goals that are taught everywhere from Harvard's MBA programs to my son's middle-school physical education class. These goals help different people picture the future in similar ways, allowing them to coordinate their actions.

But the reason that goal setting is taught everywhere is because it is so often done poorly. And that's because there's a hidden tension between clarity and importance. The most important goals are abstract. The United Nations' admirable "Grand Challenges," for example, include improving human rights, reducing poverty, spreading democracy, and providing peace and security. Very important, but not specific and measurable.

The inherent clarity-importance tension makes it difficult to organize effective collaboration around important goals. University of Pennsylvania professor Andrew Carton has studied the clarity-importance tension extensively, noting that "the very features that make ultimate aspirations meaningful—their breadth and timelessness—undermine the ability of employees to see how their daily responsibilities are associated with them." The solution, Carton suggests, is for leaders to use language that paints a picture of what the future will look like when we achieve the goal. For example, in 1980, Bill Gates imagined a future with "a computer on every desk and in every home," animating the group that became Microsoft. President John F. Kennedy reenergized a failing National Aeronautics and Space Administration (NASA) by asking them to put a person on the moon by the end of the decade. If Coach K wanted to take things a step further, he might have asked players to imagine standing on the podium with the world watching, receiving their gold medals with the US national anthem playing in their ears. A vivid shared picture of the future helps us manage the tension between clarity and importance.

Collective goals need one final ingredient: They need to be challenging. But that challenge needs to come with specificity.

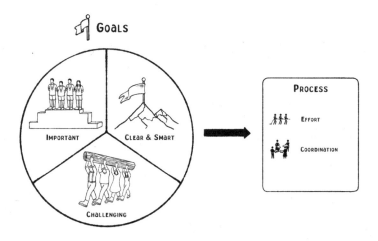

Organizational psychologists Ed Locke and Gary Latham discovered the depth of this principle. Across many studies, they compared "do your best" goals to specific, measurable, challenging goals. The funny thing is, if you take it literally, "do your best" is the most challenging goal you can set. It means that you need to meet or exceed whatever you've achieved in the past. But "do your best" doesn't produce that result. Research has shown that, as long as a person feels the numeric goal is possible to achieve (even if it is extremely difficult), a specific, challenging number helps them outperform "do your best" goals.

In 1975, Latham had left academia temporarily and was working for the Weyerhaeuser logging company in Tacoma, Washington. Latham and his colleague James Baldes designed a study to put this goal-setting theory to the test at Weyerhaeuser. They noticed that the company's thirty-six logging trucks were usually loaded only to 60 percent of their capacity before they were driven off. This was a big inefficiency for the company. But the drivers thought little of it; they were paid a flat hourly rate, regardless of how much wood they chucked onto their trucks.

Latham and Baldes arranged for the drivers to be given a "do your best" goal to set a baseline. Even though their "best" was measurable and self-evident, the "do your best" goals didn't move the needle—drivers continued to drive off at around 60 percent of their trucks' capacity. But Latham and Baldes talked to the drivers and got their take on what a challenging yet attainable goal would be. They agreed on 94 percent.

The impact was immediate. Within a month, trucks were hauling more than 70 percent of their capacity. After another month, it was more than 80 percent. And after four months, trucks were near their 94 percent target. Although there were small fluctuations in the following months, they stayed right around 90 percent for the remaining six months of the study.

Challenging numeric goals motivate us by tapping into our need to feel competent, like we are masters of our environment. They transform important yet abstract concepts into something that we can work on right now.

But goals aren't simply vehicles for task completion. All groups have both task and relational goals. It's just a question of their relative importance. Friendship groups are almost entirely relational (with the occasional task, like helping one another move or bringing food when one is sick). Work groups and teams prioritize tasks over relationships but still need to foster relationships and not be so horrible that everyone quits. Families are mostly about relationships but also have tasks like managing the household finances, getting everyone fed and clothed, or growing happy and healthy children. Social groups like book clubs are somewhere in the middle.

Hopefully, you can see the collective perspective starting to take shape. To this point, we've covered three critical conditions that promote effective groups: tasks, composition, and goals. These are three of the four core aspects of what we'll call **group structure**—the DNA of your group.

Group structure shapes group process. Good goals and well-designed tasks are motivating and aid in coordination. Well-composed real teams have an easier time coordinating. Because groups are aligning their efforts effectively, they often improve upon their initial goals and tasks, further improving their process. It's no wonder they're more effective.

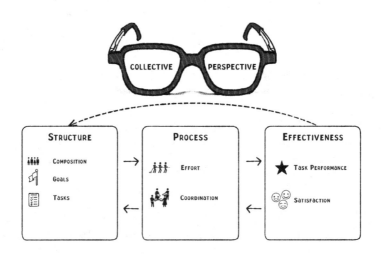

These benefits lead to a virtuous cycle. Teams that are trying hard and coordinating efficiently are much more likely to perform their tasks well. And people like that! They're more satisfied by their membership in the group. These more-satisfied members are then more likely to exert even more effort on behalf of the group. Over time, effective groups retain their members—and attract valuable new ones. And the members often learn and change from being a part of the group, increasing their knowledge and skill base. They collectively set new goals. They improve upon their initial structure. Being part of an effective group—your organization, school, or family—can make you better; you learn more and enjoy it more.

And the reverse is true when group structure is flawed. Unclear goals and unmotivating tasks are dissatisfying. You don't get the competence boost from being a member of the group. Members don't give it their all. The group struggles to attract capable new members. No one bothers to fix the flawed goals and poorly designed tasks. The group falls into a cycle of dysfunction from which it struggles to emerge. And it sucks to be a part of it. Members leave, and the group falls apart.

That's why launch is such a critical time in a group's life—it is the time when structure blooms into group process. If you are a formal leader, you can help your group maximize its chances of synergy by composing the team thoughtfully, articulating its goals, and designing motivating tasks. If you are a member, you can help bring structure to life by discussing—and even questioning—the goals, tasks, and composition. These discussions keep everyone on the same page and are easily sparked by any member asking a question. You don't even need to go to that off-site ropes course!

But the fun is just beginning, because even when we have a

well-structured team, group dynamics can still go awry. They can be derailed by cooperation's volatile companions: conformity (Section II) and competition (Section III). So you better keep reading!

GROUP THOUGHTS ON COOPERATION

"Group Thoughts" are nuts-and-bolts applications related to the research-based insights in each chapter. Managing group dynamics doesn't lend itself to little "tips and tricks" that dominate the self-help and management genres; there's no silver bullet to managing groups and teams. But there certainly are issues that have come up over and over again in the decades I've been teaching students how to manage collective work and life. Group Thoughts detail the most common ways you can use the science of group dynamics to improve your work or your well-being, or do your part in building a more just, peaceful world. Okay, maybe Group Thoughts are tips and tricks.

Thought 1: Clarify Boundaries to Foster Real Teams

Problem: A lot of the main problems in teamwork come from understanding the boundaries of the team—it's hard to work together if you don't know who you're supposed to work with.

Solution: How do you avoid confusion about who is in a group? Tell people! Over and over. Ask people if they're willing to join, and tell them when you consider them a member. List all team members on agendas and memos. Create online groups, using platforms like Teams, Slack, or WhatsApp, for only your team members. Email the whole team rather than subsets of members. If you do these things consistently, they may seem unnecessary. But think of them as insurance. Once people get confused about the boundaries of a team, working together becomes very, very difficult.

Thought 2: Make Goals Explicit

Problem: A group in which members have different—but unstated—ideas about the group's purpose is doomed to dysfunction. A group like that can have fundamental disagreements on how to balance task accomplishment and member satisfaction. For example, you might be on a soccer team where some people are there to win and others are just there to hang out and have a few beers afterward. Or like me, you could be on committees at work with unclear purposes and grumble over calendar invites to meetings that seem unnecessary and really don't require your presence. That makes it hard to coordinate and hard to be motivated!

Solution: Groups always have multiple purposes; the question is how to balance them. Whenever a group assembles, the balance of these purposes should be explicit. When you get to the locker room, how much is it "Let's have fun out there" versus "Let's kick their ass"? The first time a group gets together, someone needs to announce why everyone is there and why it's important.

When I kick off a new group or facilitate a meeting, I articulate my version of (a) the purpose of the group and (b) the goals of the meeting. This is short, no more than a few sentences. I then invite others to share if they have a different perspective. Yesterday, for instance, we launched a "half-baked research idea group." I offered that the purpose was not only to help one another vet and develop our new, half-baked ideas (a task goal), but also to catch up and feel more of a sense of community (a relational goal). And then I asked what other people wanted to get out of the group.

Sometimes, the goal of the first meeting is to figure out what the group's purpose should be. That's fine—but say that. Out loud. If you're just getting together to hang out and enjoy one another's company, say that. It can be as simple as, "I'm so excited to see you guys and catch up! Woo-hoo! Is there anything else we need to do?" The bottom line is this: Make explicit both the purpose of the group (why the group exists) and the goal of the meeting (the specific objective that should be accomplished by the end of your time together).

Thought 3: When You Make Decisions, Write Them Down

Problem: Even though we talked about our goals and how to cooperate, our group doesn't stick to them. The kids don't do their chores when they agreed to. My coworkers don't track changes like they agreed they would. Bob is still always late!

Solution: When you discuss your goals and processes, write down what you agree on! Researchers call these "team charters"—documents that clearly spell out the team's purpose, SMART goals, everyone's roles, and initial norms. (More on norms in Section II.) Charters shouldn't be immutable law, though—you should adjust them about halfway through any task, after you've reached major milestones or accomplishments, or if they seem to be creating more problems than they solve.

Another good practice at launch is to try to identify likely obstacles to achieving your goals. A useful way to do this is a premortem. A premortem is a discussion in which the group imagines things have gone horribly wrong. Premortems work because groups are surprisingly good at intuiting potential problems like overfull calendars or a lack of underwater basket-weaving skills—if they take the time to think about them. Premortems help the group adjust its structure and process to avoid these likely obstacles.

Thought 4: Negotiate Your Roles, Tasks, and Jobs

Problem: In a group we adopt roles. And those roles come with expectations for how we'll behave. The drummer keeps the beat, the piano provides the harmonic nuance, and the bass player holds the two together. At work, jobs have titles and descriptions. The same is true for families, where roles like wife, mother, husband, father, or child come with expectations. We often want and need to break out of these restrictive roles, but it is hard to do!

Solution: In a real team, everyone's role is negotiated. Experts like Yale professor Amy Wrzesniewski call this "job crafting," in which people carve out idiosyncratic ways to think about and enact their roles. We don't know how others think about their roles unless we ask. And others don't know how we think about ours unless we tell them. Have regular conversations about people's formal and informal roles. Again, beginnings, midpoints, and endings are good times. Make time for people to reflect on what they like and what'd they'd change. If you have power over others'

73

roles, make sure you don't hog all the well-designed, interesting work for yourself, delegating only the menial and repetitive tasks. Making space for reflection and conversation will help all group members craft well-designed tasks for themselves—generally, that's what people want anyway.

SECTION II

Conformity

Conformity sounds bad, but it has a purpose. Our tendencies toward conformity are embedded in our Paleolithic brains, which keep groups together and coordinating smoothly. The surprising differences in what's normal between different groups manifest through hidden forces known as "social influence"—the ways that other people alter your thoughts and behavior. Chapter 5 will explore the light side of social influence: why we sometimes need to go along to get along. This leads us to the final condition embedded within group structure: "social norms." Chapters 6 and 7 will examine the dark side of our tendencies toward conformity—the times when we're subtly and not-so-subtly pushed to conform to the will of the collective. The structures from Section I that promote good cooperation are the same things that prevent these dysfunctions. But there are some principles that uniquely apply to avoiding dysfunctional conformity pressures, which you'll learn in Chapter 8.

CHAPTER 5

Go Along to Get Along

The Influence of the Many on the Few

After one of their early games, several of the younger players on the 2008 USA Men's Basketball Olympic team went out to celebrate a victory. They came back late from their revelry . . . or rather, very early the next morning. Shortly before five a.m., they were passing through the lobby of their hotel and bumped into teammate Kobe Bryant. Bryant had gone to bed early and was on his way to begin training. Bryant greeted his teammates cordially but with a hint of derision that changed everything.

Bryant was one of the Redeem Team's biggest assets, not only for his talent but also for his influence. Although they were young, his teammates were some of the most competitive people in the world. They worked hard—but Bryant's work ethic was legendary.

Now, standing face-to-face with Bryant as a teammate and a mentor, they felt that little hint of derision for what it was—peer pressure. Before long, the whole team was going to bed early and getting to the weight room by five a.m.

In the back of almost every self-improvement book is a caveat encouraging us to join a group in which good behavior is the norm, in which talent is honed on the whetting stone of dedication and perseverance. In *Atomic Habits*, James Clear tells us about the British Cycling team that dominated the 2008 and 2012 Olympics; the Polgar family, in which all three sisters grew up to be chess champions; and the MIT class of ten that spawned four astronauts. All these groups were essential to the extraordinary success of their members.

Whether it's your workplace, your school, a twelve-step group supporting one another through addiction, or an Olympic team, becoming a member of a group that is devoted to a cause changes your perspective on what counts as normal. And "normal" for each group is more different than you might think.

Social Norms

Social influence is a necessary part of group life. We get information from observing others' behavior. Our evolutionary programming encourages us to mimic the behavior of those we identify with—who we see as members of the same group. At an individual level, that helps us satisfy one of our biggest evolutionary imperatives: Don't get separated from the group! If you copy the herd, you'll end up in the same place everyone else is going.

Moving in the same direction isn't enough. We want synergy—

for our groups to dance to a hidden beat, able to anticipate each other's steps and adjust on the fly. All the examples of real team-work we've talked about—basketball teams, jazz ensembles, and project teams—require a deep understanding of "how things are done around here." And that deep understanding emerges be-cause we have a radar for the unwritten rules of social life that silently help a group stay together—**social norms**.

Social norms are the rules that govern how one behaves in a particular group. What's totally normal in one group may be for-bidden in another. Whether it's putting your phone away during a family meal, never clicking Reply All to a departmental email, or not dating your second cousin, a group's social norms deter-mine what we think, what we do, and who we do it with.

Within a group, situations also determine which norms apply. In most cultures, we can't shout as loud as possible near other people—unless we're at a concert or sporting event. We can't take off our clothes in public—unless we're in a locker room or at a swimming hole. Circumstances determine whether a behavior is appropriate or inappropriate.

When norms get passed down through generations, we call them traditions or rituals. At work, they might get formalized as policies or procedures. At a societal level, we agree to enforce some norms so strongly that we encode them as laws.

You can see social norms clearly when contrasting different cultures—in the foods, clothing, and little rituals of interaction. In many cases, norms align with the values and purpose of a group. A "no phones at dinner" norm in a family reflects the parents' value of attentive conversation. Many norms about dress and appearance have religious roots. Uniforms at work or school reflect a value for unity and discipline. Even norms for waiting in line (or queuing, the national pastime here in the UK) reflect values for equality, patience, and perseverance.

Norms also have specific task functions. In a jazz jam, norms keep the music listenable and the musicians coordinated with one another. The same is true at work. IDEO, for example, has norms for brainstorming plastered all over the walls, like, "Defer judgment," "Stay focused on the topic," and "Go for quantity." In the famous Shopping Cart Project mentioned in Chapter 3, IDEO team leader Peter Skillman declared that those who violated the brainstorming norms would suffer the indignity of a little bell ringing to signal their wrongness. "You'll get the bell," as he put it.

These aren't arbitrary norms. They were formulated not only to reinforce IDEO's values, but also to help with the specific task of group brainstorming. If you've ever been in a brainstorming session, you'll probably recognize the function of these norms right away. If we judge each idea as it's suggested, that will not only eat up time (leading to fewer ideas), but also make people fear being evaluated, so they'll be less willing to make suggestions. And getting off topic or talking over one another is self-evidently undesirable. The specific norms are even based on research that aids in generating creative ideas, like deferring judgment and going for quantity. Putting these norms up on the wall and making sure they're mentioned in media coverage are symbolic acts that send a message to both group members and outsiders about what is valued.

Norms are powerful, invisible influences on our behavior. They subtly shape what we do and what we don't do. What we openly discuss and what is off-limits. Who makes decisions for the group and how they do it. As organizational scientists and norms experts Kenneth Bettenhausen and J. Keith Murnighan put it, "Social norms are among the least visible and most powerful forms of social control over human action." (That doesn't mean that you, as an individual, can't influence social norms—we'll discuss that in detail in Chapter 8.)

Some norms don't have an obvious task function and seem unrelated to the group's values and purpose. For instance, in both countries that I've lived in (the US and the UK), shaking hands is the polite thing to do when you meet someone. I was taught to put out a firm, willing hand when introduced to a new person. Limp handshakes were frowned upon. And failing to offer a hand or take one when offered? That was unspeakably rude.

But if you go to another country, shaking hands isn't always the way to greet someone. People bow in Japan, press noses among the Māori people in New Zealand, or kiss on or near the cheeks in France. And during the COVID pandemic, many people gave up their physical-contact greeting rituals altogether but were no longer considered rude. Even within a country, how you greet someone tells them something about the groups you belong to (or aspire to) and your relationship with the other person—fist bumps, half hugs, or the TikTok dance of the day all convey different identities, relationships, and group memberships. The point is, while greeting people is universal, the precise form that greeting takes is specific to a group or circumstance—and a bit random.

This randomness has a hidden purpose. Norms help us identify fellow group members—you belong when you learn the secret handshake. Adherence to norms can include how you dress, your accent, or how you act. If you think like a prehistoric human, it's easy to see why groups often developed strong norms about clothing, hairstyles, makeup, and jewelry, which you can observe clearly and quickly from afar.

Norms about appearance helped our ancestors decide whether they wanted to approach or avoid a new person. In prehistoric times, when a person approached, you could assess whether the stranger was a viable cooperative partner. Knowing the proper greeting, along with a similar accent and other mannerisms, signaled the stranger came from a related group and was thus less likely to be a threat.

We make similar inferences today. Logically, we infer that those who know one proper way to behave also know other appropriate behaviors. Therefore, we think we're more likely to be able to cooperate effectively with them for work, friendship, or romance. Those dedicated enough to wear the right clothes—or more permanent markings like tattoos or piercings—could be reliably identified by both in-groups and out-groups. Adherence to norms marks you for friend and foe alike.

These symbolic norms do more than help us sort friend from foe; they also add predictability to interactions. When you meet someone, you shake hands and say something like, "Nice to meet you" (even if it isn't that nice). Those were decisions your brain didn't have to make. Social norms give your brain time off from figuring out what to do. Because we humans dislike uncertainty, we value anything that limits the little decisions and awkwardness pervading the social world. How do we politely end our conversation? How much do we tip? Knowing the norms means we don't have to make these decisions about how to behave. Meeting someone new, beginning and ending conversations, paying at a restaurant—these are all transitions in cooperative behaviors. Knowing how they'll unfold lubricates the gears.

As the all-knowing meme gods tell us, "Traditions are just peer pressure from dead people." That makes it sound like traditions and norms aren't useful. But these small, shared rituals provide information about our group memberships and help those who participate in them build affinity and trust. That makes social norms essential to effective cooperation—and the right norms are a great catalyst for synergy.

But where do they come from?

The Origins of Social Norms

Looking through the telescope, one saw a circle of deep blue, and the little round planet swimming in the field. It seemed such a little thing, so bright and small and still, faintly marked with transverse stripes, and slightly flattened from the perfect round. But so little it was, so silvery warm, a pin's head of light! It was as if it quivered a little, but really this was the telescope vibrating with the activity of the clockwork that kept the planet in view. As I watched, the little star seemed to grow larger and smaller, and to advance and recede, but that was simply that my eye was tired.

—*H. G. Wells,* The War of the Worlds, *1898*

When you look at the night sky, the stars deceive you. These ancient pin's heads of light traveled millions of miles to dance on our retinas. But is their dance the illusion that Wells believes?

Back in 1799, German polymath Alexander von Humboldt discovered "swinging stars," which he believed reflected the actual movement of heavenly bodies. It wasn't until 1857 that it was discovered that each person saw the movement of the same swinging star differently. In the darkness, our brains have a predictable problem: We perceive movement where there is none. Without any frame of reference, our visual system misfires and interprets eye movements and muscle fatigue as movements of the light. Stationary points of light seem to quiver, advance, or recede. The cause of many reports of UFOs, this visual illusion is known as the "autokinetic effect."

In 1935, legendary Turkish American social psychologist Muzafer Sherif (born Muzaffer Şerif Başoğlu) capitalized on the autokinetic effect to delve into the origins of social norms—and maybe even truth itself.

Born in 1906, Sherif lived among many groups with seemingly incompatible realities. His childhood was marked by wars between groups eager to establish their place in the ashes of the fallen Ottoman Empire. The expulsion and killing of one million Armenians, as well as thousands of Assyrian and Greek Orthodox Christians. The occupation of his town by the Allied forces during World War I. The clash between Turkish nationalists and Kurds, which continues to this day.

Sherif fled his home country, was eventually stripped of his citizenship, and became a stateless immigrant to the US. His early experiences fueled his fascination with group dynamics. As he put it:

> *As an adolescent with a great deal of curiosity about things, I saw the effects of war: families who lost their men and dislocations of human beings. I saw hunger. I saw people killed on my side of national affiliation; I saw people killed on the other side. In fact, it was a miracle that I was not killed . . . I was profoundly affected as a young boy when I witnessed the serious business of transaction between human groups. It influenced me deeply to see each group with a selfless degree of comradeship within its bounds and a correspondingly intense degree of animosity, destructiveness, and vindictiveness toward the detested outgroup—their behavior characterized by compassion and prejudice, heights of self-sacrifice and bestial destructiveness.*

Sherif realized that being a member of a group changed how people saw reality. Two groups can see the same event but believe wildly different things about it. Groups are a lens through which members view what is true.

He devised a study to show the role of groups in our perception of reality, using the autokinetic illusion as a tool. In his "autokinetic experiments," Sherif brought university students into his lab, armed with a primitive light projector, a timer, and a totally dark room. The task was for participants, randomly assigned to groups of three, to estimate something objective and verifiable: how many inches the light moved during several repeated trials. (The correct answer was, of course, zero, but the autokinetic effect made the light seem to dance.)

Many versions of the study exist, but I'll tell you about a particularly important one with two experimental conditions. In the first condition, study participants estimated how far the light moved on their own in the first trial but then in groups of three for subsequent trials. In the first independent trial, the three participants disagreed on how much the light moved; a typical group of three would have one member estimate a quarter inch and another eight inches. But as trials went on and members made their estimates as a group, their estimates converged, with most people trusting the group rather than their own perceptions.

In the second condition, participants made their first estimates in groups. Hearing other members' estimates had a profound effect—members' estimates clustered around whoever spoke first. Everyone was unsure how much the light was moving, so whatever the first person said seemed pretty good to everyone else. The most surprising thing happened in the final trial. Participants now made their estimates alone, free of the influence of the group. Yet the norm that had emerged remained—the individuals continued to follow the norm, even when the group was gone.

The autokinetic experiments have been replicated, challenged, and extended numerous times. In one variation, experimenters actually moved the light a set distance (two inches or eight inches) in the first trial and found that the norm persisted even months later when the light wasn't moving. Members could be replaced one at a time until the original group members were all gone, yet the initial norms continued to hold sway.

When a situation is new and uncertain, norms emerge quickly and most people fall in line rather than sticking up for their own (weakly held) points of view. In fact, many people adopt group norms so quickly, they don't even realize they changed their own views.

Tuckman got at least one thing right in his -orming model: In a group with no norms, we're all looking for information about what is appropriate. Do we make small talk or silently look at our phones before the meeting? Do we start on time or a little late? Like in the autokinetic experiments, whatever happens first has a disproportionate influence on what happens next. Where we sit, who speaks first, who never speaks—groups tend to follow these norms from the very beginning. In short, norms are sticky.

Although we're constantly in new groups in our daily lives, those groups are embedded within a network of larger groups. And large groups like nations and religions were originally separated enough that their norms hardened into unique traditions and rituals. Over days, years, or generations, members internalize the implied values of those norms. We don't just behave like fellow group members; we also think more like them. We know how to behave in each situation. We can differentiate fun from boring, important from trivial, or right from wrong. As Sherif had guessed, our groups define our truth. We develop a shared reality.

We need some conformity to cooperate. Having a shared reality helps us cooperate effectively, especially in a stable environment. We can predict other group members' behavior, infer their intentions, and understand new events similarly. Sometimes, that's as simple as adhering to social norms, which allows others to see you as a fellow group member and helps make your actions more predictable. Other times, it means going along with the views of others to keep group actions coordinated and the group together as a unit. As the old saying goes, you need to go along to get along.

With clear norms and a shared reality, communication gets easier and the chances of synergy go up. Norms make our fellow group members' behavior more predictable and understandable. They allow us to coordinate wordlessly, recognizing not only when the no-look pass is coming, but also getting ourselves in the position to make it in the first place.

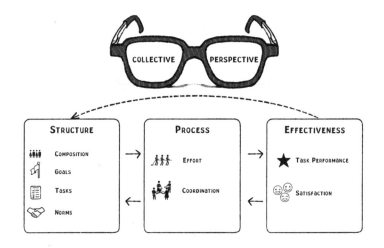

That's why norms are the fourth condition for promoting group effectiveness. They are part of the scaffolding that keeps group process humming along, the final ingredient of group structure. Some norms are changed by group process itself—like a game of telephone over time, the secret handshake morphs a bit into something different. Other norms are crystallized by their habitual repetition, making them more powerful than ever.

Norms Are Sticky

If you have an iPhone, there's a hidden lesson about norms in your general settings. In the Keyboard settings, if you choose English, you'll find several keyboard options, including the default QWERTY keyboard most people use. But you'll also find Dvorak.

The QWERTY keyboard wasn't designed to make it easy to find letters. The legend that the QWERTY layout minimized typewriter keys sticking by spacing apart common letters isn't true, and it doesn't make much sense if you think about it. In fact, the QWERTY configuration arose in response to telegraph operators' outdated Morse code habits. Through trial and error, QWERTY allowed early users who were accustomed to telegraphs to type faster and more accurately.

University of Washington professor August Dvorak thought there was a better way. In 1936, he created an alternative layout for letters and numbers that he claimed increased speed because it reduced finger motion. The main difference is that uncommon letters, like *Q*, *J*, *K*, and *X*, are in the bottom row, so most words require only the top two rows. And there's some reason to think he was right. In 1976, Barbara Blackburn earned the *Guinness World Records* "Fastest Typist" title—two hundred twelve words per minute—using the Dvorak layout.

You probably haven't ever used, or even seen, a telegraph. So why do most of us still use QWERTY? If the original reasons to use QWERTY are gone, why don't we all learn on the most efficient keyboard? Well, a lot of people have learned to type on these nonsense keyboards. It might be a little better for humanity if we changed them. But not better enough for any one person to relearn typing. Innovation researchers call this "path-dependence." Over time, other technologies, platforms, and users learn and make things that depend on the status quo.

So how did the little-used Dvorak system end up as an option on iPhones nearly ninety years later? Dvorak had a few loyal converts, including Apple cofounder Steve Wozniak. Given that the iPhone's keyboard layout is only digital, it cost Apple little to provide a Dvorak option.

But the funny thing is that Dvorak doesn't do you much good on an iPhone. It only has an advantage over QWERTY if you type with ten fingers, not two thumbs. It's really just about what you're used to—digital keyboard layout doesn't matter very much for speed.

Norms are the same. Like keyboard layouts and greeting rituals, most norms aren't good or bad. But they are comforting in their familiarity. Even if we were real anarchists who wanted to free ourselves of all social norms, we'd just develop new ones. Even being an anarchist requires conforming to norms of nonconformity! So group norms—and some peer pressure to conform—are inevitable.

Because norms are usually comforting and useful, many people shield them from change. As social science teaches us, the status quo has an inherent advantage over change in our minds. We have a soft spot for the familiar, so much so that it has its own name: "status quo bias." For the most part, people don't want to make changes unless there's a clearly better alternative or a big problem—and sometimes, they don't want to make changes even then. It's often more trouble to speak up in favor of change than it is to just go along with the crowd.

That makes norms really sticky. Some groups have norms permissive of being five minutes late or breaks that go on longer than planned. Most quickly develop norms about where people sit and who speaks first. None of these norms seems important enough to talk about. After all, we can't discuss every little thing, can we?

When most people follow norms, it is tough for any one individual to change them. Thus, like Isaac Newton's first law of motion, groups tend to be inertial—they follow similar interaction patterns across time until something big happens. We continue to follow the rules of social proof—that others' behavior is a good guide to our own. The desire for change is weaker than the cost of speaking up. Inertia keeps norms, rituals, and processes in place. Indeed, we go along to get along.

Although we often overlook them, social norms are a boon to humanity—we've managed to make the world safer and more prosperous largely through social norms toward prosociality. People are more virtuous when they treat others with kindness and generosity; they are more evil when they use violence or otherwise harm others. You can thank social norms for being able to walk around with far less fear of other humans than at almost any point in the past.

As time passes, these norms can drift away from their original functions. We participate in the little rituals of interaction without knowing why because it's just how things are done. At their worst, norms promote obedience without any benefit. That's scary. In our individualistic minds, it's sometimes so scary it becomes the protagonist in sci-fi horror.

CHAPTER 6

You Will Be Assimilated

The Dark Side of Conformity Pressures

For fans, *Star Trek* is a refreshing antidote to dystopian visions of the future like *Dune*, *Mad Max*, and *Black Mirror*—a techno-optimistic vision in which people's basic needs are met and we are free to explore space. That optimism has already led to changes in the real world: Google's search function was born out of its founders' desire to realize the near-omniscient *Star Trek* computer.

But people love *Star Trek*'s universe for more than its cool tech. The show also depicts a particularly effective collective—an extremely diverse society, composed of species from all over the universe. They're constantly learning from this diversity, adopting new technologies and ideas without that pesky in-group/out-group bias. There are no secrets or political games; they share all their knowledge and goods freely. Sounds like a recipe for synergy!

The only problem is that this effective collective is the villain. The Borg—the powerful group in question—are hell-bent on assimilation. They conquer other groups, using cybernetics to link them to a collective "hive mind," stripping them of their individuality. This allows the Borg to instantly share an assimilated individual's knowledge with the entire collective. They have the best weapons and technology, allowing them to dominate almost every new place they encounter. Great for the collective, but not so great for the individuals assimilated into it.

The Borg have an earthly analogue, even if it doesn't assimilate other species: ants. Ants have colonized almost every corner of the earth. They're the most numerous insects on the planet (scientists estimate there are twenty quadrillion of them) and collectively weigh about twelve megatons—more than all wild birds and mammals combined! From a strictly evolutionary perspective, ants have been around a lot longer than humans and have a good chance to outlast us.

Ants, humans, and the Borg have more in common than you might think. Harvard biologist Edward O. Wilson won two Pulitzer Prizes for his work comparing ant sociality with our own. Ants farm, build communities, and wage war. They communicate, take on differentiated roles, and help one another altruistically. The commonalities between humans and ants, Wilson argued, explain why the two species have outcompeted all others and become what he called "superorganisms."

Our individualistic brains find the idea of humanity as a superorganism, as cogs in a vast machine serving its own ends, to be repulsive. Science fiction is replete with stories of villainous hive-mind collectives intent on assimilating or destroying humanity. From the Borg to *The Matrix* to *Doctor Who*'s Ood, it's clear we have a deep-seated enmity toward single-minded collectives. Especially in the wake of the Cold War, the Western World feared that, if push came to shove, a well-organized collectivist society could defeat our more individualistic one.

We have an innate need for autonomy and individuality. The problem with superorganisms is that they resolve almost any conflict between individual and collective needs in favor of the collective.

In this chapter, we'll discuss the dark side of conformity—the times we act as if we have a hive mind in ways that invite process losses and destroy the potential for synergy. At worst, these forces combine to produce groups that mindlessly herd together, making catastrophic decisions and making members feel coerced and controlled.

More Vision Tests from Psychologists

Imagine you've signed up for a research study to help the noble enterprise of science (and you're being paid to do so). After arriving, you and seven strangers sit in a completely dark room for a vision test. It isn't a normal vision test, though. Instead of reading increasingly small letters off a chart, you and your compatriots are asked to match the length of a short line to one of three options, as in the image that follows.

95

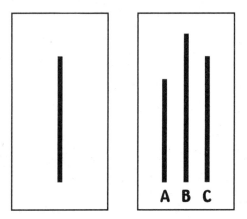

These researchers have a very odd way of testing vision—they ask each person to answer the question aloud. The first person responds that the line on the left is obviously the same as B. The second subject concurs. And down the line, all seven people before you confidently answer that B is the same length as the line on the left. You are the last to answer.

At this point, you're pretty confused. The answer is obviously C—isn't it?! But if seven other people unanimously and confidently said B, there must be some kind of optical illusion you're missing. And even if your instincts are correct, do you want to be the only one who says something different? And how is this supposed to test vision, anyway?

Social psychologist Solomon Asch ran this classic experiment in 1951 not to test vision, but to test conformity. The other seven people giving estimates were part of the research team (known as "confederates," but not the American Civil War kind). These confederates had preplanned to give a clearly wrong answer. And 76 percent of the actual research participants (like you) went along with the incorrect majority at least once, even if they privately disagreed.

Asch and other group dynamics researchers at the time were unpacking how so many "normal" people could have conformed to the will of Nazi Germany, going along with evil thoughts and deeds. They found that people distrust their own senses (at least publicly) when the group has expressed different opinions—people would say that green dots were blue, that short lines were long, and that still objects were moving if they heard others say so first. Sometimes they were suppressing their own views; sometimes they actually believed others' instead of the evidence of their own senses. These studies in conformity helped demonstrate that, when they feel uncertain, people often prefer to stay with the herd. They go along with the crowd—even when they think the crowd is wrong.

When we're unsure (or don't care very much), we like to blend in with the crowd. It's more trouble to argue to convince others than it is just to go along with it. Internally, the desire to belong makes us want to conform, to find commonality with those we identify with, so we copy them, often unconsciously. We seek common ground and look to other people for information on what is appropriate.

But sometimes, going along to get along leads to catastrophe.

Groupthink: When a Group of Smart Individuals Pressures One Another to Make Stupid Decisions

In the 1960s, John F. Kennedy and his advisers in government were the darlings of the Western world. Full of seemingly smart and charismatic young men (only men), they heralded a new, wiser age of governance that drove out the stale parochialism of the postwar era. But early in its tenure, the Kennedy administration made a shockingly foolish decision: It ordered the invasion of Cuba in hopes of triggering a popular uprising to take its communist leader, Fidel Castro, out of power—despite the recent popular uprising that put Castro *in* power in the first place.

To psychologist Irving Janis, it seemed like all the individuals involved must have gotten stupider from being in a group together. It seemed crazy that the highly educated Kennedy administration could decide to invade Cuba in the Bay of Pigs fiasco when it was so obvious that the invasion would fail. Which, of course, it did. Why didn't Kennedy's expert advisers speak up more strongly? Why didn't the rest of the group see the naysayers were clearly right? As Kennedy himself asked, "How could I have been so stupid?"

In analyzing this and other high-profile, avoidable political debacles, Janis took inspiration from *1984*, George Orwell's dystopian, yet prescient, novel in which authorities ruthlessly police citizens' thoughts. Janis proposed that group members analogously police each other's thoughts. His book *Groupthink* popularized the term, explaining how conformity pressures allow seemingly smart, capable groups of people to make spectacularly bad decisions.

Groupthink, along with its negative connotations, has held the popular imagination for a long time. It's one of the few terms from group dynamics research that has made its way into the popular lexicon. It's used to describe the errors of political leaders, sports teams, and businesses—a catchall for the wrongheaded decisions that seem easily predictable. For instance, government leaders across the world—from JFK to George W. Bush to former UK prime minister Boris Johnson—have been accused of groupthink when their decisions go awry. And it rings true to us because we've all gone along with a group and kept our doubts to ourselves or been carried away by others' convictions and enthusiasm toward a foolish end. Indeed, it is human nature to try to fit in with a group we identify with.

The idea of groupthink resonates for people because we all feel the subtle conformity pressures of group life every day. Imagine five friends are meeting for lunch. Someone starts off the conversation by saying, "I'm reading this wonderful new book about group dynamics!" The next speaker is probably going to agree or ask a question that implies agreement, like "Oh, what's it called?" If someone were to immediately chime in with, "That Colin Fisher book? I hated it," we'd probably find that person a bit unpleasant. These subtle norms toward agreement help us build rapport and shared identity—we look for common ground in most conversations. But these same norms allow similar information and views to dominate group discussions. Within groups, particularly those in which members share similar worldviews, getting contradictory perspectives and information out there takes effort.

Even when new information and perspectives manage to make it into conversation, people still need to interpret them. Unfortunately, that interpretation process is further biased by member preferences—our opinions, likes, and dislikes. We better remember information consistent with our preferences and forget or rationalize away information that's inconsistent with them. That's what social psychologists call "confirmation bias."

Confirmation bias stems from how our memory is organized: When we have a hypothesis, like "The death penalty helps deter crime," our brain starts marshaling arguments to support it. When confronted with new information—for instance, the many studies showing that the death penalty doesn't do much to deter crime—our brain doesn't listen. It's too busy preparing to convince others that we're correct. We thus end up overlooking information that contradicts our preferences and beliefs—our brains are a lot better at confirmation than disconfirmation. Evolutionarily, this isn't such a bad thing—we are actually right about most things; we correctly intuit that jumping out of a third-floor window is dangerous and things that smell bad usually taste bad. If every new piece of information made us reconsider our beliefs, we'd be paralyzed. But this confirmation bias isn't so great for making group decisions.

Taken together, these forces lead groups to "biased information processing," a phenomenon that compounds social influence pressures toward conformity. Group discussion is dominated by things we all know and agree on. The things we disagree with, we tend to overlook or forget. People who disagree stay quieter.

Through biased information processing, groups act as filters for information. When left unchecked, this leads groups to overlook crucial evidence, resulting in all kinds of spectacular failed decisions. The 1986 explosion of the *Challenger* space shuttle, Ford's disastrous release of the safety-challenged Pinto in 1971, and Coca-Cola's decision to change the flavor of Coke and release New Coke in 1985 have been linked to these problems.

What if you disagree with the crowd? If you are the person in Asch's study who knows C is the correct answer, after everyone else says B? If everyone else wants to go get pizza, but you just had pizza for lunch a few hours ago? It's an uncomfortable position— no one wants to be the only person who refuses to go to the new restaurant everyone else wants to try, or to argue against a new policy we think others favor. So we stuff our disagreement down deep. For now, belonging trumps getting our way. As Asch's studies found, we censor ourselves or convince ourselves that we're wrong to go along with what we imagine to be the will of the group.

This is the dark side of social influence. Conformity pressures us to repress our unique knowledge and perspectives, unconsciously prioritizing harmony and belonging over the task. We thus lose the benefits of diverse groups—and our chance at synergy. Groups become "echo chambers," where members share only information and ideas they think other members want to hear, not what will help them accomplish their goals.

Socialization

Famously, there was a moment leading up to the Bay of Pigs invasion when Harvard professor and JFK adviser Arthur Schlesinger Jr. brought up his reservations about the proposed invasion plan. But Robert Kennedy, the attorney general and John's brother, took Schlesinger aside. "You may be right and you may be wrong, but the President has made up his mind. Don't push it any further," Robert told Schlesinger. "Now is the time for everyone to help him all they can." Schlesinger said, "I didn't feel like we could speak up," later writing, "our meetings were taking place in a curious atmosphere of assumed consensus and not one spoke against it."

Peer pressure isn't just self-censorship and questioning your own judgment. Groups enforce conformity, censuring members who step out of line. That might be something as small as Robert Kennedy and Schlesinger's conversation, or even just Kobe Bryant's hint of derision for his teammates' staying out late.

When we're uncertain about whether we belong, we're on high alert for cues about whether we're getting approval from others. We interpret a look, or something someone didn't say, as signals that we're doing it wrong. This is our Paleolithic brain in action, protecting us from ostracism.

Conformity pressures are crystallized into formal, repeatable group processes through socialization, in which norms are taught to new group members. Conformity pressures can be coded into formal processes like orientations (or "inductions," as we say in the UK). Every university, job, sports team, and sorority has one. At one end of the spectrum, a new job might play a short video to welcome you to the company and direct you to the website for more information. At the other end of the spectrum, we have hazing, indoctrination, and abuse.

In 2017, Penn State student Timothy Piazza died at nineteen years old from injuries sustained during his "pledging" to a fraternity, leading to the biggest criminal trial against a fraternity or sorority in US history. According to media reports, after the fraternity encouraged absurd amounts of alcohol consumption, Piazza's blood was 40 percent alcohol—500 percent of the legal limit to drive. He injured himself falling down the stairs. When another fraternity member tried to call for medical assistance, three other members allegedly slammed him against the wall to prevent him from doing it.

Although over-the-top socialization processes seldom end in death, all kinds of groups are famous for them. Fraternities, sports teams, and military academies have "hell weeks" or "rush," replete with hazing both good-natured and abusive. Proponents believe pledging and hell weeks bring groups together, that they are shared traditions marking symbolic transitions to from nonmember to member. Critics worry that the power the group has over newcomers leads to cases like Piazza's all too often.

Most groups aren't so extreme but still subtly demand tolls from those seeking admission. These can be traditions like newcomers buying coffee or carrying luggage, or leaving individuality at the door with strict dress codes and uniforms. Like norms, a lot of these tolls are symbolic, ways through which prospective members demonstrate their willingness to join a group by subordinating their individuality to the group's authority. We say "Do this unpleasant or embarrassing thing!" and you do it.

Like other normative behavior, socialization processes are good when they're developmental—when they're aimed at helping new members prepare for group membership. But socialization can turn coercive, seeking obedience to the group and its leaders as its main purpose.

Is there a better parody of pointless bureaucracy than the movie *Office Space*? In it, the character Joanna (played by Jennifer Aniston) works at a fast casual restaurant called Chotchkie's Bar & Grill. One of the restaurants' policies is that staff wear "flair" on their uniform—decorative buttons to convey fun and personality to customers.

The policy is that all staff should wear a minimum of fifteen pieces of flair. Noticing that she has exactly fifteen, Joanna's manager asks what she thinks of people who only do the bare minimum. After all, Brian is wearing thirty-seven! After her third time being criticized for lack of flair, Joanna gives her boss the middle finger and walks out. The flair norm that may have started off as an opportunity for employees to personalize their uniforms becomes merely another avenue of control and conformity.

Amusingly, *Office Space*'s parody of corporate life influenced flair policies in the real world. *Office Space* creator Mike Judge noted he'd been told that TGI Fridays had discontinued its real-world policy of forcing waitstaff to wear buttons on their uniforms. "About four years after *Office Space* came out," Judge told Deadline.com, "TGI Fridays got rid of all that [button] flair, because people would come in and make cracks about it. One of my [colleagues] asked once at the restaurant why their flair was missing and they said they removed it because of that movie *Office Space*. So, maybe I made the world a better place."

We calcify norms and procedures into laws and institutions that are so decoupled from their original purpose that they aren't in anyone's interests; they're merely "flair" that's no longer allowing staff to express themselves, nor helping the group's image. It's just another thing that we do because that's what we've always done. But like Joanna's manager, group members still try to enforce it. Policies and procedures become ends in themselves, rather than means to an end.

Extreme rules and enforcement are common in the real world, too. There's a secondary school my kids applied to, not too far from my house, that gets extremely strong academic results. It also has extremely strong norms and policies. Students need to wear a jacket and tie every day—and receive a detention if they wear it improperly. There's a one-way walking system in the school. The penalty for deviation is again detention. And most outrageously, physical contact with other students inside school buildings is forbidden. Any touch leads to a detention.

We all could come up with some logic behind these rules and punishments. But the truth is, you could easily replace these rules with different ones because these rules aren't ends in themselves; they are meant to teach "discipline." In this case, *discipline* means conformity to the way school leaders think things ought to be done.

Another way groups enforce conformity is through formalizing their norms. *Law* is just a word for a nation's formalized norms—those it cares about enough to punish people for breaking. Although most groups don't have the power to imprison members who deviate from the norms, they can withhold rewards like bonuses or promotions at work or give punishments like detentions in school. Or simply ridicule or yell at nonconformers—after all, part of what we want from groups is a sense of belonging. Withholding that sense, or subtly threatening ostracism, is a form of punishment our Paleolithic brain takes very seriously.

Usually, formalized norms like rules, laws, and policies start from a good place like a desire to prevent costly mistakes or to capture "best practices." But too often, these end up like flair at Chotchkie's—rules that are enforced without purpose. Moreover, doing too much freezing of best practices into policies and procedures is a dangerous game. People and situations change, leaving outdated norms in their wake. Before long, the handbook is decoupled from its original purpose.

Using norms and socialization only for symbolic purposes is an example of "coercive control"—trying to alter people's behavior through monitoring, rewards, and punishment. And it is all too common in groups. In coercive systems, members focus on avoiding punishments. One of the biggest lessons from social psychology in the last fifty years is: Bad is stronger than good in the brain. We remember negative experiences about five times more strongly than equivalent good experiences. On average, people feel worse losing one hundred dollars than they feel good finding one hundred dollars. We've also learned that people who are working hard to avoid punishment aren't necessarily working hard to achieve goals.

In fact, avoiding punishment takes up so much of our mental energy that we struggle to learn or be creative. We don't take risks or try new things. Our brain prioritizes familiar pathways, making it hard to establish new neural connections. Therefore, the chances of synergy plummet in coercive groups.

And powerful groups have the ability to monitor our behavior like never before. Many of us carry listening devices with us wherever we go. Online, we publicly record data about our preferences and opinions that anyone can purchase. Many of us fear technology companies and governments are trying to control us (and a few worry that aliens or lizard people are doing the same). We might not need cybernetic brain implants to become the Borg.

The same systems that build a shared reality (and help us cooperate!) often suppress dissent and reject members who don't play by the rules. Those who step out of line too much get pushed down the hierarchy and have less influence. They often get pushed out.

Just like Chotchkie's Bar & Grill, groups lose when they become unattractive for those who don't want to follow every norm mindlessly. When a group becomes known for a certain way of doing things, people who might question that way don't seek admission.

Even if you do convince new and different people to join, socialization and coercive processes will make it hard to get the benefit of their new and different perspectives. Our Paleolithic brains convince us to mimic others until we think and act more like the people who are already there.

Over time, this forms a cycle in which groups become more and more concentrated versions of themselves. New members are those people for whom the group's reputation is most appealing. The group selects those who are most likely to conform to the group's norms. Through socialization, it begins to enforce those norms. Those who don't fit leave. The group's ethos hardens, becoming change resistant.

In 1961, famed social theorist Hannah Arendt watched the trial of Adolf Eichmann, one of the major architects of the Holocaust. Along with the rest of the world, Arendt, who was among those rescued by the ERC (see the Introduction), was shocked by Eichmann's apparent lack of dislike for Jewish people like her. Over and over, he argued that he shouldn't be held responsible for his actions during World War II because he was only "doing his job."

Arendt's book *Eichmann in Jerusalem* is best remembered for its poetic subtitle: *A Report on the Banality of Evil.* That phrase, "the banality of evil," captures the danger of conformity pressure. Arendt rightly saw beyond an individualistic perspective that would cast all Nazis as motivated by malice and hate. Rather, they were motivated by dedication to the group and a need to belong. As Arendt put it, "Going along with the rest and wanting to say 'we' were quite enough to make the greatest of all crimes possible."

Groups get a bad rap because of conformity pressure. But we need social influence and socialization because social norms are essential to building a shared reality and cooperating effectively. Yet these same processes that foster harmony, identity, and coordination are often turned toward stupidity and evil. Groups that mindlessly conform to tradition or coerce members into acceptance are among the most dangerous of forces—the Borg set on assimilating or destroying all in their path, brooking no dissent, difference, or individuality. We'll discuss how to avoid these issues in Chapter 8. But first, we need to look even deeper into how and why conformity can push groups to the extremes.

CHAPTER 7

Red and Blue

How Groups Get Polarized

On January 23, 2023, the official Twitter (now X) account for M&M's candy made an unusual announcement: "In the last year, we've made some changes to our beloved spokescandies. We weren't sure if anyone would even notice. And we definitely didn't think it would break the internet. But now we get it—even a candy's shoes can be polarizing."

A candy's shoes can be polarizing? What happened to elicit this befuddling message from a brand of button-shaped chocolates? "Spokescandies," anthropomorphic animated characters depicting individual M&M's with cartoon faces and rubbery limbs, have been longtime mascots for M&M's. Spokescandies have appeared in ads on the sides of buses, before movies, and on television. In addition to colorful personalities, each M&M was either stereotypically male or female. In the original depiction, the brown M&M wore high-heeled shoes, and the green wore go-go boots. In the new advertising campaign, their shoes were lower heels and sneakers.

Conservative media went crazy—hence, M&Ms' claim to breaking the internet. Last I checked, the original statement had been viewed more than fifty million times and retweeted more than twenty-six thousand times. For days, commentators on Fox News sought to link these changes in imaginary footwear to societal efforts to promote equality and inclusion. Infamous ex–Fox News commentator Tucker Carlson raged, "M&M's will not be satisfied until every last cartoon character is deeply unappealing and totally androgynous; until the moment you wouldn't want to have a drink with any one of them. That's the goal. When you're totally turned off, we've achieved equity. They win." Now, opinions on the fashion choices of animated sweets have become a proxy for political beliefs.

These kinds of "culture war" issues in politics are a fantastic example of "group polarization." Polarization has become another group-based bogeyman in the popular press—especially in the US. Everyone from politicians to celebrities to your black sheep cousin is expressing more and more extreme views on almost everything, from politics to spokescandy fashion. People are clustering to one extreme or the other, and there seems to be no way to cross these group-based divides.

Unfortunately, this isn't just a feeling. Researchers have found that polarization is increasing in the Western world. In the US, for example, members of each major political party disliked the other party almost twice as much in 2020 as they did in 1980. In the UK, Brexit exposed stark divides, with "Leavers" and "Remainers" drifting farther apart. You can't open a newspaper or go into a bookstore without seeing a lot of armchair theorizing on different groups' journey toward the extremes of every political and social issue until we all need to take a stand on M&M's sartorial choices.

Although polarization may be more obvious now (thanks, internet!), it isn't new. In 1961, graduate student James Stoner stumbled upon group polarization accidentally. Stoner believed that conformity pressure would make groups risk averse. Although every group might have a Tucker Carlson or two, Stoner believed that group interaction would bring collective decisions toward the middle, not the extremes. In his master's thesis, Stoner thus predicted that groups would make more cautious decisions than the average of individuals who composed the group.

But to everyone's surprise, he found the opposite: Group interaction seemed to pull the collective toward the extremes. Social psychologists replicated this effect hundreds of times, trying to figure out why. In one study, they found that, individually, college students were willing to bet $3.20 in today's money, given a one-in-ten chance of increasing their money tenfold. But after those same individuals discussed it in a group, they were now willing to bet $3.73—an increase of 17 percent.

Decades of research have shown that, despite their penchant for conformity, groups rarely regress toward the mean. Actually, it's partially because of pressures for conformity. When a group leans a certain direction, interacting with one another pushes them even farther in that direction. If the average of individual members' preferences initially favors risk, group interaction makes both individual views and group decisions even riskier. And if members initially favor caution, interaction makes them more cautious. Interaction tips groups not toward the middle but in the direction of the average of their initial preferences—toward one extreme or the other. In other words, it polarizes them.

As we learned in Chapter 5, when we identify with other people, we want to affiliate with them. We tend to focus our discussions on areas of agreement, which makes us feel closer to others and gives us a greater sense of belonging. After all, it's tough to build rapport without common ground! But if you're merely observing other group members talking, you're likely to hear information and arguments mostly from one perspective. Perhaps you learned something and were persuaded to change your own view. Once convinced, you chime in, too. Yes, M&M's have gone too far this time! Yes, the Cuban people just might greet us as liberators if we invade! Yes, NFTs (non-fungible tokens) sound like a good investment! If you disagree, you probably stay quiet. You don't want to stand out, like Schlesinger, who worried about becoming a "nuisance." This hopefully sounds a lot like the last chapter—the majority view gets more airtime. Those speaking believe the group is behind them and grow more confident in their position.

For the most part, "persuasive argument theory"—that polarization is mostly about people being logically convinced by the information available to them—isn't so terrible for humanity. From an evolutionary perspective, it might even be useful. Groups that move farther in the direction of members' initial preferences should be more decisive. Thus, prehistoric groups could quickly take advantage of opportunities and avoid threats. You hear that there's a new fishing hole that's unexplored? Let's get everyone motivated and grab some fish! A big storm is on the horizon? Take shelter in the caves!

But as I'm sure you guessed, polarization doesn't stop there and ends up doing more harm than good.

Love Has Won

On April 29, 2021, police found a nightmare in a house in Crestone, Colorado: a blue human corpse. The forty-five-year-old woman's body was wrapped in a sleeping bag adorned with fairy lights and glitter, with her mummified skin an otherworldly periwinkle. Although she'd been dead for several weeks, the seven adults and two children in the house never called a doctor as her health deteriorated, nor reported her death to police. In fact, they didn't believe she was really dead. They believed she'd "ascended to the fifth dimension."

Amy Carlson was the founder of Love Has Won, a cultlike spiritual group. Carlson claimed to be the 534th messiah reincarnate, known to her followers as "Mother God" or "Mom." Her past lives included Jesus, Cleopatra, and Marilyn Monroe. Her wisdom came from "the Galactics"—supernatural beings who walked the earth as celebrities like Robin Williams, Michael Jackson, and Donald Trump. The Galactics confided in her that our mundane reality—the "3D world," as they called it—was an illusion propagated by a shady cabal of liberals and Jews. QAnon conspiracy theorists had a lot of it right. Mother God would soon shatter that illusion for precisely 144,000 of Carlson's followers, who would then ascend with her to the fifth dimension.

At its peak, Love Has Won grew to about twenty members living together in remote cabins and RV parks, followed by thousands of internet fans. Carlson had begun posting YouTube videos in 2009, streaming her teachings into thousands of homes around the world. For those ready to abandon the false trappings of 3D (that is, real) medicine, she and her followers sold wellness products and spiritual healing. One of their bestsellers was "tinctures" of colloidal silver—particles of silver suspended in liquid.

Now, it's important to note that silver is toxic. It isn't a necessary mineral like iron or magnesium. Ingesting a lot of it can lead to liver failure. And a quirky side effect is that it turns your skin blue.

Carlson believed in the products she sold. She frequently felt ill, as she battled with addiction and anorexia. More and more, she took tinctures to heal herself. Likely because of silver poisoning, she eventually lost the use of her legs.

In her few lucid moments as her health deteriorated, Carlson expressed doubts about the story she'd concocted and whether she was truly Mother God. For the first time in nine years, she called her 3D family and asked them to come visit. She wrote to her three children, whom she'd abandoned, and told them she loved them. She asked to be taken to a hospital—a real one.

But her followers, on whom she now depended for everything, refused to take her. "Mom would never go to a 3D hospital," one said. Even when Carlson asked, her followers viewed her requests to see her family or go to a hospital as hallucinations—extensions of the painful process of "ascension."

As she got sicker, Carlson couldn't feed herself. Some of her followers upped her dosage. They competed to show their dedication by bringing her tincture after tincture. After all, what could be more important than healing Mother God? They explained her frailty as a sign that her ascension was near. Even after she died, they couldn't believe that any of it had been wrong. (Seven suspected members of Love Has Won were arrested at the house and charged with abusing a corpse and child abuse, but the charges were subsequently dropped.)

All groups—from cults to political parties to boards of directors—have a tendency toward polarization. The catalyst is homophily—the human tendency to flock toward our in-group. Only those who were open to Carlson's message joined Love Has Won. Like the members of Love Has Won, we are most likely to seek membership in groups where we see like-minded others—homophily influences where we go to college, what jobs we take, and what clubs we join.

In the US, political homophily is now driving geography. Race, religion, career choice, penchant for hiking—these were things that used to drive decisions about where to live. But people are now choosing where to live based on politics, moving to locations with higher concentrations of those with similar political beliefs. For instance, it has never been harder to find a Democrat in Corpus Christi, Texas (75 percent Republican), or a Republican in Baltimore, Maryland (87 percent Democrat)—the two most politically homogenous US cities in 2022. According to polarization expert and Stanford political scientist Shanto Iyengar, 85 percent of American married couples share a political party; that figure was 60 percent in 1965. That's part of what we mean when we say American society is increasingly politically polarized. The political and ideological boundaries are getting stronger because birds of a feather flock together.

According to Harvard social psychologist Amit Goldenberg, there's another force that explains polarization besides homophily, which he calls "acrophily." Acrophily is a love of the extreme. Unfortunately, we like to listen to people with slightly more extreme versions of our own views. In one study, Goldenberg and his colleagues asked both liberal and conservative Americans about their views on divisive political issues, like affirmative action, gun control, and remedies for police brutality. Participants were then shown six other people espousing a wide range of views on the topic. Just like on social media, participants chose which of these people to add to their network—who they wanted to hear more from in the future. Regardless of which side of the issue they were on, participants disproportionately chose people who agreed with them—but were just a bit more extreme in their views.

Acrophily explains why news and social media amplify extreme content. It's because we want it! We like consuming opinions we agree with but that are a little bit louder and stronger than our own. Those social media algorithms we complain about are structured to fit our brains.

This helps explain polarization in all kinds of groups, not just politics. Once we're embedded in a flock of our fellow group members, we start to give more credence to more extreme voices. Because more extreme views attract more attention, they gain influence. The Tucker Carlsons and Nigel Farages of the world have the microphone. They are confident, and they are loud. In groups of all kinds, the most passionate (and extreme) are likely to speak the most and try the hardest to persuade others. The rest listen.

We now get to the ultimate irony of polarization. Because extreme views gain influence, group members develop a warped sense of what is "normal" in the group. The increased attention and airtime given to extreme voices make other members falsely believe the loudest view is in the center. After all, it's the one you hear the most. It's like a group of kids egging each other on to ride their bikes down a dangerous hill, even when almost all of them don't want to. What are you, chicken?

Thus, most group members (and definitely members of other groups) overestimate how extreme the average member's views really are. People holding more extreme views are seen as more prototypical of the group. Because we identify with the group, we want to bring our own views into alignment with its norms. Over time, members' views shift gradually toward the poles because members think that view is normal for the group and, consciously or unconsciously, they want to fit in.

We can thus see how Love Has Won slipped away from reality. A group of people who were already predisposed to distrust institutions and society got together. They liked to listen to those a little louder and more confident in how screwed up the 3D world is and how plausible Mother God's promise was. Over time, what was "normal" got more and more extreme. One tincture every once in a while grew to ten a day. Until there was nowhere left to go.

Echo Chambers and What We Want to Hear

The internet was supposed to be the great equalizer that gave all humanity access to all the world's information. It connects people around the world, allowing them to communicate, regardless of distance. Shouldn't that provide the diversity of information and perspectives that ward off conformity and polarization?

Predictably, people seldom use the internet to change their minds. They use it for entertainment and belonging. We devote most of our attention to things that give us a momentary hit of dopamine. And our tastes are heavily influenced by our Paleolithic, tribal brains.

It's thus easy for the internet, and social media specifically, to become perfectly tailored echo chambers. The echo chamber is exacerbated because we get that hit of dopamine from a somewhat sinister side of ourselves: We love to hear people talking smack about out-groups. Social psychologists Steve Rathje, Jay Van Bavel, and Sander van der Linden analyzed 2.7 million posts on Facebook and Twitter (now X). Regardless of political affiliation, nothing predicted shares and retweets better than out-group hate. Recently, out-group hate has gotten even more popular than in-group love; that's a worrying new trend.

There are a couple reasons for this. As we've discussed, our brain has a bias toward bad over good; in the contest for attention, negative emotions are destined to win. Because expressing negative emotions about your own group might get you kicked out, you need a different target—other groups. Being outraged or angry about other groups strengthens in-group identity and pride. Casting your in-group as a victim also works extremely well. Posting words like *hate, attack, fight,* and *destroy* are among the most potent predictors of getting your message those sweet, sweet likes and shares.

Collectively, outrage about out-groups is a surefire way to get attention and approval from your own group. In his book *Outraged: Why We Fight about Morality and Politics*, social psychologist Kurt Gray explains why group-based outrage perpetually seems to be at the center of public discourse: "We have a harm-based moral mind," Gray writes. "Our evolutionary past makes us worry about harm, but people today disagree about which harms are most important or most real, creating moral outrage and political disagreement."

The second problem is that we get trapped in echo chambers or "information bubbles" where we're exclusively exposed to information from our fellow group members. Homophily tells us we are likely to hang out with people who think similarly to us. And by interacting, we'll think more and more similarly over time. The information and opinions we hear are thus likely to reinforce what we already think. If we fail to have a steady diet of diverse groups (or be a part of groups with diverse perspectives and information), we get exposed to more and more of the same. Our social life becomes dominated by people who generally agree with us. Our information sources become part of group identity—we seek information from organizations that cater to "us," not "them."

Luckily, people aren't stupid. Most of us realize that we can be fed misleading information by those with a political agenda. We distrust tabloids and explicitly political organizations, knowing they may be giving us a warped view of the world. After all, misinformation is as old as humanity. Before "fake news," there was propaganda and good old-fashioned lying.

But there's something different going on in the US today—a partisan gap in trust for news outlets. Historically, most people trusted "traditional" nonpartisan news and distrusted explicitly partisan ones and tabloids. But in the US now, there's a large divide for almost everything. There are very few information sources that people in both parties agree are trustworthy. In other words, your political group determines what information you believe more than ever before.

Polarization leads many groups to view information that doesn't originate within the group itself with suspicion. For Love Has Won adherents, doctors weren't reliable sources because they were prisoners of a 3D mindset. The same forces are at work in many groups. Truth becomes relative and a matter of identity, rather than verifiable reality. The group's shared reality becomes more idiosyncratic, drifting away from the rest of the world. Information that comes from outside can't penetrate this shared reality. Even perspectives that come from inside can be disregarded if they deviate too far from the group's identity and values—even when it comes from Mother God herself.

People intuitively know all this. The unscrupulous among us use this knowledge to gain influence and make their echo chambers ever more appealing and strong-walled. Once the walls are up, they can say almost anything.

Proving Your Worth

In groups where everyone leans a certain way, you get ahead by being a bit more extreme than the average person. M&M's were wrong to change. Boycott M&M's! Burn the M&M's you already bought at home—and your Mars bars, too, just in case!

This leads to a race to the poles within a group—the most enthusiastic members compete to prove what true believers they are. The most committed member of Love Has Won proves it by giving Mother God the most doses of colloidal silver. By cutting off their family forever instead of calling twice a year and going to holiday gatherings. By giving not just some, but all of their money to the cause. The enforcers of our groups' shared reality aren't randomly selected either. They're those who have risen to power on our penchant for extremes. The gatekeepers and their minions model and enforce a view more extreme than the average member, asking for thirty-eight pieces of flair, rather than the required fifteen.

Extreme polarization doesn't happen overnight. Pizzagate, QAnon, Love Has Won, and even the Bay of Pigs didn't happen all at once. They were gradual drifts that took place over months and years. Those who deviated from the orthodoxy were ridiculed by those in power. The more moderate members were pushed out or left, leaving behind a more extreme, homogenous group. People increasingly feel like their views on diverse issues like climate change policy, racial inequity, and spokescandy footwear are interdependent—one cannot be a "true" member of the group without conforming to the norm on all of them.

Extreme beliefs gradually become normalized, and those who

hold them rise to power. Without a significant minority with a countervailing view, members keep pushing one another closer and closer to the edge. Crazy political views, conspiracy theories, and cults all emerge through this process.

Highly polarized groups live and die through coercion. Punishments for deviation get more severe, yet increasing extremes make it harder for the group to attract new members. The group usually gets smaller and smaller.

But even small, extreme groups can do a lot of damage. Terrorist groups willing to give their lives to kill out-groups are seen by believers as martyrs for the cause. And groups on the receiving end of these increasingly extreme acts harden their opposing views in response. Both groups dehumanize the other, concluding, "We can't reason with them."

There are always a few extremists in a group who dehumanize out-groups. Letting their views go unchecked is dangerous. It leads to these views getting traction on both sides. That one person who says, "We can't reason with them" becomes a handful of people. Then views can spread.

So what can we do?

CHAPTER 8

The Idea Meritocracy

Winning the Battle Against the Dark Side of Conformity

Avoiding the dark side of conformity, like groupthink and polarization, is an ongoing battle against our Paleolithic brain that's seeking safety within the herd. As we've seen in the last two chapters, that prehistoric part of ourselves is a well-intentioned, but dangerous, foe.

In our battle, the Paleolithic brain's advantages are that it's quick and stealthy. It exerts its influence automatically, often without our conscious awareness. To defeat it, we need to get outside perspectives, foster a psychologically safe environment, and collect information systematically. When we do, we can keep conformity's dark side at bay. Unfortunately, the enemy is so stealthy, we often ignore it. We grow complacent and forget to deploy our arsenal.

I've never seen an organization prepare for the battle as thoroughly as Bridgewater Associates.

Bridgewater Associates is the world's largest private hedge fund and an unusual place to work. Your coworkers use tablets to grade you in real time. Are you being assertive, open-minded, and creative? You'll find out from the company's internal feedback tool, Dot Collector, which is constantly aggregating your coworkers' views of you. Are you arguing with a colleague about what was actually said in a meeting? Don't worry, you can literally check the tape: Every meeting is video-recorded and archived in a searchable database. All this effort is in service of what founder Ray Dalio calls "an idea meritocracy," which uses radical transparency to make sure everyone questions their own opinions and assumptions in making collective decisions.

But is this foolproof armor against conformity or a dystopian nightmare of a workplace? You can't argue with Bridgewater's results—it has outperformed most of its rivals and made obscene amounts of money. But it's also true that about a third of new employees leave in their first two years. And that's only the people who applied and were hired—it's not the place for everyone.

Bridgewater is clearly doing some things right in the fight against conformity. Leaders consistently ask for everyone's input—and don't start the discussion by sharing their own opinions. Bridgewater's evaluation processes demand that people share their ideas, information, and perspectives. And Dalio constantly preaches that he doesn't have all the answers and expects everyone to contribute.

Bridgewater's approach to fighting conformity is a bit different than most people's go-to: the devil's advocate. A devil's advocate argues for a contrary position, ostensibly to help expose potential flaws in reasoning for the dominant position. Research shows devil's advocacy is better than nothing—by calling explicit attention to conformity pressure, almost any intervention will help a bit.

But devil's advocacy is an imperfect weapon because it contains part of the problem: advocacy. Advocacy is usually a step in the wrong direction, especially early in a group discussion. The alternative is to approach group discussions as shared problem-solving. We should think like detectives or, as Adam Grant advises us, like scientists (not that we, as social scientists, are biased or anything). Scientists may have hypotheses, but they collect evidence to test them and update their views as new evidence comes in. Good scientists also search for information that contradicts their hypotheses to make sure they can withstand scrutiny. And if the evidence fails to support their view, a good scientist will think again.

Groups seeking to avoid conformity's dark side should do the same. We're all on the same team, trying to discover a way forward together. If members have opposing views, there's probably a reason; we'll learn something if we try to understand those reasons. When there's disagreement, members should ask: "Why did you think that? What led you to that view?" Don't fall victim to the conversational norm of agreement cascades, where we all pile on information and opinions in the same direction.

Think about how the Bay of Pigs might have unfolded differently if someone had followed up the "Cuban people will greet us as liberators" claim with some of these kinds of questions. The discussion might have taken a very different turn if everyone who had doubts had been invited to express them.

If fact, that's what Kennedy learned from the Bay of Pigs fiasco—that we need to run group discussions differently. During the Cuban Missile Crisis, the world teetered on the brink of nuclear war. The Soviet Union had moved ballistic missiles into Cuba, a mere ninety miles from Florida. How should the US respond?

Kennedy and his team had learned from their mistakes during the Bay of Pigs fiasco. They proposed and developed a wide array of possible responses without endorsing any one of them. Instead of a discussion that was either yes or no to invasion, like the last time, the pros and cons were weighed for each option.

They also were more careful to consider the perspectives of other groups. During the Bay of Pigs, Kennedy's advisers relied heavily on the opinions of Cuban immigrants—who had left Cuba because they disliked Castro. The view of the US as liberators came from them. Few of Kennedy's advisers considered that the Cubans who left might feel differently than those who stayed. But during the Cuban Missile Crisis, JFK's team focused on understanding the motives of Cuba and the Soviet Union.

There's some good stuff there. Devil's advocacy often positions decisions in terms of two options and asks members to argue for or against, trying to win people to their side. But group decisions shouldn't be a contest. And that's where leadership like Dalio's or Kennedy's can help. Research by London Business School professor Randall Peterson shows that groups make better decisions when leaders direct "how," not "what." Effective group leaders orchestrate the process of decision-making. They require groups to seek out all the information before trying to make sense of it. The best leaders also avoid advocating for specific options.

That way, members don't try to mimic or suck up to the leader by choosing their preferred option—they instead gain favor by following the process.

This is an exception to General Patton's maxim about never telling people how to do their jobs from Chapter 3. Leaders can and should direct information-sharing and decision-making processes. We all know that group discussions and decisions often seem chaotic and inefficient, so people generally appreciate leaders bringing a bit of structure to them. But don't go around telling people how to do their jobs the rest of the time unless they want your help.

Fortifying Your Lines

For decades, researchers tried to stave off dysfunctional conformity by changing things inside groups—they experimented with devil's advocacy, complex decision-making techniques like the Delphi method (with its multiple rounds of expert forecasting and updating), and many others.

MIT professor Deborah Ancona realized, however, that research was overlooking an equally important battlefield—what lay beyond the groups' boundaries. Ancona and her colleagues discovered that the most innovative and effective teams aren't solely focused on the challenges they face internally, like warding off conformity pressures. Instead, they look outward. Groups that look outward adapt faster to an ever-changing world.

"Boundary-spanning" groups, as Ancona called them, can have a lot of advantages if they play their cards right. Most groups—your work team, nuclear family, and friends—are part of broader networks of other groups. And diverse teams tend to be connected to a more diverse array of other groups.

That positions many boundary-spanning group members as "brokers" who connect two parties that aren't otherwise connected. Brokers offer what organizational sociologist Ronald Burt calls a "vision advantage": They have access to the rare combination of different groups' shared realities. Take IDEO, for instance. It has worked for hundreds of clients across dozens of industries. It has designed everything from Oral-B toothbrushes to jet engines to the mechanical whale from the movie *Free Willy*. And working with all these different clients gives the company the ability to take ideas from one project and apply them to totally different ones. The diversity of its social connections helps fuel its creativity.

Diverse groups are thus well equipped to ward off dysfunctional conformity pressure because they're more likely to contain a variety perspectives and information. That means members have more opportunity to learn from one another—and less chance of starting off with homogenous opinions that lead to polarization. Groups with deep-level diversity usually have a lot of opportunities for boundary-spanning and brokerage because those differences in perspective come from outside the group. All that's left is to make sure groups take advantage of it.

Probably the most famous example a group composed to ward off conformity pressure was put together by Abraham Lincoln, who famously assembled a "Team of Rivals" to serve as his advisers. As historian Doris Kearns Goodwin documented, Lincoln was determined to recruit the most capable candidates, even if they disagreed with him and each other. So he recruited his opponents from the presidential race into his cabinet, where they disagreed with him on everything from slavery to immigration.

After the Bay of Pigs fiasco, John F. Kennedy did the same, shuffling his cabinet and populating it with a more diverse array of advisers. Perhaps more importantly, he revamped the administration's decision-making process to allow discussion that welcomed dissent.

Research suggests that Lincoln and Kennedy were on the right track. In their studies of norm formation, organizational scientists Kenneth Bettenhausen and J. Keith Murnighan found that when group members have similar experiences prior to interaction, they adopt norms thoughtlessly. When they have diverse experiences, they're more likely to discuss and negotiate their norms. That doesn't always improve the norms, but it's better than when we mindlessly proceed based on habit or the way things have always been done.

But as we learned in Chapters 6 and 7, diversity of perspective doesn't always last forever in groups. Natural pressure to collaborate and affiliate means groups will develop more of a shared reality and get exposed to similar information and perspectives over time. That's just a consequence of being a part of the same group.

That's why newcomers are essential in the fight against conformity. New group members aren't just newbies to indoctrinate; they are great opportunities to learn. The Emergency Rescue

Committee (see the Introduction) didn't try to simply indoctri-nate new members into the way things were done; they actively recruited members with useful new information and skills. And they learned from them. The best groups do the same.

Even if you don't have the power to assemble your own team of rivals, you can still do your part in fighting off conformity and polarization. First, you can think like a broker. I'll bet you are a member of at least two groups that don't know each other. That positions you to offer both groups a different perspective. To take ideas from one group to another. To connect people from differ-ent worlds who might otherwise stay separate. Making sure that you step outside one group's reality and learn about another one is a healthy inoculation against conformity pressures. Second, you can go out and join new kinds of groups. Take a class on street dance. Join a band or choir—even if you don't (yet) have much musical know-how. Volunteer for a cause that you care about. In doing so, you are giving yourself a vision advantage and inoculating yourself against conformity's dark side.

The Mystery of the Adverse Drug Events

Back in the 1990s, Harvard Business School professor Amy Ed-mondson was a doctoral student, working under the guidance of groups guru Richard Hackman. Edmondson was studying nurs-ing teams that were charged with administering medications to patients in hospitals. The hospital was interested in using Hack-man's theories to reduce "adverse drug events"—harms patients suffered from medications the nursing teams administered. At the time, adverse drug events were also the hospital's main measure of nursing team performance.

When she analyzed data on team effectiveness, Edmondson discovered something alarming: The teams with the best conditions, who should be the most effective, according to Hackman's theory, were reporting the most adverse drug events. In other words, the well-structured teams seemed to be performing the worst.

I've told thousands of students about this finding in my classes. "How could this be?" I ask. "The well-structured teams were overconfident," some students suggest. "They grew complacent." "They took more risks." "They were more concerned with getting along than getting it right."

But these aren't the correct explanations.

After a while, someone suggests the correct answer: The hospital's performance metric was flawed. Well-structured teams didn't *make* more mistakes; they *reported* more mistakes. The poorly structured teams were probably making more mistakes but didn't report them.

In her interviews with nurses, Edmondson found evidence for this hypothesis, which has since been supported by oodles of research. In well-structured teams, nurses talked openly about their mistakes, with everyone contributing and trying to improve their performance. As a nurse on one of these teams told Edmondson, "Mistakes are serious because of the toxicity of the drugs [we use]—so you're never afraid to tell the Nurse Manager."

But in poorly structured teams, speaking up wasn't the norm. A nurse on a different team in the same hospital said, "You get put on trial. People get blamed for mistakes . . . you don't want to have made one."

The contrast is clear. In one team, it was normal for everyone to discuss their errors. In teams like this, members tend to share their knowledge, suggest ideas, and ask questions. In the other team, people kept their ideas to themselves because they knew they'd be blamed for mistakes and ridiculed for suggestions.

The foundation of avoiding conformity's dark side is what Edmondson calls **psychological safety**—the shared sense that members can admit mistakes, suggest new ideas, and ask questions without fear. In a psychologically safe environment, people aren't so worried that the group will ostracize them if they say something people disagree with or admit they aren't perfect. And along with the four elements of structure, psychological safety is the fifth essential condition for truly effective collectives.

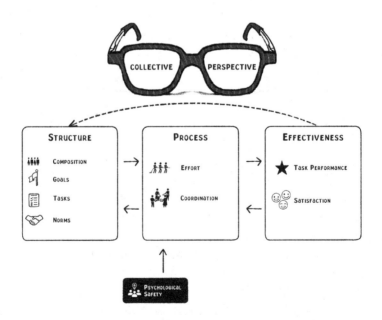

Psychological safety isn't an individual feeling. The same person can behave wildly differently in two different groups. Think about your own experiences. If you recall some of the most effective and least effective groups you've been a part of, it's likely that they differ in psychological safety. Among the best groups, you know it's okay to voice your frustrations, call attention to things that aren't going well, or ask for help when you need it. In the worst groups, you hesitate to speak up or ask questions, knowing there's a risk you'll be made to feel small when you do.

Psychological safety allows groups to develop norms and behaviors that keep conformity pressures at bay. A key predictive factor of team effectiveness are norms about how much everyone speaks. Carnegie Mellon University professor Anita Woolley and her colleagues found that groups with roughly equal speaking time perform better across a variety of tasks. Norms encouraging everyone to weigh in equally appear to help. Other norms, like quickly responding to messages, such that communication is "bursty"—meaning that groups cluster their communication closely in time—also appear helpful.

The main misunderstanding I encounter when teaching about psychological safety is that it's comfortable, like a warm bath. A group with psychological safety should be harmonious, right? But it's often the reverse, where decorum is the enemy. A psychologically safe group can sometimes look combative, with members constantly poking at the status quo. What's working? What's not? Why do we do it this way? Are there alternatives we aren't considering? It's a group that will openly disagree—because members have developed the skill and trust to do it effectively. They can tell one another when it's time to stop disagreeing and get on the same page, too.

Poking at the status quo can be uncomfortable and threatening for those charged with maintaining it. That's what gives leaders and members the incentive to snap in irritation when someone makes one too many suggestions or asks a question you thought you'd answered. But remember, bad is stronger than good in psychology. That little snap, like Kobe Bryant's hint of derision, is four or five times more memorable than all the praise you might give that same person. Psychological safety is fragile because we're so sensitive to ostracism. Our Paleolithic brain fears that ridicule is a precursor to being kicked out of the group. So even minor threats to our sense of belonging lead us to swallow our ideas and questions.

Psychological safety is most important when we're trying something new—when we need to learn and be creative. But every group is trying something at least a little new because today is different from yesterday. And so there's novelty, discovery, and learning in every moment of group interaction, making a culture of psychological safety one of the most important things for a group to nurture. (We'll come back to how to do this in a minute.)

Pro-Communication Norms Like Voice and Listening

If we think all the way back to the ERC, you might remember Albert Hirschman, the young economist who helped get refugees like Hannah Arendt across the mountains. Like Arendt,

Hirschman went on to a celebrated academic career. Most of his work on political economics wasn't directly related to power and group dynamics—he didn't follow Arendt's or Sherif's path. One exception, though, was his masterpiece, *Exit, Voice, and Loyalty.*

Hirschman posited that when members of a group see a problem, they have two options: They can either speak up (voice), or they can leave the group (exit). Back in Germany, Hannah Arendt had begun by speaking up to try to halt the country's slide into a bigoted, authoritarian Nazi state, but eventually she decided the situation was untenable and she needed to leave.

We all face similar decisions on a smaller scale. No group is perfect, and there are always things that need changing. Our job is to speak up when we see the need for change and to encourage others to do the same—especially the less powerful. But there is always a cost-benefit analysis to speaking up. Is the time we'll spend discussing this issue time well spent? How much do I care about this issue—or this group? If I'm the one to speak up, will I be put in charge of fixing the problem? Maybe it's better to stay quiet.

Even though I teach this stuff, I stay quiet more often than I speak up in many groups at work. Universities are run mostly by faculty. If I voice an issue or suggest a new initiative, the chances I'll be expected to lead the change effort are high. That means extra work for me. And if I say something is a problem (like my many tirades against long lectures and exams, which I believe are in Edward O. Wilson's category of "medieval institutions"), I often alienate my colleagues who don't agree. The deck is stacked against speaking up.

That's why groups like Bridgewater Associates and Edmondson's nursing teams need to praise those who speak up and create norms and structures to enable it.

But to make such a system work, leaders of groups need another critical skill: listening. As my research with Simon Fraser University professor Jeffrey Yip suggests, real listening means the speaker feels understood in meaning and intent. If members speak up but don't feel heard, they'll eventually stop speaking up. And if they feel like they aren't understood, their sense of belonging and loyalty to the group will wane. If that happens too often, the group begins to disintegrate.

The Wisdom of Crowds

Another way to fight conformity is for your group to interact less—or rather, more strategically. And the way we can do that is by aggregating members' information, preferences, and opinions without interacting. Everything from sports-betting markets to political forecasts are more accurate when they average across many independent opinions. Research shows that methods that do this are surprisingly effective, leading to an interesting phenomenon: the wisdom of crowds.

One area that benefits from the wisdom of crowds is predictions. Research has consistently found that when predicting things like how many jelly beans are in a jar, how the stock market will do next year, or who will win an election, crowds (that is, not-so-groupy groups with little to no interdependence or meaningful interaction) often outperform even the most talented individual prognosticators. That is to say that averaging a bunch of independent judgments is a pretty good bet. That's because independent judgments can't fall victim to agreement cascades or herding. We can't conform if we don't know what other people are saying.

Crowds outperform individuals and interacting groups when judgments are independent, but they fall victim to social influence once they see the judgments of others. So the stock market, political polling, or sports betting might be valuable for a while, but they can also fall victim to bias. Moreover, the wisdom of crowds is most effective with well-defined problems, like how many jelly beans are in the jar, but not so much for creative work or goals we haven't yet determined.

The problem is that, once we see other people's judgments, the crowds get less wise and turn to madness just as often as wisdom. Crowds become mobs. Economists refer to this as "herding," when investors follow one another, assuming that the crowd must be onto something. Efficient markets become faddish bubbles. Depending on what century you're from, tulips, Beanie Babies, or NFTs might be irrationally overpriced by people jumping on the bandwagon.

That's why information systems and the process by which individual judgments are collected, stored, and aggregated are so important. At Bridgewater, Ray Dalio knew that attempts to harness collective wisdom require systems to store and organize information. That's why Bridgewater created Dot Collector—the system that collected everyone's opinions and recorded every meeting—to gather the dots for people to connect. People are incredibly lazy about looking for information. Anything that decreases friction in finding out what we need to know is good. Groups with shared stores of information and norms about how to use them are at a big advantage.

A Quick Guide to Effective Dissent

My colleagues who teach about groups and teams often show students the 1957 movie *12 Angry Men*. This movie depicts a jury deliberating about the murder of an abusive father by his teenage son. Of the twelve jury members, eleven initially vote to convict, but Juror 8, played by Henry Fonda, argues for the defendant's innocence. Spoilers, but during the course of the movie, Juror 8 convinces all eleven jurors to switch their positions and vote to acquit.

I don't show this example in class because this situation is nearly impossible: Conformity pressures are too strong for a minority of one to overcome a determined majority of eleven. Thankfully, even if we think we're alone in our view, we may not be. As we discussed in Chapter 6, we tend to overestimate the size of majority positions. If we privately disagree with the majority, chances are that someone else does, too. Statistically, if we assume that information is randomly distributed among people, but there's an objectively "correct" decision, it is unlikely that there could be an overwhelming majority that is incorrect. (Although Galileo and others would like to point out that it does happen.)

If you're in the minority trying to influence a majority, you have two options for expressing your position. One is to be a loyal member of the group in all other respects so you earn what social psychologist Edwin Hollander calls "idiosyncrasy credits." Loyal group members get an occasional pass to deviate from a few norms or disagree with the majority. As long as you aren't violating the most sacrosanct norms of the group, you're likely to be taken seriously when you dissent.

Idiosyncrasy credits allow an individual to deviate within a group, but they only translate into changing other group members' minds when they're used by those in power to advocate for change. Unfortunately, this isn't as common as we'd like. We all think "I'll do things differently" when we gain power and influence. But our time in a group changes us. By the time we get near the top, we understand why we do things the way we do—and we need to pick our battles in where to advocate for change. Silent warriors for change who pledge to do things differently after they've paid their dues are rare.

The other approach is to openly challenge the status quo or majority—and to do so respectfully but consistently. Over time, the group accepts that you're that person who thinks that thing no one else does.

Take longtime US senator Bernie Sanders. Sanders has long been a thorn in the side of Democrats. He refused to identify with the party, labeling his party affiliation as "Independent." He argued for positions that few others would. He was the lone holdout from the Democratic Caucus many times. His dissent was so consistent and predictable that comedians around the world parodied his New York–accented stump speech of "The one percent of the one percent . . ."

Yet Sanders ran for the party's nomination for president of

the United States and got closer than anyone predicted—twice. And he's a classic version of what sociologist Dan Forsyth calls a "tolerated deviant"—a member of the group from whom dissent is expected and accepted.

The secret to becoming a tolerated deviant is to be consistent in your position over time. Research has found that we respect people who espouse consistent values and positions but are suspicious of the motives of those who change their views too often. Like Sanders and Juror 8, consistency allows dissenters to win respect from other members.

But tolerated deviants can't dissent on every issue—if you disagree with the group about everything, why are you in the group? Effective dissenters support the group's core values and norms and use their dissent strategically. Sanders caucused with Democrats for years and voted with the party the vast majority of the time.

And it is hard to influence the majority without a friend. Lone dissenters, like Juror 8, have a poor track record. Research tells us that you need at least one fellow dissenter to have a decent chance to convert a majority. Moreover, like Bernie Sanders, you need to dissent consistently and visibly. Whenever your issue comes up, you have to voice your position and make sure others are aware of your dissent. Although converting the majority is still an uphill battle, you have a chance if there's a consistent, visible subgroup of dissenters.

Sanders's relative success in building a minority coalition and extracting policy concessions from the majority is unusual in the competitive world of politics. And that's because minority influence is difficult in the real world. When groups are stressed—by time pressure, competition, or threat—tolerance for dissent goes down. Wars, alien invasions, and deadlines all increase conformity pressure and our desire to see unity in our groups.

Conclusion: Decisions Are Processes, Not Events

Have conformity pressures turned us into sheeple in need of waking up? Although the conspiracy theory flavor to "Wake up, sheeple!" has turned it into a meme, there's some truth to the idea that we need regular wake-up calls to remind us to fight our conformity-loving brain.

Being accepted within the herd was a matter of life and death for our ancestors, but we can handle a bit more disagreement now. A lot of writers (including me?) may overstate some of the power of conformity pressure. In Asch's study, groups researchers throw around the statistic that 76 percent conformed by stating at least one wrong line length. But if you count each trial individually, participants still gave the correct answer 64 percent of the time in the face of unanimous opposition. And nearly one out of every four participants never went along with the crowd, voicing the opinion that they felt was right. That's double the proportion that always went along with the crowd. The optimistic take on these findings is that, most of the time, someone will speak up when the group is wrong.

So the trick is to make sure we're listening and that we're using dissent productively. Social psychologist Charlan Nemeth found that groups that make good use of dissent are more creative and do better in complex decisions—even when the dissenter is wrong. Hearing another point of view breaks conformity's spell—the illusion that no one thinks differently is shattered. And that's often enough to turn our critical thinking back on and give us the confidence to speak up.

Fostering psychological safety and productive dissent, while maintaining the bonds that hold us together, is crucial. And very, very difficult. There isn't one weird trick that allows you to do this. Instead, like Bridgewater Associates, it is about putting in the work every day. Every meeting, every charged family dinner, is a process. It's an ongoing battle within ourselves that separates us from cults, ants, and the Borg.

GROUP THOUGHTS ON CONFORMITY

Thought 1: Check on Your Norms and Shared Reality at Beginnings, Middles, and Ends of Tasks

Problem: Conformity pressures make it difficult to establish healthy norms. They also can lead your groups' shared reality to fall out of step with the outside world.

Solution: Have explicit discussions about the alignment between your groups' values, goals, and norms at regular intervals. Based on Connie Gersick's groundbreaking work on group development, I recommend three moments to schedule these discussions: beginnings, midpoints, and endings. At the launch of a new task, the leader or facilitator should state their understanding of the group's values and main goal (inviting questions or alternative views). If groups do this regularly, that exercise is mostly insurance against misalignment. The group should then analyze the main tasks that need to be done and discuss what norms would support them. (More on that below.)

Assuming you set SMART goals, you have a clear deadline for your task. Halfway between launch and the deadline, schedule a quick group check-in about how your norms and strategies are working—are we sticking to them? Do they need changing? The Start-Stop-Continue rubric is a good heuristic for these meetings. (I start with Continue so we talk about what we are doing well first.)

Immediately after the task is done, have a debrief, where you reflect on the same ideas but with a broader future in mind. It is tough to ask a group for meaningful reflection when heat from the deadline is on, so the end is the best time.

Thought 2: Approach Group Decisions Like You Are Solving a Problem Together, Searching for Unique Information and Perspectives

Problem: Group discussions are biased against unique information and minority perspectives. If a group is just going to discuss things everyone already thinks, what good is a group discussion? Group decisions only have the potential for synergy when they focus on stuff some people don't know. Also, too many people treat group decisions like a contest, where it's your preference versus mine.

Solution: Group decisions should be us versus the problem. As I mentioned, simple reminders help us take this view. Here's an example: "Let's make sure we approach this decision like collective problem-solving. We all want to get these elephants out of the building and into the hot-air balloons. We all want the best for our group, The Banana Squad, even if we might have different views on the best way to do it. Please focus on sharing all the relevant information before we start advocating for any particular course of action. And we may need to take time to brainstorm as many potential ways as we can before we reach any decision on how to move these elephants." My own research suggests that the best time to say this is just after interaction begins. We've already talked about asking for different perspectives and counterfactual information, so keep doing that, too. You can substitute the part about elephants and hot-air balloons, of course, but for it to work, you do have to call your group The Banana Squad.

Thought 3: Keep Communication Channels Open and Information Storage Obvious

Problem: Most groups don't have Bridgewater Associates' Dot Collector. At best, they have a messy shared drive, where it isn't clear which documents are up-to-date or whether they are all there. Most group members communicate by email and text, but some chat in the halls or on the phone. When you actually need information, it isn't clear where it is or who to ask.

Solution: I can't even tell you how many problems in new groups could be avoided with a discussion of communication and information storage norms—this is in the top five for easy fixes that most groups still don't do. The basic questions are: How will we communicate? How quickly should we expect a response? (And how long until we worry?) How will we store information where everyone has access to it and can find what they need?

For instance, when I'm leading a group, I share that I communicate best via email and try to reply within two working days for active collaborations. But I struggle with very long emails and email threads with tons of responses—and research suggests I'm not alone in missing things in such situations. If you need my attention quickly, WhatsApp is your best strategy. (But if I wake up to one hundred messages from the group, I might mute it.) I'm a stickler for organized shared folders and file names (version, date, editor in the file name, please). I assiduously archive documents that aren't the most current version. My groups have dedicated notetakers for meetings who send around the summaries and add them to the shared drive. The point isn't whether these are the best norms, but that this is the level of detail at which to have the conversation.

Thought 4: Build a Culture of Psychological Safety

Problem: Psychological safety is fragile. Our default with strangers is to approach others with caution, wary of revealing potential flaws. Our brain spotlights negative emotions, like when we feel inadequate or singled out. You have to go out of your way to establish psychological safety and keep it going when the pressure is on.

Solution: Honestly, you should probably read Amy Edmondson's voluminous work on this subject. Here are a few of her tips to get you started:

(1) *Frame the work accurately.* As Albert Einstein reportedly said, "Anyone who's never made a mistake has never tried anything new." If we're Einstein or IDEO, for whom trying

new things is essential, we're going to have to make some mistakes along the way. But if work is routine and errors are life-and-death, as for safety officers at a nuclear power plant, minimizing mistakes is crucial. So we need to agree: Is this a creative or learning task, where we'll need enlightened trial and error? Or is it a routine, high-reliability task, where there's no room for mistakes?

(2) *Ask for input.* If you want people to ask questions, discuss errors, and speak up when they have an idea to improve things, ask them to. No, not like that—like you really mean it. Otherwise, you are doomed to communing with the Galactics and drinking tinctures.

(3) *Take interpersonal risks.* Trusting others is a paradox—you need trust to take risks, but you need to take risks to build trust. So go first! Admit your mistakes and ask your questions that you worry are dumb. It helps to have a few idiosyncrasy credits banked, so it tends to be the more powerful and high-status group members who can start this norm. If you are a leader in the group, it is that much more important that you model the kinds of behaviors you want others to exhibit.

Thought 5: Keep Your Boundaries Semi-Porous

Problem: Groups need clearly defined boundaries. Yet fighting conformity pressure means staying open to information and ideas from outside those boundaries. There are so many issues inside the group, it can be easy to forget to go outside and get some fresh air.

Solution: As discussed earlier, use newcomers as an opportunity for learning. Ask what they are thinking and what they find confusing, and try to understand their points of view. This is especially important before newcomers are fully socialized. (This is one of the reasons I like working with PhD students; I have them capture their ideas before they get too deep into academia.) It also helps newcomers feel they belong. How people are treated at the beginning will shape whether the group benefits from new and different perspectives.

Further, make sure you have a strong network of outside advisers. In mentoring research, they talk about the importance of a strong "developmental network"—people with your best interests at heart who can offer outside perspectives and expertise. Groups need the same. Who can you ask for help or a reality check? Clearly, you don't want to share things with outsiders your group isn't comfortable with. But it can be helpful to run important things by a few trusted outsiders.

Thought 6: To Avoid Echo Chambers, Keep Your Information Diet Healthy and Balanced

Problem: We love to consume out-group outrage—to give our attention to people talking about all the ways our group is victimized and other groups are to blame. That's polarization fuel. But resisting the urge to consume out-group outrage is pretty difficult: You are fighting against the world's biggest companies and most powerful algorithms. When you are tired, lonely, or otherwise grumpy, you'll probably lose that battle more often than you win.

Solution: Bestselling food science author Michael Pollan's simple dietary advice is to eat a variety of unprocessed foods—mostly plants. Your information diet should be similar. Social media is the junk food of information. If that's most of your information diet, you won't have a healthy brain. *Processed* means that you are hearing information thirdhand—an influencer talking about something they heard from another influencer who read the headline but didn't read the article. Wholesome, unprocessed informational diets come from consuming expert reporting and research. (You're reading this book, so I probably don't need to be telling *you*.) Variety, in this case, can simply mean reading books and articles and changing up the kinds of media you consume— newspapers, magazines, podcasts, and TV. But being a member of different kinds of groups, interacting with different kinds of people, and really listening to them is best.

Competition

In Section III, we're going to talk about competition and conflict within and between groups. Within a group, competition acts as a foil to conformity, pushing us to get ahead, stand out, and get recognized. In Chapter 9, we'll discuss the light and dark sides of group competition: Competition is a powerful motivator, but you need to know when it helps and when it hurts performance. In Chapter 10, we'll move on to conflict, competition's dangerous, hotheaded cousin. Unfortunately, most research on reducing the harms of conflict has focused on individualistic solutions, which have, at best, a mixed track record. In Chapter 11, we'll discuss how to reap competition's benefits while minimizing its dangers—to compete with yourself, avoid relationship conflict, and recognize that those who seek to divide us and foment conflict between groups are the real enemies. That knowledge can help you use competition to better your groups—and yourself.

CHAPTER 9

Always Competing

How Competition Shapes Us and Our Groups

At the outset of the Harry Potter series, the Slytherin house has dominated the fictional sport of Quidditch. Slytherin used superior broomsticks and tactics of questionable legality to win the coveted "Quidditch Cup" a record six consecutive years. But Harry Potter changed all that when he joined Slytherin's rival, Gryffindor, buttressed by a Nimbus 2000—a state-of-the-art broomstick. And in the first book of the series, that broomstick helps Harry lead Gryffindor to a nail-biting victory over Slytherin.

But Slytherin doesn't take this lying down. The next year, Slytherin enlists Harry's nemesis, Draco Malfoy. Draco's wealthy father buys even better broomsticks for the entire Slytherin team.

Gryffindor's job just got a lot harder! Luckily, Harry soon manages to secure an even newer model of broomstick that runs circles around the older ones.

Throughout the series, we see an arms race in broomsticks between the teams. Each team scrambles to get newer, faster, more maneuverable models to get an edge on the competition. The teams push one another to increasingly higher Quidditch heights.

The real world is full of similar examples. For instance, North Carolina is home to not one, but two powerhouses in men's college basketball. The University of North Carolina (UNC) and Coach K's Duke University are right down the Tobacco Road from one another. The teams have won several national titles in close succession: Duke in 1992 and then UNC in 1993. UNC in 2009 and then Duke in 2010. Duke in 2015 and then UNC in 2017. Overall, the teams are third (UNC) and fourth (Duke) of all time in Men's Basketball NCAA championship wins. Is there something in the water in North Carolina that makes eighteen- to twenty-three-year-olds better at basketball?

Research by New York University professor Gavin Kilduff helped rule out my water theory with a much more logical one: Competition with a rival helps group performance. In one study, Kilduff and Columbia University researchers Brian E. Pike and Adam Galinsky asked whether a rival's postseason success in one season improved the team's performance the next season. Did Duke's 1992 Championship, for instance, really spur UNC to perform better in 1993? Or were they both just good teams that coincidentally won in consecutive years?

The researchers collected a ton of data—not only from NCAA

Men's Basketball teams, but also the four biggest American professional sports leagues (National Football League, National Basketball Association, Major League Baseball, and National Hockey League), covering more than five thousand six hundred observations of team-rival performance. That's a huge number for a study of real teams competing in the wild! And they found that competition between rivals indeed spurred teams like Duke and UNC to excel: In all these sports leagues, teams perform better the year after their rivals perform well in the postseason.

That's the power of competition. You probably don't need much convincing that competition can motivate and focus. Your rival's performance gives you a clear goal to aspire to—a perfect vivid, SMART goal out of Gary Latham's dreams (Chapter 4). If your rival can do it, why can't you?

Competition has some sneakily cooperative properties, too. Its Latin root, *competere*, means "to meet" or "strive in common." In competitive situations, we can, quite literally, bring out the best in one another. Like UNC and Duke, Olympic athletes often spur one another to set new records and personal bests in the same contest. For instance, in the 2016 Olympics, Ethiopian runner Almaz Ayana ran faster than anyone ever had, shattering the ten-thousand-meter dash world record by more than fourteen seconds. Yet in the same race, Kenya's Vivian Cheruiyot also ran faster than she ever had, taking home silver while setting a new national record. The Kenya team told *Sports Illustrated* that they strategically trained to beat Ayana, so Cheruiyot's drastic improvement was at least partially thanks to competing against her rival.

Things are similar in competition between groups. The Space

Race between the US and the Soviet Union spurred both countries to pour resources into developing new technologies, including satellites and rockets, at a faster rate than they would have without that competition. Fierce competition among car manufacturers gives us ever more powerful, safe, and fuel-efficient cars—or at least ever more cup holders and phone chargers. Competition among streaming platforms like Netflix, Amazon, Apple TV, and Disney gives us ever more lavishly costumed, expensive spin-offs of fantasy novels and sci-fi stories. Just like competition between individuals, competition within and between groups motivates innovation, achievement, and efficiency in ways that have benefited humanity.

In the throes of competition, we often have a physiological "challenge" response: Energizing hormones—testosterone and cortisol—fire into our bloodstream. Our blood vessels open to allow better circulation, letting these hormones and a ballast of oxygen reach our brain and muscles. When it goes right, we're more physically and mentally able to perform at our best.

Given the power of competition, it's no wonder that it is everywhere in modern society. Nations go to war. Political parties compete in elections. Businesses compete for market share. Even our entertainment is often competitive, whether it's Quidditch, basketball, or *Survivor*.

Given that competition is used so much, it must be pretty helpful in pushing you to perform your best, right?

Not so fast. Although competition can sometimes bring out the best in you, its overall track record in improving human performance is mixed. In their meta-analysis, psychologists Kou Murayama and Andrew Elliot summarized sixty-five studies of the competition-performance relationship, capturing the experiences of 14,721 people. Their headline from this comprehensive study: Competition and performance have barely any detectable relationship.

That's because competition also brings out the worst in us. We hoard resources and information, making it harder to cooperate. It can lead those who don't see a path to winning to give up or fail to participate at all. It sometimes pushes competitors to win even at the cost of their friends and values. Those who lose or fail to achieve their goals can get so discouraged they stop trying. And too often, competition can spill over into conflict that, between groups, is the most dangerous force humanity has to offer.

To understand the effect of competition on groups, we'll first take a step back from our collective perspective and find out what happens to us as individuals when we compete.

What Happens to You When You Compete?

Competition is stressful. And stress can be good or bad for performance. In a no-stress world, I might just sit around watching *The Office* reruns and snacking. Most of us want a bit of pressure to keep us motivated to satiate our need for competence.

But when we're competing for something we care about, we're under a lot of pressure. And in contrast to the headline from Murayama and Elliot's research, that pressure affects our performance in predictable ways.

In fact, research on evaluative pressure—the pressure we feel when being judged that emerges in any kind of competition—has been producing mixed results since the 1960s. In some studies, when people were put in stressful situations, like competing or performing in front of an audience, they did better than they did in isolation. Yet other studies showed the opposite—people performed better alone than with a crowd. Why?

Most 1960s researchers were individualists. They took these mixed findings about how people respond to pressure as a sign that there was some kind of competitive personality trait, a clutch gene, that determined whether you blossomed or wilted under pressure.

But psychologist Robert Zajonc was no individualist. He noticed that the studies showing a positive effect of pressure used simple tasks like riding an exercise bike as fast as you can. But studies that showed a negative effect used more complex tasks like doing algebra problems in front of an audience. In his research, Zajonc showed that the key to understanding how pressure affects people is their mastery of the task at hand. For well-mastered skills, like riding an exercise bike, evaluative pressure should improve performance. But if the task isn't well mastered, like saying every fourth letter of the alphabet in reverse order (Z . . . W . . . uh . . .), amping up the heat will harm performance. Unfortunately, Zajonc was terrible at naming things, calling the positive effect "social facilitation" and the negative effect "social inhibition."

Social facilitation and inhibition allow us to predict when people will blossom or wilt under the heat of competition. The same is true for anything that raises the stakes, like a million-dollar reward or an audience of thousands. Whether or not you get the psychological and physiological benefits of competition depends on whether you think you're up to the task. When, deep down, you don't believe you have a chance to win, you don't get the "challenge" physiological response that amps you up. At worst, you might get the "threat" response, telling you to retreat or keeping you from trying in the first place.

This helped Murayama and Elliot explain why competition has such confusing effects on performance. For those who believe they can win (or otherwise achieve their goals), competition improves performance. But those who are just trying not to embarrass themselves have the avoidance-oriented "threat" response, so competition harms their performance.

In sum, competition has a complicated relationship with human performance. When you are doing well-mastered tasks, competing can spur you on to new heights. But when you are still learning, competing is likely to hurt you. That's something to keep in mind when choosing to participate in competitions to stretch yourself, encourage your children, or motivate your work team.

But people don't compete merely to perform better. We also compete because it provides an addictive reward: winning.

Social Comparison, or What You Give the Man Who Has Everything

In 2021, Russian billionaire Roman Abramovich, the former owner of the Chelsea Football Club, had a one-hundred-forty-meter yacht called *Solaris* built for himself. According to reports, the yacht has eight decks, a helipad, and can house thirty-six guests. But unbelievably, Abramovich owns an even bigger yacht—*Eclipse*. *Eclipse* is 162.5 meters long, includes two swimming pools, a cinema, two helipads, and a built-in submarine. Despite being used for maybe a quarter of the year, both yachts require a full-time live-in crew. And other superrich compatriots are plotting to outdo Abramovich. There are rumors that "an anonymous Malaysian businessman" purchased an even more extravagant yacht, *History Supreme*, which is made from ten thousand kilograms of gold and platinum at a cost of $4.8 billion. Other oligarchs are working on yachts fashioned into islands and cities. No matter how pointlessly extravagant one superyacht is, the next seeks to surpass it.

Even people who have everything want to be at the top of their social hierarchy. It isn't just about having a great yacht, house, or car. It's about having the best. Being a little bit better than our peers always gives us a warm feeling. Economists have sometimes wondered why the superrich continue to work to accrue wealth that they can't even use. But social psychologists have long known the explanation: social comparison. People will compare themselves to one another on basically any dimension imaginable and compete to come out on top. Often it isn't about the actual money, power, or function. The eternal competition in our minds is about something far more ephemeral—status.

Status is the respect and esteem of others. It's the Machiavellian cousin of belonging; both make us feel valued, but status wants to climb on the backs of our fellow group members and live there, whereas belonging just wants a hug.

Your place in these hierarchies doesn't just affect your psychology—it also affects your physiology. Having low status is stressful—losing status changes your blood pressure and hormonal balance and can even shorten your life. The stress from perpetual low status actually makes you less capable over time. Although high status does make people happier and healthier, it also means constantly fending off challenges from those below (like having to build another, bigger yacht once again). But at its worst, high status causes people to start imagining challenges and building structures meant to deprive potential challengers rather than elevating fellow group members.

To understand social comparison and status, you have to understand groups. We usually don't compare ourselves to random strangers. Instead, we selectively compare ourselves to fellow group members, real or imagined—someone we share, or aspire to share, an identity with.

Unfortunately, a lot of our social comparisons make us less happy. In a famous study that exemplifies this, Cornell social psychologist Victoria Medvec and her colleagues found that Olympic silver medalists were less satisfied than the bronze medalists they beat. Silver medalists were on the verge of winning, so they compared up. But bronze medalists were on the verge of watching the medal ceremony from the audience, so they compared down. It's the "I could have won gold" effect. More recently, researchers replicated this finding using automated facial expression coding of photos from the Olympics from 2000 through 2016. The silver medalists were less smiley than the gold and bronze medalists—and when they did smile, the silver medalists were more likely to have fake-looking smiles.

Social psychologist Susan Fiske summarizes our social comparison tendencies as "envy up, scorn down." And these tendencies are poisonous, pushing us apart, regardless of which direction we compare. As Fiske wrote, "Envy says, 'I wish I had what you have,' but it implies 'And I wish you did not have it.' Scorn says, 'You are unworthy of my attention, but I know you are down there somewhere.'" Comparing up makes us feel inadequate, and comparing down makes us mean.

Research shows that people spend a lot more time thinking about social comparisons that make them feel bad than those that make them feel good. In the new era of constant social media and curated online personas, our brains are programmed to focus on comparisons that fundamentally undermine our well-being. We all want to keep up with the Joneses, whether we think of the Joneses as owning island-sized platinum yachts, having eight-pack abs, or getting a thumbs-up from the boss. In short, try to avoid social comparison; it's mostly bad for you and the world. But that's very hard to do because our brains are programmed to compare ourselves to other group members.

Humans aren't unique as voracious status seekers. Many animals have clear status hierarchies that help organize their social lives, from alpha wolves to queen bees. Wolf packs, primates, and even some insects have a strict hierarchy, with a single alpha leader perched atop a pyramid-shaped ladder.

Like many animals, we're hypersensitive to signals about everyone's place in a status hierarchy. To infer high status, we use small cues, like speaking confidently, making eye contact, and having relaxed, open body language. We use fleeting glimpses of others' faces and posture to make these judgments. Like our evolutionary cousins, the great apes, lowered eye gaze or a raised chin give us lightning-fast cues about who's in charge. This can happen in as quickly as 0.33 milliseconds—literally in the blink of an eye.

Because of our ability to quickly detect status cues, we'll spontaneously produce hierarchy in a group without it. When others display dominance cues, like talking loudly, behaving angrily, or even raising their chin or making uncomfortably intense eye contact, we have two potential responses: Either we stare right back and raise our chin, mirroring these cues and challenging their dominance, or we complement these cues with submissive ones, averting our eyes.

It makes sense that we're so sensitive to status cues. Our ancestors were competing with real stakes for the resources they needed to survive. The stress juice that competition evokes has helped humanity accomplish things no other species has thought about. Blue whales have big brains, too, but they're not as worried about status as we are. They're just floating around, sippin' water and eating krill. Most of them don't even have side hustles!

Yet considering you bought this book, you probably aren't competing for food and water. You have some disposable income. So for the relatively privileged, the impulse to compete gets routed into competing for status. Which is weird, because status is just a mental construct. You can't eat it, spend it, or see it. At least not directly.

The result is that even the most egalitarian groups still develop informal hierarchies. Members disproportionately go to certain people for help and advice. Those helpers' voices carry a little more weight when making collective decisions. They gain status and influence.

At the very least, I hope your group's hierarchy isn't based purely on primate-like social dominance. It's hopefully based on assessments of competence—getting done what the group needs done.

Because status is baked into our evolution, we can't avoid status competitions and hierarchy entirely. And evolution is right—hierarchy is good for something. Indeed, we need some hierarchy for coordination and collaboration. Social hierarchy can help peacefully settle arguments between members. It can also speed up decisions as we all look to our superiors to guide us.

But in most groups, we end up with more hierarchy than we need. A decent chunk of the population really likes to be on top of at least a small pyramid. Even if you aren't the CEO, it's still nice to have some people to boss around. This is a personality trait that actually matters—"social dominance orientation." How important is it to you to move up in the hierarchy? There's some evidence this trait is linked to genes and testosterone levels (which also predict aggressive behavior) and varies quite a bit between people.

Regardless of whether you are competing to be on top, you will likely be pretty motivated not to be on the bottom of the pyramid. Everyone wants to be higher status than someone. The easiest way to achieve this is to create more rungs on the ladder. Over time, therefore, we got more and more hierarchy. It wasn't enough to have a king and queen. We needed dukes and duchesses, barons and baronesses, and lords and ladies. And it's the same in the world of work today. You don't just have the CEO, you also have the various C-suite positions, senior vice presidents, vice presidents, senior managers, all the way down to assistant managers and assistants to the regional manager. Big companies have dozens of rungs on the organizational ladder, and the number of rungs is going up, not down.

That's because humans are happy within a hierarchy only when they stay put or move up. Research shows that people at the top are happier and less stressed than those at the bottom. Status even affects people's health and lifespan—even after statistically controlling for wealth- and health-related predictors, people who think of themselves as lower status actually die earlier because of stress's effects on cardiovascular health! But even those at the top can get stressed out when they think there's a threat from below. University College London social psychologist Pranjal Mehta has found that high-status people who believe their position is precarious fail to get the health and happiness benefits of status.

Once you have a new rung on the ladder, it's pretty difficult to get rid of it. If your workplace decides to flatten its hierarchy and your job title disappears, you either get promoted or demoted. People hate demotion so much that most groups would rather keep a rung that's outlived its usefulness than risk the chaos that ensues when too many group members feel disrespected. Just like

top management teams from Chapter 3, hierarchy keeps growing to the point that it starts to impede coordination.

That's why research increasingly shows that too much hierarchy is bad for group effectiveness. Synergy often means being
flexible in who takes the lead on what and adapting to use the
knowledge and skills most appropriate to the situation. In practice, hierarchies are often rigid and slow, like the bureaucracy
that's ridiculed on *The Office* or in *Office Space*. And the person on
top isn't always the person with the most relevant knowledge and
skills. But according to research by Harvard professor Heidi
Gardner, when the heat is on, groups tend to look to the person
at the top of the hierarchy. Even when that keeps them from listening to the person who knows best.

Flexible hierarchies have their own problems. As we discussed with norms and roles, groups need some predictability to
coordinate effectively, and stable hierarchies help people know
their roles and reduce conflict. Just how much stability is needed?
This is a question research is still working on, as it's clear that
hierarchies can't be so rigid that those at the bottom are doomed
to live the life of an omega wolf or monkey, one who lives on the
outskirts of the group and tends to be the most stressed and least
healthy.

The individualistic thinking fallacy leads people to believe
that those at the bottom of a hierarchy are inherently less worthy.
But being pushed down over and over also causes people to become temporarily less capable. Those at the top always want to
believe that they're smarter and more capable. But the truth is, if
they were at the bottom, they might not seem so smart and
capable.

Hierarchy does two other interesting things to groups. Okay, *interesting* probably isn't the right word. Hierarchy does two other *bad* things to groups.

First, being at the top of the hierarchy changes people. There's some truth to the saying "Power corrupts." One reason it corrupts is psychological distance—the metaphorical space between you and someone else. A lot of things make us feel more distant from other people, including physical distance, virtuality (like talking over video call instead of face-to-face), and having very little in common. But some important ones are power and status. People at the top of a group's hierarchy develop a sense of power that distances them from those at the bottom of the hierarchy. And that leads them to see the bottom-dwellers as tools more than people. For example, one study using the classic "trolley problem," in which one person is sacrificed to save the life of five others, found that 69 percent of study participants said it was more acceptable to sacrifice the life of one person experiencing homelessness than a middle-class person.

Over time, status and power infuse our social identities to the point that they become their own sorting category. We distance ourselves from group members lower in the hierarchy. We might even see ourselves as more akin to the powerful in other groups—fellow yacht owners—rather than our own colleagues. We become the pigs at the end of George Orwell's *Animal Farm*, no longer identifying with the other animals and making peace with the humans.

If you're lower in the status hierarchy, you also may find yourself eager to please and obey those higher up. In one of the most famous series of experiments, social psychologist Stanley Milgram tried to see how far he could push obedience to authority in 1963. Participants were asked to administer shocks of increasing severity to another participant when that person made mistakes on a memorization task.

Or so they thought. Shock receivers were trained to pretend they were in pain. The experiment was to see how many people would go along with experimenters' questionable requests—how high a voltage would they go to just because an authority issued a command? The answer was too high. Milgram and subsequent researchers found that more than 70 percent of people obey experimenters' unethical requests. The study's even been replicated for TV a few times, making the nightly news whenever atrocity and torture are doled out by a cult, army, or government.

People of that time saw the Milgram studies as an explanation of Arendt's "banality of evil." Those embedded in the middle of a hierarchy could tell themselves they were just doing their job. They didn't need to believe in the cause—evil without malice could be explained by boring, banal bureaucracy.

Subsequent research, though, raised questions about Milgram's interpretation. Social psychologist S. Alexander Haslam and colleagues found that people needed to identify with the broader cause in order to obey; no one ever went along with a straight command from the experimenter, even in Milgram's original study. Yale has since released the original transcripts of Milgram's work from the archives. In a reanalysis, social psychologist David Kaposi noted an overlooked aspect of these classic studies: "If people do not simply obey but do so visibly against their inclinations, then there is a moment of reluctance that even technically fully obedient participants need to overcome." What is surprising in these studies isn't that people mindlessly went along with whatever the experimenter told them. Instead, they had the moment of conflict—they knew something was wrong with the experimenters' request to go on. Yet authority and iden- tification with the broader goals of the experiment allowed them to harm their true peer—the person being shocked.

Competition for status in groups is natural, but it's also fraught with danger. But that danger pales in comparison to the most powerful force the earth has ever known—conflict between groups.

CHAPTER 10

The Escalator to Hell

The Conflict Within "Us" and Between "Us" and "Them"

Before Socrates took the number-one spot on the "Top Forty Ancient Greek Philosophers" charts, the most popular thinkers were the Sophists. Sophists were the professors of their time but were more like traveling debate coaches for hire than the professors we know today. And Sophists philosophized through competition. According to Plato (who wasn't a Sophistry fan), they held stylized rhetorical contests that were more rap battles than debates— you could score as many points by dissing your opponent's character as by critiquing their ideas. The goal of their debate wasn't to find truth but to persuade for personal gain. In fact, many Sophists were moral relativists: They didn't believe there was any such thing as objective, knowable truth. They were advocates of a "might makes right" philosophy—if you were strong enough to enforce your view, your view was correct. The only goal of arguing was to gain power and status—to win.

But Socrates disagreed. He had a wild idea: We should focus on the ideas themselves rather than the person saying them. The Socratic method we know today constantly challenges ideas to probe their underlying assumptions and seek their truth.

The nature of conflict mirrors the ancient debate between Socrates and the Sophists. Conflict is the behavioral manifestation of disagreement or dislike. But conflict isn't always hotheaded. At its best, conflict sticks to disagreement about ideas, like Socrates debating with some Sophists about the nature of truth over ouzo and grape leaves, or Victorian salons, where people shared their views on the issue of the day by the fire after dinner. Conflict can be quite civilized when it wants to be!

When it keeps its temper in check and sticks to ideas, conflict can actually be a welcome guest. It's often searching for the truth or the best course of action. Just as we saw in Chapter 8, pitting ideas against one another helps us keep the dark side of conformity at bay. We call this productive side of conflict "task conflict."

Task conflict is any action that indicates disagreement. When members of a group express different preferences or ideas, that's task conflict. Where should we go for dinner? Which companies should Bridgewater invest in? Which prototypes should IDEO build? Should we toilet train our cat like jazz master Charles Mingus did? If we publicly disagree about questions like these, we have task conflict.

Within groups, task conflict should help the group make better decisions and be more creative, as well as offer individuals the chance to learn from one another. In theory, at least. Unfortunately, within-group conflict doesn't always stay focused on the task. Instead, disagreements spill over into Sophist rap battles that we call "relationship conflict." Vigorous task conflict can get heated and angry. We may lash out at our fellow group members rather than sticking within a collective problem-solving frame. "You always say things like that" or "You're the kind of person who . . ."—these types of statements are hallmarks of relationship conflict.

Relationship conflict isn't just disagreement about ideas—it's visible dislike. As you might suspect, that's unabashedly bad for group effectiveness. Groups with even moderate levels of relationship conflict struggle with trust. Relationship conflict takes time and energy away from other goals. And perhaps most importantly, relationship conflict is a threat to members' sense of belonging—one of the key reasons that people join groups in the first place.

When conflict turns personal, the group is in real trouble. Relationship and marriage guru John Gottman found that one of the strongest predictors of divorce is contempt. And contempt is similar in groups. Because it's about you as a person, relational conflict puts belonging at risk. Your primitive brain fears that the group may kick you out—ostracizing you and leaving you vulnerable to saber-toothed tiger attacks. And so it usually responds with anger. Which makes other group members angry. And so on.

CONFLICT IN GROUPS

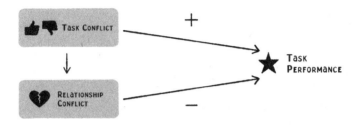

So when conflict arises, don't make the disagreement about the person. Make it about the issue. (Check out Section III's Group Thoughts for some tips about how to do this.)

Throughout the book (particularly in Chapter 8), I've encouraged you to foster dissent in your groups. Form a team of rivals like Abraham Lincoln did, in which people have diverse perspectives and information. That way, they'll disagree productively! But it isn't so easy. (Which, again, keeps me in business . . .) Research suggests that task conflict frequently spills into relationship conflict. That makes it hard for researchers to detect the theorized benefits of task conflict. And once relational conflict emerges, we're in deep trouble—especially if it happens between groups.

Family Feud

If you learned American history from Bugs Bunny like I did, you may remember that one of the most famous intergroup conflicts is a decades-long battle between two families who lived on opposite sides of the Big Sandy River on the Kentucky–West Virginia border. The Hatfield-McCoy feud kicked into gear in 1878, when both families claimed ownership of a pig. The local judge, Anderson Hatfield, ruled the pig belonged to . . . the Hatfields! Shocking.

Imagine being a McCoy. Your father, Randolph, calls you and your twelve siblings to the house. We don't know what was said there, but I imagine Randolph would have said something like, "Those Hatfields think they're so high and mighty—they stole that hog! It had McCoy markings clear as day. But they've got connections. Hatfields are all over the West Virginia law enforcement. The law won't help us, and it's only a matter of time before the Hatfields steal from us again . . . if we don't do something about it."

According to legend, shortly after the hog trial, the key witness, Hatfield relative Bill Staton, was killed by brothers Sam and Paris McCoy.

Now imagine being a Hatfield. Your father, William Anderson "Devil Anse" Hatfield, calls over you and your twelve siblings. "Those McCoys killed Cousin Bill!" Devil Anse might have raged. "All over a stupid pig. Something has to be done!"

During the next decade or so, the families traded murders, each in retaliation for the last. Ellison Hatfield was killed by Tolbert, Phamer, and Bud McCoy, who were then killed for the killing by assorted Hatfields. A few more reciprocal murders spiraled into the New Year's Massacre of 1888, when the Hatfields opened fire on the sleeping McCoy clan, killing several McCoys, including a young child. And that led to an all-out battle, known as the Battle of Grapevine Creek. It took intervention from the US Supreme Court to bring the conflict back down to a simmer.

Conflict between groups has an unfortunate tendency to escalate. It's self-reinforcing, intensifying through a series of feedback loops. And you probably don't need research to tell you that. Each group gets all the good and bad stuff from having a clear enemy—a rival group that pushes us to try as hard as we can. We get the motivation but also the conformity pressure and polarization. We band together, pool resources, and see off the enemy.

The world is full of stories—both real and fictional—about two groups with a history of conflict waiting for any excuse to hurt each other again. The memory of the pain one group inflicts on another persists for generations. Everyone knows someone touched by the conflict, so it becomes personal for almost every member.

I think of intergroup conflict like a forest fire that creates flammable ashes. Even after the fire is out, it's just a bunch of dry kindling waiting for another spark. To understand why, we need to explore two key concepts: escalation of commitment and revenge.

Intergroup Conflict Is a Dollar Auction

As I mentioned before, World War II was a big catalyst for research on group dynamics. Norms, conformity, polarization, group development, and obedience to authority all got their start during the war. But another war sparked interest in escalation of commitment, our tendency to invest more even when the evidence says we are failing: the Vietnam War, or the "War Against the Americans to Save the Nation," as the Vietnamese people call it. The fighting killed more than fifty-eight thousand American troops, one million Vietnamese combatants, and two million Viet-namese civilians. In 1960, the US had about eight hundred military personnel in Vietnam, largely in training and support roles. The number gradually rose as US involvement in the conflict escalated, yet US commitment of ground troops remained relatively small until 1965. That's when the first US prisoner of war was taken by the Vietcong following a US air strike. Then-President Lyndon Johnson sent fifty thousand more ground troops in response—and increased the draft to thirty-five thousand per month. By 1966, there were four hundred thousand US soldiers in Vietnam. By 1967, it was five hundred thousand.

In 1976, Vietnam reunified under communist rule. The US—the most powerful military in the world—had utterly failed. How did the US end up investing so much for so long to gain so little?

There are two main ways in which conflict is sustained, especially between groups. The first is rooted in our psychological tendency not only to keep doing what we've always done (inertia from Chapter 5), but also to escalate commitment even to a failing course of action. And competition and conflict intensify this tendency.

When I teach about this phenomenon, I often use a game called the "dollar auction." Popularized by economist Martin Shubik in 1971, it's an unusual auction used to demonstrate just how irrational we get in the throes of competition. Auctions tend to get people's competitive juices flowing as they try to outbid one another for some lovely trinket or another. But instead of auctioning off a painting or vase, Shubik auctioned off a crisp one-dollar bill. Now, this is an odd item for an auction because its name tells you how much you should pay. If we were rational economic creatures, ninety-nine cents should always be the maximum winning bid.

But it never is—because this auction has a twist. The highest bidder gets the dollar, and the second-highest bidder gets nothing but still has to pay what they bid. And the late, great organizational psychologist J. Keith Murnighan has perhaps the best story I've ever heard about running a dollar auction.

Murnighan was teaching seventy students in an executive master's degree class on negotiations at Northwestern University. When I've taught in these kinds of programs, students are often new executives, managers tipped for promotion, or professionals like lawyers and doctors who have found themselves running a business rather than doing what they were trained to do.

It was 1998, and because of inflation, Murnighan decided to auction off a twenty-dollar bill instead of a one-dollar bill. As always, the auction hit nineteen dollars. And then came the big decision. Do you bid twenty dollars for a twenty-dollar bill? To the person who bid nineteen, it seems inconceivable that someone would do that. But the other person stood to lose their eighteen-dollar bid and would get nothing for it. Why not bid two dollars more to avoid that? Surely, the other person won't bid twenty-one?

The winning bid turned out to be fifty-four dollars, with the loser on the hook for fifty-three—a slightly high cost, but within the normal range. That isn't what makes this a good story.

Murnighan was more dedicated than I am to driving home the lesson. He immediately started a second auction to prove that somebody would make the same mistake again because it's wired into our psychology. "When the bidding gets past $30 or so," Murnighan wrote, "monetary outcomes sometimes become secondary. Both bidders are now clearly losing . . . They now focus on avoiding being seen as the big loser."

On this day, the bidding reached two hundred dollars in the second auction. Tired of counting by ones, Murnighan asked for sealed "best and final" bids, which were two hundred fifty and two hundred ten, respectively. Lesson learned, right?

But Murnighan held a third auction. This time, the bidding for the twenty-dollar bill flew past two hundred . . . five hundred . . . even one thousand dollars. By the end, the loser committed to pay $1,950. But the winner bid two thousand dollars—and thus stood to lose $1,980 when counting the twenty they won. That's right—the "winner" lost thirty dollars more than the "loser."

After the auction, Murnighan talked with the bidders. "They were in shock, literally," he recalled. "They both mentioned that they did not remember a thing that I had said in the class after the auction." A while later, the winner—a company president—reflected on his experience, writing, "My ego took over and my competitive juices began to flow. I had won a $20 bill for $2000! Why me?" The loser, an engineer, recalled, "My internal stress level had reached a point where I was not thinking clearly . . . I was more concerned with 'winning' and 'not giving up.'"

Unlike most escalating conflicts, this story has a benign ending. Murnighan didn't make his students pay what they bid. All first- and second-place bidders instead agreed to pay fifty dollars each, which was given to charity.

But the lesson here is deadly serious. What if your "bid" is sending ten thousand troops into battle and your opponent sends twenty thousand? You'd likely not only lose the battle, but also your troops. In an escalating conflict between groups, second place often loses, too.

Like the dollar auction and the US involvement in the Vietnam War, people are very slow to learn to avoid escalating these conflicts past the point of rationality. Too often, both parties are losers.

Escalating commitment to a failing course of action is such a well-known phenomenon now, it seems almost mundane. It starts with our tendency to stick with things because we've already invested time, effort, and money, even when it ends up costing us more in the future. This is known as the "sunk-cost fallacy." Venture capitalists, having invested three million dollars already, decide to throw another million to a start-up that hasn't made a profit in its five years of existence. A sports team overpays its own underperforming draft pick in free agency rather than admitting a mistake. You read one hundred fifty pages of a book you don't really like but you keep reading anyway. (Okay, bad example! It doesn't apply to books! Please keep reading!) The idea is: Things will turn around if we just try for a little bit longer. Everything we've spent on this can't be for nothing!

Economists and psychologists will tell you the sunk-cost fallacy is a bad way to think. If you're investing money, it doesn't matter how much you invested before. Only your cold, rational calculation of the future matters. Investors shouldn't think about how much they've already spent when deciding whether to com-mit more. They should treat every decision like a new investment. That's what the best businesspeople do—they're ruthless in avoiding the sunk-cost fallacy. If you made a mistake in the past, that doesn't mean you should double down on the mistake.

Yet double down we do. We hate admitting defeat so much that we'll pay two thousand dollars for a twenty-dollar bill. We'll send another fifty thousand troops when the last fifty thousand didn't make a difference. If we don't fight another day for control of this town, what does it mean for those who lost their lives yesterday? So we fight on.

The problem is that we often don't realize we are escalating commitment to a failing course of action. After all, we don't know the future, and we can't quit every time things don't go our way. We're taught from an early age the value of persistence—that "slow and steady wins the race" and that giving up is cowardly. But that's not what the sunk-cost fallacy is about. It's about sticking with something *because* you've already invested so much— even though you believe it will fail. Grit and persistence are good because a lot of important things in life are difficult and you won't achieve your goals on the first try. But what you've already invested shouldn't be part of the equation. "We've already invested so much, we might as well" is bad logic. If you've bid ten times and hit eighteen dollars, you should cut your losses and give up rather than bidding twenty.

But escalation of commitment isn't just the sunk-cost fallacy by another name. It is also caused by overconfidence. The US wouldn't have entered Vietnam if it didn't think it could have won. The McCoys wouldn't have challenged the Hatfields.

In-group/out-group bias suggests that we're likely to overesti-mate our group's abilities and underestimate the other group's. Both think the other will give up first.

Overconfidence also extends to our choice of leaders. Studies have shown that people who are overconfident are seen as more competent by their peers. That allows them to accrue power and influence within the group. If JFK already made the decision to enter Vietnam, he's likely to give command to a general who says he's confident about a path to victory, not a general who is skep-tical. Groups flock to those who promise they will prevail. Con-formity, polarization, and acrophily (that love of the extreme from Chapter 7) join forces to give groups overconfident leaders with more extreme positions than the average group member. These overconfident, extreme leaders are unlikely to de-escalate conflict or abandon failing courses of action.

Unfortunately, groups also make it hard for leaders to back off from their overconfident, extreme promises. I still remember co-median Dana Carvey's iconic impersonation of former US presi-dent George H. W. Bush. Carvey exaggerated Bush's nervous fidgets and nasal-toned self-deprecation, making him seem weak and timid. The "Bush-is-weak" narrative really got going after he flip-flopped on a key campaign promise. A defining moment of the 1988 presidential campaign was Bush's memeable line, "Read my lips: No new taxes." Yet the practical realities of gov-erning led him to reconsider. And he was pilloried for it. Conser-vative columnist William F. Buckley Jr. called it an "arrant act of hypocrisy." Research shows that people don't like leaders who experiment with different courses of action. They like decisive leaders who stick to their guns. Leaders who admit defeat get penalized.

Let me editorialize briefly by pointing out that it's absurd to demand consistency from our leaders. Everyone should be allowed to learn, grow, and change. Yesterday's opinion might not match today's decision—because today is different. We are different. That's okay. Obviously, we can't have capricious leaders who keep jumping from one goal to another without achieving any of them. But demanding absolute consistency is self-defeating. Politicians who recognize that a policy they proposed doesn't fit the current world should be praised, not criticized.

Alas, I have little hope that insight will do any good. Our perceptions of leadership and authority emerge from the deep caverns of our Paleolithic brains.

Groups often make escalation of commitment worse. We already learned in Chapter 5 that groups have a bias toward the status quo. Inertia is strong, and change is an uphill battle. It's hard enough as an individual to give up on something that isn't working. It's even harder in groups—we had to go through all those hard decision processes and get everyone's commitment! Change requires dissent. Continuing as planned is the default.

And so, conflicts between groups continue because that's the status quo. Because we've already invested so much. Because we punish leaders who change their minds. And if we just send a few more troops or bid a little more money, maybe it will all pay off.

And that's without even factoring in the second half of the intergroup conflict problem: Humans love an unhealthy dish that's best served cold.

The Science of Revenge

Revenge is everywhere. And it isn't unique to humans: Creatures from waterfowl to elephant seals to lions attack—and sometimes kill—even cute babies of their own kind that have stolen food from them. And it is pure malice—there's no way to get the food back.

People put tons of time and effort into revenge, even at great cost to themselves. Stories like Japan's "47 Ronin," in which a band of samurai whose master was murdered plot for more than two years to avenge the murder only to kill themselves because of their own crime, or *The Count of Monte Cristo*, whose titular character plots and exacts an intricate revenge to ruin his rival over nine years, seem believable to us. But revenge is weird if you think about it. Aren't you punishing yourself in the process? Wouldn't a survival-of-the-fittest version of evolution encourage us to forgive and forget, once whatever offended us is a sunk cost?

Revenge is one of those paradoxical groupy behaviors. It is costly for the individual dishing it out because it risks retaliation from its target. Yet out in the wilds, revenge may be the only law enforcement there is. With revenge as a deterrent, members of the herd are more likely to follow the rules. So evolutionarily, revenge is good for the group because it enforces norms but bad for the individuals who give and receive it.

Unlike elephant seals, humans want revenge most when someone violates social norms—those unwritten contracts between people. Human revenge is as influenced by culture and norms as it is by evolution and genetics. And the more unwritten the rule, the more prevalent the revenge is. Some studies have found that revenge is more common in cultures that lack reliable, institutionalized justice systems. The Hatfields and McCoys, for instance, lived across the Kentucky–West Virginia border. This area was sparsely populated, with infrastructure damaged by the Civil War. It wasn't clear which state had jurisdiction, with both states shielding their own citizens from extradition (which is why the Supreme Court got involved). Vigilantes thrive where we don't trust a higher authority to enforce justice.

According to UNC psychologist Joshua Jackson and his colleagues, people are most likely to take revenge when they perceive four qualities in a transgression: It's intentional, aggressive, severe, and morally offensive. For instance, unlike elephant seals, humans won't take revenge on a baby who steals their food because it isn't seen as intentionally malicious. But an action that ticks those four boxes elicits a very dangerous emotion: righteous anger.

Anger is an aggressive, approach-oriented emotion that brings up the "challenge" response. But righteous anger adds a moral component, stemming from breaking norms that are essential to the group's identity. And emotions like anger are highly contagious in groups.

If we go back to the Hatfields and the McCoys, we can start to unpack what happened to escalate things. The McCoys must have felt righteous anger after losing the pig trial. It seemed to them to tick every box—it was intentional and aggressive, it was morally offensive that the case was decided by a Hatfield, and through the dark side of polarization and conformity, that sentiment got stronger and stronger.

But did the severity of their response—killing a Hatfield—

match the severity of the original offense? We learned in Chapter 7 that polarization can increase a group's tolerance for risk. So the first suggestion might be to take back the pig. But that was just the starting bid. Assuming the average sentiment was toward taking revenge, the planned response in a group only gets riskier and more extreme.

Moreover, in-group/out-group bias means that the in-group's well-being is "worth more" than the out-group's. Harm to one of us is worth harm to two of them. A small slight elicits even stronger retribution. It's not an eye for an eye because our eyes are worth more than theirs. So both groups use a logic of two eyes for an eye.

But it isn't just this type of accounting that drives intergroup revenge. People exaggerate harms to themselves and their in-group. It wasn't just an honest misunderstanding of who owned a pig—it was deliberate theft, symbolizing their everlasting disdain for us. They also minimize the harms they themselves perpetrate, especially on out-groups. It wasn't murder; it was self-defense.

Groups on the receiving end of revenge feel the reverse—that the punishment was disproportionate to the crime. So everyone feels aggrieved. When both sides think this way, it's easy to see how a small harm can spiral into major conflict. And there's worse yet to come.

On October 7, 2023, terrorists affiliated with the Palestinian group Hamas attacked Israel from several directions. About one thousand two hundred people—many of whom were Israeli civilians and foreign nationals—were killed. A further two hundred forty people were taken hostage. In response, Israel declared war on Hamas and has killed more than forty thousand Palestinians— most of whom were civilians—at the time of this writing.

Referring to Palestine, Israeli president Isaac Herzog said at a press conference, "It is an entire nation out there that is responsible. It is not true this rhetoric about civilians not being aware, not involved. It's absolutely not true. They could have risen up. They could have fought against that evil regime which took over Gaza in a coup d'état."

The world has watched the unfolding war, appalled at how both sides harm civilians not involved in the conflict. It's clear from their behavior that Hamas terrorists felt justified in holding all members of the group responsible for the actions of some— they didn't care who was a civilian (or even Israeli or Jewish). And Herzog spelled it out publicly that Israel felt the same.

When we look at out-groups, we exaggerate their homogeneity. We understand the diversity in our own groups and the different motivations and experiences of each member, but we tend to see other groups as undifferentiated collectives where all members are the same. And that enables "vicarious revenge," where harm of any out-group member is justified because the whole group is seen as equally responsible. It's okay to shift accountability from specific individuals to the group as a whole. And in doing so, dehumanization rears its ugly head. "We are fighting human animals and we act accordingly," Israeli defense minister Yoav Gallant said, justifying increasing escalation of the conflict and the two-eyes-for-an-eye logic. And we don't need a quote to know that the Hamas attackers were just as willing to escalate and seek revenge, given the opportunity.

Groups that have been in conflict for a long time don't even need a trigger for revenge-like behavior. Research shows that people are sometimes willing to harm the out-group, even at a cost to themselves. History is replete with terrorists and kamikaze fighters willing to give their own lives simply to inflict harm on the out-group.

I desperately hope that, by the time you read this, this conflict will be in the past. But I doubt it. Although all wars have a host of complex causes, the forces that keep "us" and "them" locked in a fight against each other are almost impossibly powerful. We have the capacity to mutually destroy one another, and the risk we will eventually do so is very real.

What can we do?

CHAPTER 11

Of Pigs and Potatoes

What We Can Do About Competition and Conflict

My home state of Washington was the site of an almost-war between Britain and America that started because of yet another nineteenth-century pig.

The conflict was set on San Juan Island (known as Lháqemesh to the indigenous Salish inhabitants), one of the larger islands that holds the oceanic border between Canada and the US. Today, the island offers calm harbors, plenty of sea life, and secluded woodlands. But in 1859, when our story takes place, the island was a site of conflict. The vagaries of mapmaking had left the 1846 Oregon Treaty's intent for San Juan Island unclear—was it to be on the British or American side of the border? Of course, both countries exploited this ambiguity and claimed ownership.

Britain's Hudson's Bay Company set up sheep ranches. And a few dozen American settlers, weary of searching for gold, also made their homes on San Juan Island.

One of those Americans was Lyman Cutlar, a failed gold prospector who started a small homestead on the island. One day Cutlar saw an unwelcome sight out his window: A large pig was rooting around in his garden and, well, pigging out on his crop of potatoes. Defending his precious tubers from the invading swine, Cutlar shot and killed the pig. Thinking it a routine dispute between farming neighbors, he then offered the owner ten dollars recompense—about three hundred sixty dollars in today's money.

Unfortunately, the pig's owner was in no mood to be soothed. The late pig had belonged to Englishman Charles Griffin, one of the Hudson Bay Company's managers. Griffin called the pig's killing a "murder" and reported it to the British authorities, demanding Cutlar's arrest. Catching wind of this, Cutlar sought protection from the US military. With the Revolutionary War and the War of 1812 still in living memory, the US government was loath to allow the British to arrest Cutlar, sending a battalion of sixty-six US soldiers to shield him.

The British raised the stakes, sending three warships.

Both sides predictably escalated their commitment to the conflict until there were more than two thousand six hundred troops on and around San Juan Island. The standoff dragged on for a month. Finally, James Douglas, the British governor of the island, gave the order to attack the American troops.

But then something extraordinary happened—something that happens too rarely in escalating intergroup conflict. Royal Navy admiral Robert Baynes refused to carry out the order, quipping that he would not "involve two great nations in a war over a squabble about a pig."

Now known as "The Pig and Potato War of 1859," it's easy to laugh off this incident as a silly escalation between puffed-up egos. After all, only the pig and potatoes took any lasting damage. But it's a pivotal moment between the US and the UK that could have undermined the "special relationship" that has since made them powerful allies.

This conflict didn't escalate just because nineteenth-century pigs were particularly valuable (although it was apparently quite hazardous to lay claim to someone else's pig!). As we learned in Chapter 10, when there's a question about enforcing laws and norms, groups take matters into their own hands. And then it became a dollar auction with committing troops—more about winning than about whether the pig, the potatoes, or all of San Juan Island was worth what they invested.

But the interesting question isn't how this conflict escalated so quickly. It's this: How did the two countries step back from the brink? There was plenty of kindling for conflict. The UK and America had been fighting, on and off, for almost a century. Charles Griffin exaggerated the harm to a "murder" and felt entitled to more than an even trade; he wanted revenge. The two groups increased their commitment and stood to lose face by backing down. We even saw James Douglas, the extreme leader we'd expect in these times, give the order to attack.

Was it just that Admiral Baynes had the extraordinary good

sense to defy a direct order? Well, probably not. Neither Governor Douglas nor Admiral Baynes made their decisions alone. And that can make all the difference.

You might have noticed that Murnighan's dollar auction story was about two individuals bidding in front of their peers. But what happens if groups do the bidding? One study showed that, although groups still escalated the bidding beyond one dollar, they were less likely than individuals to end up with extreme outcomes. All it took was one voice of reason to break the spell of escalation, and the majority would see the foolishness of continuing to bid. Groups also learned more quickly and stopped making the mistake of bidding more than one dollar across repeated trials. So even though Governor Douglas got caught up in the heat of the moment, Admiral Baynes was there to pull him back.

Recall from Chapter 7 that groups polarize in the direction of members' initial preferences. That direction isn't always toward escalation. By 1859, very few Brits or Americans wanted actual violence between the two countries. Although they wanted to control the island and show their power, there wasn't much will on either side for a real fight. So the majority probably agreed with Admiral Baynes's view. Polarization was likely working in the direction of de-escalation.

And that was especially true for the British Navy. Could Britain truly sustain an attack on America's West Coast? Getting a navy across the Atlantic Ocean to the East Coast was one thing. But back then, ships needed to sail around the tip of South America to reach San Juan Island in the Pacific Northwest. Even if Baynes won the first battle, he was sure to lose the next few in the months before reinforcements could arrive.

And although America shared borders with the British Empire (Canada and various islands and territories), it was far away from many of the key decision-makers in London. And most of them didn't care as much about a rivalry with faraway America as with much nearer European countries. There was a lot of psychological distance for the king and Parliament in the UK. The stakes of the Revolutionary War—keeping the empire together—were gone. Instead, war with America was about this one little island—or maybe just about status.

There's more to this story than a specific individual or conversation that tipped the scales in a way that changed the world. In fact, that's a pretty individualistic way to look at things. De-escalating intergroup conflict is much more complex.

According to sociologist Randall Collins, the reasons groups in conflict de-escalate are nuanced and based on context. One reason is that they can't find solidarity within their own group—some people want to keep fighting, but others aren't so sure. In his research, Collins found that national solidarity after terrorist attacks like September 11 lasts for about six months. After that, many people's motivation to fight wanes, allowing counter-conflict movements to gain traction.

Another factor is that, like in the dollar auction, groups learn from experience to fear escalating conflict (although they forget again pretty quickly). Even the distorting lenses of in-group favoritism and out-group denigration don't lead them to see a positive outcome for their group. Again, perfectly rational. And finally, resources—material and otherwise—are exhausted.

That's not an easy recipe, but it helps explain the realities of conflict de-escalation. The Cuban Missile Crisis was resolved because both sides knew the stakes were so high—mutually assured destruction is a pretty good deterrent. Practically, this is another area in which a diverse set of decision-makers can help. If you're part of a group enmeshed in potential or escalating conflict, speaking up about the costs of conflict and escalation encourages others to speak up and breaks the illusion of solidarity and extremism. In the early stages of a conflict, that might get you kicked out of the halls of power, but it's still the right thing to do. If everyone with doubts voices them, they can pull even countries that have been fighting for decades back from the brink.

But this isn't the most well-known approach to de-escalating intergroup conflict. That approach takes us back to the author of the autokinetic experiments from Chapter 6, Muzafer Sherif.

Robbers Cave and Middle Grove

If you've studied group dynamics before, you're probably wondering why I haven't yet talked about Sherif's most famous study: the Robbers Cave experiment. I almost didn't include this in the book because it's in every book about group dynamics. But researchers aren't allowed to do these kinds of experiments anymore, for reasons that will become obvious. And even if you've heard of this study, you probably don't know the whole story.

Sherif dreamed up Robbers Cave late in his career. It was 1953, and he'd just won a Rockefeller Foundation grant for thirty-eight thousand dollars (worth about four hundred forty thousand dollars in 2024). After decades of lab experiments with lights in dark rooms, he wanted to study groups in the wild (or close to it).

At the time, the prevailing wisdom was that it didn't take

192

much to trigger intergroup conflict. Research in the minimal group paradigm, where researchers randomly assigned groups based on artificial or superficial similarities, had shown that ingroup/out-group bias emerges quickly, even in these synthetic nonsense groups. Each group would believe their group to be superior and that worthier individuals had been sorted into their group by chance. Surely eliciting conflict in real group competitions would be a piece of cake.

Most textbooks will tell you that Sherif had no problem conjuring real conflict. In 1954, he and his colleagues ran their own summer camp in Oklahoma for eleven-year-old boys. (*Lord of the Flies* was coincidentally published the same year.) The twenty-two boys were randomly assigned to one of two groups, each with its own territory in the two-hundred-acre camp. The boys named their groups the Rattlers and the Eagles. They made flags and uniforms for themselves. To set the conditions for conflict, Sherif organized competitions—tug-of-war, baseball, treasure hunts, and many others.

Conflict indeed showed its gruesome visage. After a loss, the Eagles stole and burned the Rattlers' flag. The Rattlers retaliated, raiding the Eagles' cabin. The Eagles raided the Rattlers' cabin in retaliation for the retaliation. Fistfights broke out. Sherif must have been pleased. Now they could get on with the true purpose of the experiment—reducing intergroup conflict.

The first attempt to lessen hostilities was a preacher, who offered a sermon on brotherly love. Although there's no harm in trying, it was as effective as Sherif expected it to be—not effective at all. If preaching was all it took, we'd live in a peaceful world indeed.

To lessen hostilities, Sherif then tried some fun activities for both groups. They watched movies, ate meals together, and set off firecrackers. This approach was based on the intergroup contact hypothesis, which was formalized in the 1950s by Harvard psychologist Gordon Allport (brother of Floyd, the group skeptic from Chapter 2). Proponents of intergroup contact predicted that the forces that lead us to dehumanize out-group members can be combated by, well, humanizing them. And the way to do that is to have meaningful contact with people from other groups so you can see them doing human things. You talk to them and try to understand their perspectives. If the Rattlers and Eagles did that, they'd see that their stereotypes and polarized attitudes about the other group were wrong. They aren't so bad! After all, we're all just human!

But socializing together didn't help the Eagles and Rattlers. Dinners were just a chance for mashed potato throwing and calling one another "ninnies," threatening "knuckle sandwiches," and hurling other adorable 1950s insults. And it wasn't just because they were eleven years old. It's because intergroup contact isn't all that effective at reducing conflict.

Subsequent research on the intergroup contact hypothesis isn't as dire as Robbers Cave but has had, at best, mixed success. Intergroup contact does change people's attitudes—the more time people spend with members of other groups, the more they like them. Indeed, research shows that familiarity breeds liking, not contempt. We have decades of research showing that even friends of friends from other groups can change people's attitudes, making them more favorably disposed toward the outgroup. For a little while, at least.

But intergroup contact isn't enough, on its own, to change behavior. In fact, despite people reporting less prejudice over time, intergroup contact doesn't always translate into less discrimination and prejudice. People love their own biases, especially when they become enmeshed in political ideology—they cling desperately to their beliefs in the face of almost any evidence.

Recent research suggests that increases in intergroup contact may not reduce prejudice at all, and prior research may have shown a spurious correlation. A spurious correlation is like the relationship between ice cream sales and murder rates. If you look at data on both, you'll probably find a correlation. When one goes up or down, so does the other. But that isn't because cookies and cream makes you a killer or murdering leads you to crave a tasty frozen treat. Instead, both are caused by hot weather, which does make people crave ice cream. And it also makes people more prone to anger and, simply, to be outside their homes and encountering other humans more often, heightening the chances of murderous rage.

Intergroup contact and prejudice have a tighter relationship than ice cream sales and murder rates, but there's more and more reason to wonder whether the relationship is causal. For instance, one recent study traced the prejudice of more than twenty-two thousand New Zealanders with European heritage against the indigenous Maori people over seven years. Although the researchers found that people who had more contact with the other group tended to express less prejudice, the relationship didn't appear causal. Looking at the same person over time, more contact didn't reduce prejudice.

A second study found the same thing when examining the

prejudice of white Brits against foreigners. Researchers have a promising theory for why intergroup contact isn't reducing prejudice. They found that people who value obedience to authority (known to psychologists as "right-wing authoritarianism") and believe society should be organized hierarchically, rather than equally (or "social dominance orientation"), avoided contact with out-groups more than people who are low in these traits. In other words, increases in intergroup contact come from people who weren't very prejudiced in the first place—the most prejudiced people avoided contact with out-groups and didn't benefit when they had it.

People have made many failed attempts to reduce the problems caused by conformity and conflict. What these attempts have in common is that they sought to alter our psychology and behavior through process alone, without changing the structures that reinforce many of the dangers of the group-focused parts of our brains.

Those who benefit from intergroup conflict erect and protect barriers between groups. They impose structures that gradually reinforce unequal access to power and resources. Although intergroup contact should be part of any effort to reduce prejudice, stereotypes, and conflict, it can't be the whole solution. We also need to change those structures.

Back at Robbers Cave, Sherif didn't give up when, predictably, his dinner-and-a-movie approach didn't work. He took the "in the wild" part of his experiment a little too seriously. To bring the Eagles and the Rattlers together, Sherif did something dangerous:

He sabotaged the camp's water supply by turning off the main valve and burying it under a pile of rocks.

The campers didn't know how or why the water had been shut off. The counselors asked the boys to follow the pipes back to the source to see if everything was all right. Hot and thirsty in the Oklahoma summer, the Eagles and Rattlers worked together for forty-five minutes to clear the rocks that Sherif and his team had placed there. After clearing the rocks and turning the water back on, the two groups celebrated as one. According to Sherif, the Rattlers even let the Eagles drink first because the Eagles hadn't brought their canteens with them.

The experimenters later arranged for the boys to "accidentally" encounter a truck carrying their food stuck on the road. Using their tug-of-war rope, the boys again collaborated to pull the truck free.

Jeopardizing their most basic resources created shared goals between both groups of boys that Sherif called "superordinate goals." Superordinate goals should reduce intergroup conflict by focusing both groups on the big picture—we both need food and water! They inspire the groups to collaborate. Our petty struggles over trophies and bragging rights need to take a back seat.

Superordinate goals are an important tool in reducing intergroup conflict. When something important happens to both groups, it can disrupt local social identities ("I'm a Rattler") and shift the focus to shared identities and shared goals ("I'm a camper and need food and water").

But superordinate goals are rarely as sudden and obvious as they were at Robbers Cave. They're often lurking in the background of conflicts that de-escalate or never happen at all.

Look at the Pig and Potato War. By 1859, the US and the UK had several shared goals and interdependencies, in addition to their shared language and cultural roots. The US sent the UK cotton and grain, subsidized by slavery, which was outlawed in the UK. The UK provided the US with manufactured goods and financial investments. So there was a lot to lose if a war broke out in 1859—the rich and powerful textile manufacturers and bankers of the UK would have been pretty unhappy if the flow of slave-harvested raw materials had been cut off.

They also had common foes. Both the US and UK were fighting China in the Second Opium War (in part, to expand the opium trade, which the Qing dynasty had restricted). In France, Napoleon III was causing trouble for America by intervening in Mexico, and France's imperial ambitions also worried the UK. And the US was sympathetic to the UK's fight against Russia in the recent Crimean War. There were plenty of common enemies during the years that had lessened their focus on one another.

Superordinate goals that focus groups in conflict on their commonalities are extremely powerful. Right now, we have a lot of conflict between groups in the world. But imagine that an alien spaceship came out of the sky. Out of the ship come ominous, formless shapes that begin to destroy whatever lies in their path— trees, buildings, people. Would humanity unite to fight off these alien invaders?

I've just outlined the setup for a lot of sci-fi movies (I had *Independence Day* in mind) because it illustrates one of the main ways to, at least temporarily, overcome intergroup conflict and social divisions. The easiest way to stop human conflict is an alien invasion—if we have a common enemy, be it COVID-19 or little green people, we might stop fighting among each other long enough to cope with it. Intergroup conflict can temporarily be put aside when we find common causes that allow us to see ourselves as part of a larger, shared group.

Attempts to rally people to superordinate goals are actually pretty common. For instance, the United Nations (which is itself an organization meant to overcome group boundaries) has come up with a list of the most pressing "Grand Challenges" facing humanity, including eliminating poverty, climate change, and disease prevention. Although they may be hard to turn into SMART goals, these challenges inherently require crossing national, organizational, and disciplinary boundaries. Even beyond these societal Grand Challenges, superordinate goals have the ability to bring people together. Think, for example, of Mark from legal and Tina from marketing putting aside their differences when the company is facing a lawsuit. Or the Elves, Dwarves, and humans putting their squabbles aside to fight an army of Orcs toward the end of *The Hobbit*. Both truth and fiction are full of stories of intergroup conflict taking a back seat because a superordinate goal has created a common purpose.

But even superordinate goals, on their own, aren't enough to end intergroup conflict. These goals need to translate into lasting collaboration and interdependence, where the stakes of conflict are so high that the majority has a lot to lose if conflict escalates.

Some now call this kind of situation "coopetition," a portmanteau of *cooperation* and *competition*. Rival pharmaceutical companies briefly collaborated to rapidly produce COVID-19 vaccines. Rivals British Airways and Virgin Atlantic put aside their longtime, heated rivalry when COVID pushed the entire industry—and the world—to a breaking point. In a symbolic gesture, both airlines ended the ban on travel from Europe with departing flights to America taking off simultaneously on parallel runways. But solidarity with other groups tends to wear off after a few months if strong cooperation structures aren't built. We all saw during COVID that US cooperation with China quickly turned to blame, polarization, and prejudice against Asians and Asian Americans.

Sherif also gave us more room for optimism with his lesser-known predecessor of Robbers Cave. Although it isn't in most textbooks, Sherif had attempted a similar experiment at an upstate New York campsite known as Middle Grove. Instead of turning off the water and marooning a food truck, Sherif had planned . . . a forest fire. Yes, his original plan was to bring a bunch of eleven-year-olds to upstate New York, persuade them to hate one another, and then set a fire around them to bring them together. Ah, psychology in the 1950s!

The problem was that Sherif couldn't get the two groups—the Panthers and the Pythons—to hate one another. Posing as camp counselors, Sherif's research assistants stole clothes from the Panthers and cut down their flag, encouraging them to blame the Pythons. One of Sherif's assistants even vandalized the Panthers' tent and broke a boy's ukulele.

But the two groups stubbornly refused to take the bait. The

Pythons swore on a Bible that they hadn't been responsible for the shenanigans, and the Panthers believed them. Afterward, the Pythons helped the Panthers clean up their tent. And both groups rightly grew suspicious of their "counselors." Because there was no conflict to solve, the forest fire never came. Sherif and his team had failed.

But there are lessons in Sherif's failure. Why was Middle Grove so much more peaceable than Robbers Cave?

First, the boys at Middle Grove spent time together before competing—some had kindled friendships by the time they were split into groups. But the Robbers Cave groups were unaware of one another for the first day or two.

This complicates the picture of what "intergroup contact" really means. As we've learned, once groups are enmeshed in conflict, intergroup contact isn't that effective. But relationships formed before competition—or before groups even form—are quite different. These connections buffer against conflict emerging in the first place. Connections aren't a panacea, however. There have been plenty of wars—like the American Civil War or the War of the Roses—where family and friends fought one another. But close, preexisting relationships help reduce the chances of conflict turning ugly.

Sherif and his team also subtly egged on the conflict at Robbers Cave. But their attempts were so obvious at Middle Grove that the boys could identify the true enemy: the research team. They were fomenting conflict all along! Once they noticed, the boys banded together to prevent the researchers from accomplishing their nefarious goals. As author Gina Perry, who wrote *The Lost*

Boys about Sherif's work at Middle Grove and Robbers Cave, said, "I do think it is a kind of optimistic view. It makes you smile, doesn't it? The fact that [the Middle Grove boys] mutinied against these guys . . . and refused to be drawn into it."

I think this gets at the most profound lesson of Middle Grove. Today, we have a lot of common foes who, like Sherif's research team, are trying to stir up trouble. Those foes are within every group. They're the ones who try to keep groups apart and encourage prejudice and conflict. Those who look to blame any problem on the other group and stoke anger. Those who demonize and dehumanize others. Those are the common foes we all face today—the politicians, bullies, and small-minded who prey on the dark side of our Paleolithic brains. If everyone who wanted to get along would see them for what they were, we might live in more of a Middle Grove world—where intergroup conflict never gets off the ground in the first place.

GROUP THOUGHTS ON COMPETITION

Thought 1: Compete Against Your Past Self

Problem: Although competition is motivating, it often directs our attention to others. And then it can spur dysfunctions like social comparison ("envy up, scorn down"), sabotaging opponents, and relational conflict.

Solution: Competing against yourself is the safest way to harness competition's benefits while minimizing its risks. Work on beating your personal bests, which, if you track them, can be vivid SMART goals. Journal every day, use apps that help you track your performance, or keep records of your personal bests. And join groups of people similarly interested in competing against their past selves. Or form a group if you can't find one to join!

I keep records for lots of things—which of my goals I achieve, how many words I write, and how much time I spend on various tasks. When I set a new record, I celebrate with a little yellow highlighter and note in my journal. I might buy myself a cheese scone for lunch! When I start new things—playing music, embarking on a research career, or writing a book—I join groups of others with similar interests.

Of course, it's only human to occasionally compare yourself to others. Just try to keep it healthy. You can compete against others as long as you keep in mind that the most important adversary is the one distracting you from improving. If you must compare, use it to learn how to improve yourself. If you can do that, winning will take care of itself.

Thought 2: Keep Conflict Focused on the Task

Problem: Disagreement about ideas is good in theory but hard to keep under control.

Solution: Start with everything we've said about good group decision-making in prior chapters: psychological safety, process leadership, clear goals, and productive dissent. The one thing I'll add is that you should have strong norms against anything resembling relationship conflict—especially when it is masquerading as task conflict. The main signs of relationship conflict I look for are personal attributions, or when members start talking about others in terms of traits or dispositions rather than the specific issue at hand. "You always say things like that" or "You are such a touchy person" are red flags. I will interrupt a discussion if I hear these kinds of statements. I'd say something like, "I'm worried this discussion is getting a little too personal. Let's take a break. When we come back, let's focus on getting these elephants out of here; we all want them in the hot-air balloons before the end of the day."

Thought 3: Work on Your Integrative Negotiation Skills

Problem: When people have different preferences or interests, their best solution isn't usually fighting it out. It's to negotiate! But many people have wrongheaded ideas about what it means to negotiate. They think negotiation means haggling, where one party gets more and the other less. We call this a "fixed-pie mindset."

Solution: When you have a fixed-pie mindset, it is easy to overlook win-win solutions. Most parties (individuals or groups) have multiple issues they can discuss simultaneously. When one party values an issue more than the other, that's an opportunity for mutual gains. If A is most important to me and B is most important to you, we can probably both get what we want. We're not arguing over how much of the pie we get; we're looking for ways to enlarge it.

Skilled negotiators look for opportunities for mutual gains. They negotiate multiple issues simultaneously, and they share information and discuss preferences rather than making offers or demands.

When negotiation is done this way, it looks a lot like group decision-making. In fact, it is. All collective decisions are negotiations between multiple parties' preferences. And all negotiations are collective decisions. The same basic rules apply.

Thought 4: Get a Mediator to Help Diffuse Dysfunctional Conflict

Problem: One of the most common questions I get is: How do I deal with two teammates who can never seem to get along? There's no quick answer because, as I've repeatedly pointed out, bad is psychologically stronger than good. Once the dark side of conflict escapes, it is difficult to put it back in the bottle. Relationship conflict erodes the trust that we have each other's best interests at heart. And two parties who don't trust one another are going to have a hard time solving a problem.

Solution: A starting point is to have a skilled third party get involved—a mediator. Good mediators help people name their problems and come up with ways to rebuild trust and cooperative capacity. That takes clinical skill, so it's best if this person has some experience and the trust of both parties.

But mediation—especially between groups—is difficult and slow. With larger groups like nations, you can have some members trying hard to solve problems through mediation and negotiation while other members are out there escalating the conflict! But that doesn't mean we shouldn't try mediation, which can be very powerful when done right. (There are references in the endnotes if you want to learn more.)

SECTION IV

Leading Groups

Section IV is about putting a collective perspective into action. In Chapter 12, I'll explain the most common mistake that people make when trying to fix a struggling group: coaching a group to change its process without fixing its structure. And in Chapter 13, I'll tell you why group leadership isn't just for formal leaders. Instead, group leadership is a team sport, not a single individual sitting atop a pyramid-shaped hierarchy. All members of groups can exercise leadership—if they know where to look. And finally, in Chapter 14, we'll talk about what the future holds for groups and what groups can do to shape the future, including how new technologies change collaboration (and vice versa). Even though this book spends a lot of time describing dark sides, challenges, and paradoxes, groups that challenge themselves to get better every day are still humanity's most powerful tool. Whether you are a C-suite executive or just want your book group to be a little more fun, you can share in the leadership of your group. And in doing so, you can make the world a little better.

CHAPTER 12

The House Always Wins

When to Structure and When to Coach Your Groups

I'm just old enough to remember when documents were copied by writing extra-hard on top of purple carbon paper. But then came Xerox. Xerox dominated the early days of photocopying, and photocopies were synonymous with the brand, like Kleenex, Band-Aids, and Hoovers (at least here in the UK).

At the time, photocopiers seemed like magic—but there was a high risk of a paper jam, empty ink cartridge, or inscrutable error message. I remember many times in the 1990s when I stood in a white button-down shirt with ink-stained hands, yanking a mangled sheet of paper from the maw of the photocopier. And I'd wonder why it was so hard to keep these damn things working right. Broken printers and photocopiers were such a cliché that the climactic moment in the movie *Office Space* involves the main characters clubbing a machine with a baseball bat. Xerox machines were both saviors and tormentors.

A photocopier's boxy exterior hides its Swiss-watch-like precision inside. These machines are so complex and were updated so frequently back then that even technicians were sometimes befuddled when they opened them up. To cope with these challenges, the best technicians shared underground knowledge of how to fix them, learning the latest tricks not from the company, but from one another. Xerox tried to foster this learning, dividing its technicians into teams of between three and nine, covering a geographic territory or set of clients. These teams needed to collaborate to keep the machines working well, learn about new problems and how to fix them, and respond to customer issues.

But some teams were better than others. Some kept clients happy and machines humming; others struggled. Some were real teams, while others were teams in name only and it was every technician for themselves.

It was clear that there was synergy in the truly superb teams, who were performing better than any combination of individuals had a right to. Xerox worked with organizational psychologist Ruth Wageman to find out what these regional managers, the external leaders of these teams, could do to help the ineffective teams become more like the effective ones.

In her research, Wageman investigated two broad classes of leader behaviors: structuring and coaching. First, leaders could intervene by **structuring** the group—they could work on the goals, tasks, composition, and norms of the team. Second, they could intervene by **coaching** the group—trying to manage conflict productively, facilitating problem-solving sessions, and offering advice. Coaching interventions directly target process. They try to head off process losses and catalyze synergy. Motivational speeches, feedback sessions, strategic planning meetings, and advice are all examples of coaching.

Which do you think helped teams more? Or—even better—under what conditions did these two types of interventions help Xerox teams the most? And what does this have to do with me if I'm not leading a work team like those at Xerox?

While you think about the answers, let me tell you a quick story.

My First Trip to a Casino

I made my first trip to a Las Vegas casino when I was seventeen years old. It didn't feel as adventurous as it might sound. My dad has lived in Nevada for as long as I can remember, moving to Reno when I was five, then to Las Vegas about ten years later. By age seventeen, I had grown a thick black goatee and could pass for someone in his mid-twenties. So one night on my annual summer visit to Nevada, Dad took me to a casino. To avoid scrutiny, we played video poker on some out-of-the-way machines, out of sight of the tables with live dealers.

I knew how to play poker reasonably well. Beyond Dad living in Reno and Las Vegas for most of my life, my grandparents had an old handheld video poker machine that I'd played with since I was little. I knew well what cards to hold in a five-card draw.

But these machines were "double bonus poker" with unusual odds—they paid a bonus for some four of a kinds, especially four aces. The odds were so appealing, my Dad advised me to keep even one ace and chase certain four of a kinds—even when that wouldn't normally be a good strategy. And it worked—I got four aces not once, but twice! We were caught up in it, hooting and hollering when we won, and swearing when we missed a promising draw. After a few hours, we walked out of the casino about seven hundred dollars richer.

Since that first winning trip to the casino, I've never had a better night of video poker. And as a professor who uses statistics as part of my job, betting against casino machines has lost its appeal. Understanding probabilities has ruined these experiences for me—when gambling against a machine, there's an optimal strategy and using it robotically is your literal best bet. So I don't get the emotional kick anymore because, on games like double bonus poker, there's nothing you can do besides obey those probabilities. And those probabilities show that the game is stacked against you.

But there are some smart gamblers who find real edges on casino machines. In 2019, for example, two professional gamblers, who journalist Eric Raskin identified only as "Max" and "Jay," started a group that won almost one million dollars during a single week in an online slot game called *Ocean Magic*. *Ocean Magic* featured gold-hued "wild bubbles" that could lead to big payouts. And Max and Jay noticed a flaw in the game's design: If wild bubbles were visible in certain positions before a spin, you had an excellent chance of winning—an actual advantage over the house.

This kind of edge doesn't happen very often, so Max and Jay

called their pro-gambler friends. Recognizing the rare opportunity, they all traveled to New Jersey, where the game was based. They identified a safe, winning bet and a legal strategy to take advantage of it—get the sign-up bonus for creating new accounts, make a big bet when the wild bubbles are in the proper position, and, after the spins where you had the advantage, quit playing. It worked out about as well as they could have dreamed.

Casinos, though, are on the lookout for these kinds of edges—they constantly monitor winning patterns that violate the game's intended probabilities. Within a few days, several of the thirteen casinos with *Ocean Magic* had removed it. By the end of the week, the game had vanished.

Then Max and Jay had to get the casinos to pay. Although the first part of their winnings had been paid, several casinos dragged their feet in paying the rest and claimed that some unnamed policy had been violated. It isn't clear whether all the money ever got paid out or not.

Back to the leaders of our underperforming Xerox technician teams. Should they intervene with structure or coaching?

As you might have expected, structural interventions worked like magic. Leaders who invested in group composition, task design, goals, and norms saw quick payoffs: Well-structured teams performed better than poorly structured teams by a wide margin (explaining 37 percent of the difference in how well teams performed). Wageman's results were representative of the effects of work design on team effectiveness: A 2007 meta-analysis of 259 studies including almost 220,000 people found that structure (in this case, work design) accounted for 43 percent of ups and downs in team performance and member satisfaction. So structure is a powerful way to influence how well a group performs.

The story with coaching is more complicated. First, some of the coaching wasn't just unhelpful, it was harmful. Some leaders weren't following the group dynamics textbook at all! They'd meet with individual members but rarely the team as a whole. They'd micromanage, watching key metrics like a hawk. They'd call customers themselves instead of helping the team handle problems on their own. They'd point out problems but then wouldn't work to figure out how to solve them. And they'd single out individuals to blame for the problems.

But even good coaching—advice, consulting on problem-solving, and pep talks—didn't help teams as much as leaders had hoped. Although Xerox teams that received good coaching managed themselves better, they didn't get better results. Coaching—directly intervening to influence group process—had nowhere near the effects that structural interventions had.

The picture gets clearer when we examine structural and coaching interventions in combination. When Xerox groups were well structured—when they had the SMART goals, strong composition, sensible norms, and well-designed tasks—they benefited from good coaching. However, poorly structured teams that received good coaching saw only insignificant increases in their effectiveness.

And as an added bonus, well-structured teams were inoculated against the harms of negative coaching. Although negative coaching made all teams less satisfied, poorly structured teams were harmed about three times as much as well-structured teams. The rich got richer, and the poor got poorer.

In other words, structure is king. You need the right structure in place for good coaching to make a difference.

Casinos are a great metaphor for understanding which interventions pay off and shape group dynamics, and the most common mistake people make.

Coaching is like Dad telling me to hold aces or Max and Jay looking for wild bubbles. Like gambling strategies, coaching directly targets group process. Sports coaches admonish their teams to try harder or change tactics. Governments put up signs to remind you not to litter. Parents cajole and discipline their children to change their behavior.

If you get lucky, you can win a few thousand dollars at video poker by changing your strategy at the casino. In the best of times, you find an edge in wild bubbles and make around a million (although getting the casino to pay might be tough). But those are the exceptions; coaching a rigged game won't win for long.

You know what's not the exception? Casinos winning. They consistently get not just millions but billions of dollars because casinos structure the game, setting the odds for video poker or the rules for slots. They might lose in the short term to a few sharps like Max and Jay, but they almost always win in the long term.

When you use structural interventions, you are the casino. Structural interventions allow you to stack the deck in your group's favor. Real teams with the right mix of knowledge and perspectives. Rich, motivating tasks. Vivid, important, challenging goals.

Norms that reduce conformity and encourage sharing capabilities with the group. That's a group ready for synergy—and good coaching.

Once you've stacked the deck, then it's time to coach the team. But too many group leaders seem to forget that they can change the game they're playing.

Even if you aren't managing a work team, you can still influence the structure of your groups. You can suggest and SMART-en up goals and tasks for your family and friends. Committees at work, the PTA, your band, your book group—all these are groups where structure isn't fixed. You can change it. A question like "What are we supposed to have done for next week? I'm not quite sure" can spark a discussion that clarifies goals, tasks, roles, and norms for everyone. You don't need to be a formal leader to initiate a discussion on your group's structure.

Like gambling, group dynamics involve both chance and skill. Groups have so many moving parts, composed of unique individuals all with their own hopes, dreams, and struggles, who are then affected by group dynamics and one another. The world around them is changing, and they are changing with it. It's no wonder that there is no way to guarantee an effective collective.

My glorious victory at video poker is actually a metaphor for the most common mistake in the group dynamics game. My dad and I thought hard about the way we would play and came up with a good strategy. Honestly, we were playing the game about as well as it could be played. So why was this a mistake?

The mistake was playing the game at all. If your goal is to

maximize your chances of winning money, you've already lost the second you walk into the casino. You're playing someone else's game, one that is structured for you to lose in the long run. Even *Ocean Magic*, one of the great recent examples of beating the house, didn't last for long. You can beat the house for a little while, but in the end, the house always wins.

Get the Order Right

When I talk to my students, whether they're in government or business leaders or just starting a new job, they often want to know what they can do to fix their teams. Meetings that seem pointless. Infighting and politics at work. A micromanaging boss. Unmotivated teammates. How can I fix it?

Most people want to go straight to coaching. Let's get everyone together in a room. We aren't motivated, so let's get fired up! Our strategy is flawed so I'll offer some advice. But often, these glaring problems are symptoms that you're playing a rigged game. They're the runny nose, not the cold virus. And although you can sometimes treat symptoms in the short term, it's not a long-term cure.

I've argued for the power of group structure throughout the book. That's because of how much it matters for group dynamics. We haven't had too many stories about a great leader who stepped in and saved the day. The speeches that have been used as examples—like Coach K's launch speech—are those that help clarify teams' goals and tasks, making sure we all know where we're going.

So get the order right. Before you start scheduling an off-site retreat to hash out the interpersonal problems in your group, do a careful analysis of how your group is structured. Do you have a small team with diverse, task-relevant knowledge and perspectives? Is your goal clear, challenging, important, and vivid? Is the work well designed? Are your norms aligned with your purpose? Work on fixing structural problems before you focus on fixing process. Otherwise, you're just making the best of a rigged game.

The same is true for any group. Honestly, in parenting, I often fall into the same trap, defaulting to coaching when I want to change my kids' behavior. If they are neglecting their chores, bickering too much, or glued to their phones, I give them a little speech. But even these process problems are usually symptoms of underlying structural causes. In families, people fight because they don't have enough money or they don't have a shared vision for their lives. That's a frustrating experience, so you might fight about everything from how to do the dishes to how much screen time the kids get. But if you don't analyze the underlying causes, you end up spending all of your energy on the symptoms.

I want to be clear that providing quality team coaching isn't wrong. On the contrary, it's definitely good! But the most common mistake managers, parents, or other group leaders make is to coach without considering the group's structure. Often, that mistake grows out of individualism——attributing the causes of collective performance to individuals. People think their problems are caused by a bad apple who just needs to be monitored or an unmotivated worker who needs a pep talk. Although good coaching can lead to short-term changes, bad structure exerts a slow, steady pull on processes that will overwhelm even good coaching. Often, the group member who seems not to pull their weight isn't clear on their role in the group or feels excluded by other members. People who don't understand the endpoint often wander off in different directions but then blame one another for going to the wrong place.

Richard Hackman and Ruth Wageman use what they call the 60:30:10 rule to think about what matters most for group effectiveness. I teamed up with them to apply this rule to *when* leaders should intervene. The rule states that about 60 percent of group effectiveness is determined by structural features like goals, tasks, composition, and norms. Structural features are usually in place before the team ever meets. The time to intervene in these areas is before the group gets to work. Sometimes, before the group even exists.

About 30 percent of effectiveness is determined by how the team is launched. Are the group's goals and purpose articulated clearly? Does each member feel like they're part of the group for a good reason—that they're accepted and respected for their potential contributions to the group? Are the norms that promote psychological safety, clarify communication and coordination processes, and ward off conformity and dysfunctional conflict well understood right from the start? Do we leave the launch with clear next steps? The time to intervene in these areas is at the very beginning.

And the final 10 percent is determined by expert coaching—small adjustments, advice, and problem-solving that keep the team on track. Because if you get the structure right, process and people mostly take care of themselves; they just need a little nudge now and again. Well-structured groups can benefit from the encouragement, advice, and feedback that coaching provides. That's why good coaching is the final condition that promotes group effectiveness—the cherry on top of our collective perspective.

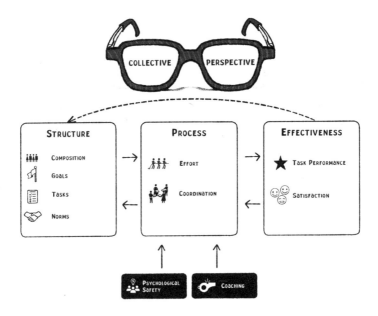

The lack of inherent structure in most of the groups in your life is a huge opportunity! All it takes is having real discussions about what your groups' goals are and the norms you want to adhere to. If you start a band, a club, a committee, or a business, you have a ton of latitude. And even if you are a member with little formal authority, you can still ask questions about structure to draw attention to it or propose ways of improving things that others may have missed. Indeed, there are so many ways you can improve your groups' structure and give them a real chance at synergy.

CHAPTER 13

The *L* Word

When and Why Leadership Matters

When I was a first-year doctoral student, my mentor Richard Hackman invited me to a panel he was serving on about leadership. One of the other panelists was a leader in a major cultural organization. (I won't say which to protect the innocent.) The panelist gave a talk titled "Leadership Lessons from Jazz." I watched from the audience as he suggested that, like jazz masters Duke Ellington, Miles Davis, and Louis Armstrong, leaders of all kinds should "listen closely," "find your own sound," "jam," "remain fresh . . . innovate," and "take risks . . . improvise!"

After the panel was over, Richard wrote to ask me what I, as a jazz musician and aspiring leadership scholar, thought of that talk. I was a bit nervous to respond. As a new grad student, what did my opinion matter? Did he like the talk? Was that panelist a friend of his?

I was honest. "I didn't disagree with much," I began. "But I didn't learn much either. You could get those kinds of lessons from almost anything. Like, I could come up with 'Leadership Lessons from Turtles': 'Have a thick skin,' 'Know when to retreat into your shell,' 'Hide your eggs carefully,' 'Slow and steady wins the race,' or 'Don't let anyone flip you on your back.'"

Richard came into my office and stood behind my desk, all six feet, six inches of him looming over me. "I got your email," he said sternly. Then he laughed and clapped me on the back. We agreed. That presentation—and a lot of other advice on leadership—was vacuous. It's not wrong, but it's empty. Like the advice you get from cracking open a fortune cookie.

I'm going to tell you about another music-derived leadership talk I attended. This time, it was led by an orchestral conductor who has a side hustle as a leadership guru. He was blathering on about what a great leader he is because he gets the best out of people. And to demonstrate, he brought along a cellist. The cellist played a short piece without the conductor. But then he started waving his arms around in front of her as she played it again. As they no doubt had planned, she now played a bit more vigorously. "You see?" he demanded. "You see how I led her to a better performance?"

I didn't see. I saw how the situation demanded that the cellist first play a tame version and then spice it up to make the conductor look good. But I didn't see much contribution from him.

In fact, orchestral conductors are one of the worst models for group leadership. Now, most conductors I've met are fantastic musicians and teachers, and many have great leadership skills. It's not their fault that they're part of an archaic organizational structure, akin to one of the "medieval institutions" biologist Edward O. Wilson warned us about.

Surprisingly, even medieval musicians knew better than to have conductors. In the fifteenth century, preclassical European musicians synchronized their performances with a constant beat from a percussion instrument like a drum. Even church choirs stayed together with a member smacking a roll of paper to create a clear, audible beat. That's what most of the musical world does.

But musical ensembles (like top management teams) started to grow in size. By the Baroque period (late-1600s until mid-1700s), conducting had a foothold; composers often played the keyboard and would occasionally wave their arms to direct tempo changes, entrances, and stops from there. Sometimes the first violin player (or "concert master") would sit in a prominent position and gesture with their bow to keep everyone together. But there still weren't specialized conductors, and those who conducted weren't necessarily considered the "leader" of the group—they were just chipping in to help the group stay together.

Orchestral conductors fully emerged in the early nineteenth century when Beethoven and his contemporaries started writing complicated music for enormous ensembles. Tempo changes and dramatic starts and stops all required intricate coordination. Not everyone was happy about the prevalence of conductors. Robert Schumann, one of my favorite composers, called them "a necessary evil."

Over time, conductors accrued more fame and influence; many famous composers were also conductors, which helped.

Audiences applauded to acknowledge the composition of the piece as much as its performance. Today conductors seldom perform their own compositions, yet they still get the bulk of the credit and applause. Audiences—and even the musicians themselves—often think of conductors as the main drivers of collective performance. It's no wonder that, like our conductor-leadership guru, many conductors start to think of themselves as heroes.

This leads to a strange state of affairs, where our conductor-guru can run his leadership seminar. The cellist he was "leading" was a highly trained professional who had secured one of the most coveted jobs in her industry—a seat in a major orchestra. She'd practiced for tens of thousands of hours and performed thousands of times. There was no one to coordinate with, so no need for a conductor at all. The cellist could have played just fine without him.

Too many conductors govern orchestras like dictators, giving world-class orchestral musicians little say over how to do their jobs. And it shows in the data. One study found that only 32 percent of orchestral musicians felt they had autonomy in their jobs—about the same as clerical workers (35 percent) and much lower than human relations workers (more than 60 percent).

Researchers Jutta Allmendinger, Richard Hackman, and Erin Lehman found something even more alarming in their study of symphony orchestras. In 1996, they compared orchestral musicians' job satisfaction to that of twelve other professions. You'd think that winning a sought-after, secure, reasonably paying job playing music—a lifelong calling for most professional musicians—would be among the most satisfying ones out there. But the orchestral musicians ranked seventh, just above industrial production teams and just below federal prison guards! And it isn't because musicians are generally moody or because classical music makes you sad; professional string quartets came in first. The explanation comes back to group structure. There is perhaps no other field in which fifty to one hundred world experts are assembled in a room and then allowed so little autonomy. Given what we've learned about the importance of autonomy in motivating work, it's no wonder they weren't satisfied.

The thinking about leadership that underlies the archaic, misguided structure of symphony orchestras is everywhere. In this chapter, I'll explain a better way to think about group leadership. But first, we need to interrogate the individualistic "Great Man" theories of leadership that permeate our society and institutions. Like the "Lone Genius," the "Great Man" takes too much credit for a group's success—but instead of claiming sole responsibility, the "Great Man" claims to be uniquely able to pull greatness from others.

Orchestras aren't the only place where "Great Man" myths have shaped our institutions. After all, I'm living in a country with an actual king! As we discussed in Chapter 1, even when the reality is that groups are the engine of progress and change, we tend to focus the story on a single hero. Leadership is no different. Even when there are many influential people in the group, we tend to look to the one sitting atop the hierarchy, like presidents, generals, sports coaches, and CEOs.

When people stop to think about it, they're smart enough to realize that any single leader isn't able to solve every group problem.

Dictators—whether a monarch chosen by God or a pushy boss who tries to micromanage every aspect of your project—aren't great at running any group. Any individual who tries to do everything for a group, organization, or nation is destined to fall short. A group that effectively relies on multiple members for leadership, however, has the benefit of more labor and more expertise. And indeed, most studies show that shared leadership improves group effectiveness.

So why do we still expect our leaders to be heroes? And why do we blame them when things go wrong? First, I'll explain why we tend to put all the responsibility on one person and then I'll show you why and how collective leadership is better. With collective leadership, anyone can be a leader—even you.

Down with the Leader!

When a group is struggling, it's clear that many people think replacing the leader is a good move. Most professional sports leagues have a "Black Monday," when a host of coaches and managers are fired—even those who have a long track record of success. In the NBA, where coaches are presumably already the best of the best, the average tenure for a head coach is five years; 25 percent of coaches are fired every year. That's about the same as the English Premier League (EPL), but the average tenure of an EPL manager is now down to a little over two years! When things go wrong, it's the leader who takes the fall.

It sure seems like we expect leaders to be heroes and saviors and blame them when they aren't—"the captain should go down with the ship" and all that. In the 1980s, organizational scientist

James Meindl and his colleagues suspected that leaders might get more than their fair share of the credit and blame. They compared how much people thought that business leaders were the cause of their groups' performance, relative to other factors like subordinates, the general economy, or anything else they could think of. They found that leaders got about 50 percent of the credit and blame when performance didn't change much (that is, slight or moderate increases and decreases in group performance). But leaders got even more blame when there was a large decrease and more credit when there was a large increase.

Given all we've learned about group dynamics, even pinning 50 percent of the outcome on the leader seems excessive. Groups are unpredictable beasts, wildly exposed to an ever-changing world. Sports teams can get a rash of injuries and unlucky bounces. Businesses can fail because of economic calamity or natural disaster beyond any leader's control. Presidents and prime ministers are lauded or blamed for economic conditions that fall well beyond their remit. Through no fault of the leader, terrible musical ensembles can become famous while great ones languish in obscurity (not that I'm bitter).

Many people believe there's a "new manager bump"—that group performance improves when the leader is replaced. After all, we've learned that leaders are likely to be more wedded to the status quo and hesitant to change. So should you replace the leader when the group is struggling?

On average, the data doesn't support leader change as a reliable method for rejuvenating groups. Research on replacing leaders has produced mixed results. Although some studies find a small new-leader bump in performance, the question is whether this can be explained by "regression to the mean," in which underperforming teams will naturally revert toward an average level of performance. So it can be difficult to tell whether new leaders are helpful or improvement is just statistical noise.

A few studies cut through the noise by looking more directly at the influence that coaches have on process. A detailed study of Polish soccer managers accounted for not only the points teams scored, but also measures of effort—how far and how fast players ran during matches. At first, players indeed ran farther and faster after the team's manager was fired, leading to more scoring. But this effect was driven not by extraordinary effort under the new manager, but by poor effort under the fired one—players' effort only reverted to the mean. And this increased short-term effort made little difference in the long run. Even after firing their managers, these teams still significantly underperformed similar teams that hadn't fired their coaches.

In another study, Norwegian researchers conducted a clever study of whether teams benefited from firing their leaders. They used data from a different NFL, the Norwegian Football League (the soccer kind), and compared teams that fired their coaches with similar teams that had the same negative performance trajectory but didn't fire their coaches. The results? In subsequent contests, teams that fired their coaches didn't do better than teams that retained them—if anything, they did worse, improving more slowly than teams that retained their coaches.

Although this kind of correlational data isn't definitive, it's consistent with other research on sports-leader turnover. Coaches are most influential when they control composition—they can change who's on the team and who plays. When they can only affect group processes like effort and coordination, their influence is reduced—usually around 1 or 2 percent of the variance in performance, rather than the 50 percent Meindl found people expected.

But people still believe that leaders should get much of the credit and blame for collective performance outcomes. One experimental study shows that, while teams get more collective credit for success, people pin more blame for poor performance on individuals like leaders. Although there's no way to know precisely how much influence leaders have, it's clear that people use "leadership" as a cognitive shortcut when trying to understand the causes of complex collective phenomena.

So what's the alternative to looking at success and failure for judging group leadership?

Functional, Shared Leadership

To understand group leadership, you need to look beyond outcomes like wins, stock prices, and whether the country is in a recession. Those outcomes are the combination of complex factors, many of which are beyond any leader's control. You also need to look beyond the person sitting on the proverbial throne.

Instead, you should think about leadership as what all group members are doing to improve group dynamics. In other words, you should think about group leadership as "functional" and "shared." By *functional*, I mean getting the most essential group functions fulfilled, whatever they are at the moment. Usually, those functions are about providing purpose and direction to the group, helping to structure and coordinate work, and creating the conditions for individual perspectives to be heard and appreciated without losing the cohesion and coordination that make the group a group.

In the Redeem Team, for instance, we talked about Coach K's textbook launch of Team USA, where he clearly articulated the team's goals. That helped motivate the team. We also learned about when team captain Kobe Bryant derisively acknowledged his teammates returning from a night of partying when he was already on the way to the weight room in the morning. That also helped motivate the team.

That brings us to the second point. You might have noticed that I've named not one, but two people who provided leadership to the Redeem Team. Coach K was the formal leader, but he wasn't the only leader. Kobe Bryant may have had just as big of an influence when he inspired his teammates to focus on their craft and work harder. We could also say that LeBron James showed leadership in responding to Kobe's hint of derision as he did and encouraging his teammates to do the same (and would Bryant's behavior have even been leadership if James hadn't encouraged his teammates to follow suit?). And what about Team USA director Jerry Colangelo, who hired Coach K and changed the selection and training process? Isn't he the most important leader of the group? He put into place a lot of the structural conditions we discussed in Chapter 12.

The answer is all the above. Group leadership is *shared*—no one person or job title should be responsible for providing all the group's leadership. The best groups don't rely on a single leader for all their leadership needs. They largely manage themselves.

Everyone should see leading the group as their job, building and maintaining structures and coaching one another as needed.

Any proactive attempt to influence group members toward achieving these functions counts as leadership. Those actions can come from formal leaders like Coach K, or informal leaders like Kobe Bryant and LeBron James, who have the admiration of their peers. Leadership actions can be noisy and public, like an orchestral conductor entering the stage to wild applause and flailing about like a drunk octopus. Or they can be quiet and unnoticed, like asking a naive question that clarifies the goals in a meeting, fixing a problem no one else noticed, or telling a joke that defuses a potentially dysfunctional conflict.

Following this logic, any proactive attempt to foster collaboration, process gains, and synergy is leadership. So are efforts to prevent the dark side of conformity and conflict from taking hold. From a functional perspective, this whole book is a stealth leadership book!

Relaunches

Fulfilling a group's needs is like being an archer on horseback, galloping at full speed while trying to shoot a moving target. So to go back to our question from the beginning of the chapter: Should replacing the head of a group be the default response when things go wrong? No. You only need leadership changes when formal leaders abdicate their duties—when they're unwilling or unable to make necessary changes to group structure and processes. Yet doing something because it worked last year isn't good enough, either; good groups think through the current situation, the current group, and the current task and then structure and coach accordingly.

And that brings us to relaunches. University of Washington professor Michael Johnson and his colleagues designed a clever experiment in which they put teams in a bad situation and then asked members what they'd like to change—group processes, personnel, and/or structure. (They could choose more than one.) When problems emerged, 84 percent of groups changed their processes and 16 percent altered their personnel. But only 5 percent made the change that most reliably improved performance—adjusting their structure.

Because people overlook structure so often, I recommend that people relaunch their groups when things go awry. This lets us go back to the beginning—to reassess the group's goals and whether the group's structure is likely to achieve those goals. If not, make the necessary changes. Then literally relaunch the team. Get the right people. Hold a meeting like it's the first day of a new group. Articulate a compelling, vivid direction for the group. Make sure that group members have well-designed, whole pieces of work. Discuss the norms you'll follow to communicate and collaborate.

I do a mini-relaunch whenever I can. After any deadline or milestone, I try to get everyone to reassess how we're doing. As organizational scientists Hengchen Dai, Katy Milkman, and Jason Riis have shown, any salient mark on the calendar—a new year, a new month, a new task—is an opportunity for change. Groups need those opportunities. Using beginnings, middles, and ends strategically gives you some of the best tools for steering the group dynamics ship.

Are You a Leader Now?

It may seem like I'm arguing that individual leaders don't matter. But that would be absurd. Clearly bad leaders can do a lot of harm. And some great leaders are unusually skilled at diagnosing what needs doing and getting it done. But individual leaders matter less than our Paleolithic brains would have us believe. Social systems are complicated. Putting all the responsibility for collective outcomes onto a single person is always an oversimplification.

So if you find yourself in a leadership position, is it better to be humble, authentic, and generous? Yes! But even if you aren't, the important thing is to do what needs doing. Clarify goals. Do your part to improve psychological safety. If you don't understand or agree with the norms, discuss them. If you have a suggestion, speak up while respecting that others might disagree. Ask others what they think—and listen well when they answer. Be proactive—don't wait around for other people to tell you what to do. Communicate clearly. And if you can't do something you think needs doing, help find someone who can. That's real group leadership.

CHAPTER 14

Groups of the Future

Or Our Future with Groups

As you're reading this, you might live in a world where commuting to the office is mostly a memory: Most office work now takes place in an augmented reality. We all wear glasses that bring three-dimensional, holographic video into our homes. Or we put on headsets and suddenly seem to be in a virtual room on a secluded island beach. Or perhaps we have an artificial intelligence (AI) avatar that can attend the meeting on our behalf. Maybe we'll have brain implants, through which we can have a Borg-like hive mind, where we share one another's thoughts and feelings.

I don't know whether any of these groupy techno futures will come to pass, although all seem within reach. And all seem alien to us, with the potential to throw our lives into flux. Writing about the future of humans and technology is a dangerous business. The chapter title, "Groups of the Future," is a little misleading. You know the future better than I do because you're reading this now, while I may have written these words years ago. I can't say with any confidence which, if any, of these worlds will come to pass.

But I can tell you with confidence that, on the surface, groups of the future will look different from the groups of today and they'll use different technologies to communicate and collaborate. But deep down, they'll be the same because they'll still need to balance our core needs for autonomy, belonging, and competence against whatever changes in convenience, speed, and realism the future may bring. It isn't for me to tell you how to adapt to any particular technology. Instead, it's to help you understand how to allow new ways of working together to coevolve with emerging technologies.

For most of my career, students, media, and managers have asked me about virtual teams. What are the best practices? How should we manage them? And I'd answer that most problems in virtual teams are the same problems you have in other teams. If your virtual team is struggling, the technology isn't the first place you should look. The same structural and process issues apply.

Still, virtual teams do differ from face-to-face groups. Importantly, they increase psychological distance among members. Many of us experienced a change in groupiness when the COVID pandemic separated us from work, school, and family. Our proximity changed, and so did our sense of connection to others. That also affected our ability to listen to one another, so many groups were retaining less information when meeting virtually.

But virtual collaboration has also been great! It allows us to compose teams with the best people from around the world. It can help with work-life balance, removing an overlooked ravager of our life satisfaction—long commutes. Virtual collaboration actually has a lot of advantages, even though it increases psychological distance and information loss. How can we have our cake and eat it, too?

The main tip I give to virtual teams is to establish communication norms and stick to them. Constantly switching communication media makes collaboration harder. A team that always meets on Zoom tends to do better than one that switches between Zoom, face-to-face, and a hybrid of the two. Most of us are getting better at using various communication media and platforms. But groups need norms, especially when a different technology is involved. How do we feel about cameras on versus off? Mics muted when you aren't talking? Can we use the chat or polls to get more people involved? Regardless of what you choose, the important thing is that you've had a discussion about what your norms should be—and that you revisit them from time to time. But when you keep mixing different communication processes, it's harder to develop productive norms.

No technology alters the fundamental challenges of teamwork. Learning how to collaborate using any new technology or trend is a moving target. Even if I wrote the best answers at this moment, chances are that the technology will have changed by the time you read these words. Most group problems are dealt with in the preceding chapters, not this one. We haven't solved these problems when we're face-to-face; using a new technology just adds another layer of complexity.

Yet if you have good group dynamics, new technologies can enable better, more diverse collaboration than ever before. So the best thing I can tell you is how new approaches to teamwork develop in concert with technological innovations—and how to get the most from this coevolution.

A Tale of Two Heart Surgeries

In the 1990s, heart surgery got a jolt with new technology. Historically, heart surgeons needed to crack open the breastbone to access the heart. The surgical team would stop the patient's heart, attaching it to a machine that kept the blood flowing to the rest of the body. Then the surgeon would fix what needed fixing, like performing a valve repair or coronary artery bypass grafting. The team then needed to restart the patient's heart, weaning it off the machine, removing air from the heart chambers to prevent embolisms, and administering small electrical shocks to get the heart beating again.

But by the mid-1990s, a new approach to the surgery was on the rise—minimally invasive cardiac surgery (MICS). Instead of cutting through the bone in the middle of your chest, surgeons performing MICS could make a few keyhole incisions to access the heart. Newly developed cameras and other instruments were then inserted through the incisions, allowing surgeons to repair the heart without splitting open the chest.

The main advantage of MICS was patient comfort. It's clear that recovery times were drastically reduced from months to days. And after the surgery, patients were in significantly less pain and didn't have a huge, permanent scar down the middle of their chest.

Despite the advantages, many cardiac surgeons initially bristled at the new technology. They had saved many lives with traditional open-heart surgery—one of the most dramatic, prestigious types of surgery, in which patients' hearts in were literally in surgeons' hands. Traditional open-heart surgery took years to master. And that mastery required the expansive view the large chest incision provided. "How could this new approach really be trusted?" surgeons might have wondered. "MICS might take years or decades to become as reliable as open-heart surgery." As one editorial in the *Journal of Thoracic Disease* asked, "Minimally Invasive Cardiac Surgery—a Fad or the Future?" One of the editorial's main concerns was whether surgical teams could collaborate well enough to pull it off.

Like orchestral conductors, many heart surgeons were quasi dictators, barking out commands for others to obey. MICS, however, required communication from the whole team. Amy Edmondson (of psychological safety fame) and her colleagues studied how two hospitals reacted to the introduction of MICS. In the first hospital, which we'll call Hospital A, surgeons found this increased communication disruptive. "In Dr. D's room, he doesn't want unnecessary chatter. Period," one nurse told Edmondson. An assisting perfusionist named Jack recalled how he was quickly shut down when he brought up a potentially life-threatening problem. "Once when we were having trouble with the venous return, and I mentioned it," he said, "the surgeon said, 'Jack, is that you?' I said yes. He said, 'Are you pumping this case [being the first rather than second, or assisting, perfusionist]?' I said, 'No, I'm assisting.' 'Well, in the future, if you are not pumping the case, I don't want to hear from you.'"

The other hospital was much more enthusiastic. At Hospital B, doctors saw MICS as a challenge for which the whole team would need to learn new ways of working together. The surgeon who led the training interviewed managers to find the most interested and appropriately skilled team members for this new approach—not necessarily those who were best at the old approach. The surgeon clearly signaled that this was an opportunity for learning—one that had clear benefits of "a transfer of pain—from the patient to the surgeon."

"The ability of the surgeon to allow himself to become a part-ner, not a dictator, is critical," the surgeon told Edmondson. "For example, you really do have to change what you're doing based on a suggestion from someone else on the team. This is a com-plete restructuring of the operating room and how it works."

In trying MICS, the team quickly recognized that because the view from the cameras and different incisions was distributed, communication norms needed to change. As one nurse put it, "When you're on bypass for the standard [open-heart surgery], there's no need for communication at all. In MICS there's a lot more . . . It is totally different. When I read the training manual, I couldn't believe it." Roles also needed to be redefined. So Hos-pital B kept the learning team intact until they were comfortable with the new technique—about ten surgeries. In each, they made subtle changes to the process, like the kinds of clamps used. They debriefed after each surgery and made small improvements.

It's no surprise that Hospital B adopted the new techniques

and technology much more quickly than Hospital A. Hospital A viewed the new technology as a "plug-in" to what they already did. Surgeons there may have used the new tech, but they made little effort to change the norms, roles, and processes. Hospital B, however, quickly recognized that adopting any new technology meant changing teamwork along with changing tech. In other words, the group dynamics needed to shift along with the technology.

The principles that Edmondson discovered from this and many other studies can help any group or organization trying to embrace innovation. The first, of course, was to set an environment of psychological safety, where speaking up and trial and error are not only tolerated but encouraged. See Chapter 8 for details!

Second, you need to acknowledge that your goal isn't just about the technology—it's also about the team. If you assume you can just plug in any new technology to your existing norms and routines, you close yourself off to critical learning opportunities. The task isn't simply learning to operate the technology; it's also learning to adapt the group dynamics around the technology. How and when we communicate (norms). Who does what (roles). You need to frame the task so people realize this is a real innovation challenge that could change everything (goals). So set a learning goal for the collective, not just a technology goal.

And third, compose your learning team carefully. This might seem obvious at this point in the book, but so many important groups are composed by a "Who's free at this time?" rubric; no one considers the knowledge, skills, or interests of those involved. If you're part of a larger organization, the learning team should contain not only those most able to learn and adapt, but also those who can teach others what they've learned.

Together, these three principles help distinguish groups that quickly and successfully adopt new technologies from those that don't.

Most new technologies aren't inherently good or bad. Instead, they offer trade-offs among multiple goals. Take communication technology, for example. We trade the richness of face-to-face conversations for the speed and convenience of video calls and text messages. Some people won't like it. But even with the invention of the telegraph and telephone, some people lamented what was lost—the art of writing letters, the nuance, the anticipation. Some from my generation lament the fact that telephone calls are now rare, replaced by brief text messages. Each technology gives us something new and crowds out something old that others valued.

Like the esteemed cardiac surgeons at Hospital A, those who already have power and status are least motivated to adopt new technology. They're often in a position to slow down or halt its adoption.

A famous management story about failing to adopt a new technology comes from Polaroid. In the 1980s, Polaroid was a market leader in cameras. Its fast, on-the-spot developing film was synonymous with the brand—and the most famous way to take pictures and see them right away. But Polaroid was also one of the first companies to develop quality digital cameras, beginning research and development in the 1960s and, by 1990, spending nearly half its R&D budget on digital photography.

At first, the investment in digital seemed to pay off. Polaroid was number one in digital camera sales for much of the 1990s. But because of its business model, the company couldn't conceive of cameras as their moneymakers. At the time, the real money was in the film, which they sold at huge margins. So top management at Polaroid wasn't so sure about the whole digital thing. They ultimately chose to slow innovation on digital cameras, which allowed competitors like Nikon and Minolta to surge ahead in the exploding market.

It was a costly decision. Polaroid filed for bankruptcy in 2001.

Polaroid's decision-makers were victims of what the late Harvard Business School professor Clayton Christensen called the "innovator's dilemma." In the 1990s, the quality of digital pictures was vastly inferior to traditional film. Top managers viewed their brand as representing high-quality images; they didn't want to pivot their business until digital images looked better. And they simply couldn't imagine a world in which people didn't care about printing pictures. To them, digital photography seemed a long way off from being taken seriously.

Whether you are a cardiac surgeon or the market leader in quick-developing film, it's threatening to think that what got you ahead might not keep you there. Successful people are motivated to disbelieve that change is coming. None more so than leaders.

So although the steps for a group to adopt a new technology aren't exactly brain (or open-heart) surgery, they are difficult to execute. For leaders who rose to power in the old world, the prospect of a new world seems both threatening and unbelievable.

To evolve with new technology requires new kinds of teamwork and collaboration—at least, that's what you should assume going in. Formal leaders are unlikely to know the correct answer. They can't be dictatorial surgeons or conductors; they need to be partners in the learning process.

How new technologies affect humanity depends on learning in groups. That's true whether you're learning to use virtual reality, artificial intelligence, or brain implants. And whether groups use new tech well depends on a learning mindset—a recognition that we don't have all the answers, but we can find them if we work together. Even adapting to remote work required us to recognize this wasn't business as usual, that it required new norms and, in some cases, new groups.

It isn't just new technology that should spur groups to organize for learning; every project is an opportunity for teamwork innovation, where we learn better ways of working together. As one of the nurses in Hospital B remarked, "It has been a model, not just for this hospital but for cardiac surgery. It is about what a group of people can do."

Groups learn through constant cycles of trial and error. David A. Kolb's famous model of learning goes something like this: You have an *experience*, like trying a new technology for the first time. You then *reflect* on how that experience went. What went well? What could have gone better? You then seek to *theorize*, looking for generalizable principles from your reflection, and you try to put those into practice by *experimenting* with your behavior. Which then leads to another experience.

That's the mantra for improving group dynamics. Whether I'm teaching, consulting with an organization, or leading a team,

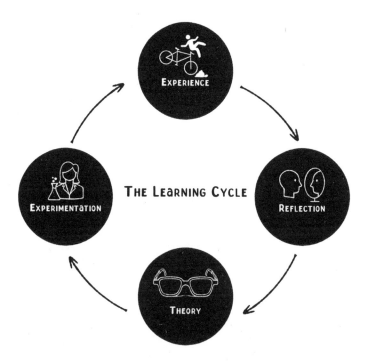

this cycle is the core of getting sustainably better. You take an experience and reflect together on how it went. You theorize about what you can learn from it and do differently next time. And then you experiment. Like IDEO's mantra that "enlightened trial and error succeeds over the planning of the lone genius," groups that embrace the learning cycle are the ones that can find synergy that lasts.

People are constantly worried that the problems of today are scarier than the problems of yesterday. And there are real things to worry about in a fast-changing world. But new technologies like remote work, virtual reality, and even AI don't have to be threats. We'll have some growing pains as new technologies enter our lives. There are huge risks of misuse, especially in the transitional period when we figure out the norms, rules, and challenges. And, yes, *The Matrix* and *I, Robot* scenarios aren't totally off the table. But there's no better antidote than sunlight and openness; banning obviously useful technology has never really worked in the long run.

The best way to assuage our worries is for groups to get together and learn. And there's simply no way around learning by doing. I'm not an expert on the risks of any particular innovation. But assuming that a technology is available, the more people who learn to use it toward shared, virtuous aims, the better.

A better world won't arise merely out of a technical breakthrough. It will emerge gradually through groups engaging with and developing teamwork innovations in concert with physical technologies, like Edmondson's cardiac surgery teams.

I really believe that groups are the solution, not the problem. In my ideal future, all groups embrace learning, constantly seeking new and better ways of working together. Members learn from one another, and the world gets a little more groupy.

The Enduring Power of Groups

The Emergency Rescue Committee (the ERC from the Introduction) was founded to rescue people from the Nazis during World War II. It had a very SMART goal—a list of two hundred people to get out of France and into America before the Nazis got them. The ERC exceeded that goal beyond any reasonable expectation. World War II ended. But did the ERC's members say, "Well done everyone! I guess we can adjourn now!"?

World War II ended long ago, yet the ERC remains. In 1942, the ERC joined forces with Albert Einstein's International Relief Association, forming what is now known as the International Rescue Committee (IRC). Today, the IRC's goal is to "help people affected by humanitarian crises . . . to survive, recover, and rebuild their lives." According to its website, the organization helped nearly thirty-three million people in 2022 alone, treating children for malnutrition, working to provide clean water, and making health care available.

The ERC isn't the only group mentioned in this book that's surprisingly still around. Although the name Love Has Won (Chapter 7) has been retired, several groups carry on its legacy. A few followers used the group's legal status as a religious nonprofit organization, changed the name, and kept doing what they were doing—selling questionable goods and services on the internet. Jason Castillo, also known as "Father God," founded his own splinter group. And these groups seem to be thriving. As journalist Christopher Moyer of *Rolling Stone* put it, "Love Has Won—in all its new forms—continues to draw in more people, receive more donations, and sell more products. They continue to sell 'etheric surgeries,' which they advertise as still being performed by Amy, albeit from the 5th dimension." They even have plans to start charter schools!

For good and ill, groups often persist beyond their founders' participation. They become something more than the sum of their members and don't depend on any one of them—even a leader who claims to be divine. Almost all the groups named in this book still exist. IDEO, Team USA, and Bridgewater are all still in business.

Today's groups are tomorrow's institutions. Today's groups of college friends can become founders of tomorrow's world-changing businesses. Today's activists for peace and prosperity can become tomorrow's ERCs.

For a group to persist beyond its current membership, it needs to make things more formal. Ad hoc roles turn into formal job descriptions. Informal processes become written-down procedures. Norms become regulations. The group becomes an entity unto itself, meant to persist beyond the involvement of any individual member. It becomes a formal *organization*.

All groups have some characteristics of organizations. The question is how formal they are. Have we explicitly agreed on how we do things around here, or is it taken for granted? Do we have a clear division of labor and well-defined roles, or do we make it up as we go along? Are our systems designed to stand the test of time, so members can come and go but the group moves on toward its purpose?

Getting into the weeds about formalizing groups into organizations would take another book. The most important thing for you to understand is that formalizing a group into an organization is a trade-off. Some steps formalize a group's existence, making it seem more legitimate to outsiders. Those might be legal steps (like incorporation), choosing a name and a logo, writing down a mission statement, or sending out a newsletter. These steps allow groups to more easily acquire resources like money and real estate that they can pass on to new members.

Other kinds of formalization allow coordination and goal accomplishment to continue, even when membership changes. Formal roles and job descriptions allow you to replace members and their contributions more easily. Official procedures, rules, and reward systems promote conformity, stability, and cooperation. These steps protect organizations from the ravages of time and allow them to continue collaborating, even if all the original members leave.

The dark side of formalization is that it makes change more difficult. New members usually are concerned with fitting in rather than sharing what makes them unique. Habits and routines are entrenched. Formal organizations tend to be stodgier than informal groups as the world changes around them. That's largely why economists see entrepreneurship as a key source of renewal—we need new groups and new organizations to supplant the old.

Many of today's organizations are smart enough to adapt. They bring in consultants and academic experts like me to help them. They acquire smaller organizations to make money when their own business models grow stale. This is so pervasive that many entrepreneurial groups don't even try to become lasting organizations—they're just trying to get acquired by an existing one.

And these old organizations contain the vestiges of the "medieval institutions." They're often controlled by powerful interests that don't want to change too much too fast, even if that change is for the good of the many, not the few (or the one).

Regardless of their downsides, organizations are one of the only ways for our groups to outlive us. All groups, even the audience at Grow or the ad hoc band on stage, are proto-organizations. They are the primordial ooze of what can become businesses, governments, and social movements. The inheritance we pass on to future generations is the groups we belonged to—our family, our friends, our school, our workplace, our neighborhood, or our nation. Have we built their capacities for good? Or have we let them atrophy on our watch?

Groups are the seeds from which new worlds grow. They're a flag for change to rally around. Old, worse social models—roving gangs of marauders, slavery, serfdom—have been gradually replaced by better ones. The change always starts with a group of people getting together and showing that a better world is possible.

But change isn't a linear process. It involves fits and starts. The powerful who benefit from the way things are resist it. Although change can often appear coercive and conflictual, that's just because conflict and coercion attract our attention. In reality, most change is just groups getting a little better every day and more people joining those groups. Groups that learn and adapt to a changing world. Groups that give voice to their members, not just the powerful at the top of the hierarchy. We lose the thread when we think that the individual is the unit of change. One person who wants change can only go so far.

As anthropologist Margaret Mead supposedly said, "Never doubt that a small group of thoughtful, committed citizens can change the world. Indeed, it's the only thing that ever has."

I promised you that this book would enable you to unlock the power of groups by teaching you *how to use the science of group dynamics to live and work together better.* The reason it took a whole book to get there is because the answers aren't simple. But there are four main themes I hope you walk away from this book with:

1. *Take a collective perspective.* If you've made it this far, you probably are already seeing things at the group level and scoffing at individualistic explanations for social behavior. But this is the most common problem for everyone around you—they aren't thinking about the group as a whole.

2. *Structure is king.* Although a lot of this book is about group process—social loafing, conformity pressure, dysfunctional conflict—you should always look at the group structure when trying to improve your group. Trying to fix process while leaving structural problems unchallenged is putting a Band-Aid over a hole in a leaky ceiling—it slows the dripping down for a second, but it doesn't solve much.

3. *Leadership isn't just for leaders.* A functional, shared approach to group leadership means that anyone can help provide leadership for a group. Asking a simple question about goals can spark a discussion that clarifies the group's goals for everyone. Questioning how things are done can promote psychological safety and lead to productive changes in norms. Even if some structures seem outside your sphere of influence, a shared, functional view of leadership helps you identify what needs doing and take responsibility for getting it done.

4. *The secret to groups is learning together.* The beginning, middle, and end of every task are opportunities to learn. Any pause in the calendar is a chance to check your group's structure for maintenance. It's a chance to congratulate one another on small wins and discuss ways to get better. Over time,

these learning cycles add up—they are the beginnings of building organizations that we pass on to future generations.

In his Nobel Prize acceptance speech, novelist William Faulkner said: "The problems of the human heart in conflict with itself . . . only that is worth writing about." Group thinking has a way of throwing human hearts into conflict. Collective life is a balancing act, a Faulknerian dilemma of "the human heart in conflict with itself." When things get out of balance, we too often blame individuals or focus on processual symptoms instead of structural causes. Our need for belonging and competence draws us to form and join groups, stitching them into the fabric of our identities. That helps us cooperate yet also leads us to conform within our group and compete outside it—often, with disastrous consequences. And our need for autonomy leads us to try to stand out and get recognized within our group and to pull away from its controlling aspects.

I hope this book has convinced you to rethink groups in work and life. If you take a collective perspective, you can unlock the power of the groups in your life. You'll achieve more of your goals and have a better time doing it.

If we all do that, there's a lot of reason for hope that *group thinking* won't sound like bad words anymore, synonymous with dysfunction. It will be the way we make the world better. It will give us all a collective edge.

ACKNOWLEDGMENTS

Behind this book about groups is a great group. Actually, it's a lot of great groups and individuals who have made all this possible.

You may have noticed that the names J. Richard Hackman, Ruth Wageman, and Teresa Amabile came up a lot. That's because these were my mentors. Richard and Teresa took a risk in agreeing to supervise some jazz musician who had no background in psychology or business as a PhD student. And I gained more than I can ever articulate from Richard, Ruth, and Teresa as advisers, collaborators, and friends. Thank you.

Then there were the actual groups in my life. Richard and Ruth brought together many of the incredible researchers whose work I've built on in their research group, GroupsGroup. It was in GroupsGroup that I learned about the research on so many of the promises and perils of group dynamics. Moreover, I've been blessed to have had amazing students, colleagues, and collaborators at Harvard University, Boston University, and University College London. I've also learned so much about writing and publishing from my colleagues in Team Onagadori, many of whom I've long admired from near and far. I'd particularly like to thank Dolly Chugh, Adam Grant, Anthony Klotz, and Drew Carton for helping me understand what the heck I was doing.

Then, there's the *Collective Edge* team. There would be no book without an email from my agent, Max Edwards. He was able to reimagine the short piece I'd written about groupthink as a book. Whatever Max saw in those eight hundred words changed my life. He helped me craft the proposal and got it into the hands of the best publishers and editors anyone could wish for. Thank you to my editors, Jacob Surpin, Caroline Sutton, and Assallah Tahir, for all the help, feedback, and encouragement—and for believing in me more than I ever had a right to expect.

And an enormous serving of gratitude to the fabulous groups and individuals who've helped the book along its journey at Avery, Simon & Schuster UK, Fortier Public Relations, Aevitas Creative Management, and Apple Tree Literary. I am forever obliged to the publicity posse of Rachel Dugan, Casey Maloney, Victoria Purcell, Naja Innis, Mark Fortier, and Lindsay Prevette; the marketing mob of Neda Dallal, Abby Stubenhofer, and Farin Schlussel; the production and design pod of Jess Morphew, Ryan Richardson, Christy Wagner, Kim Lewis, Brianna Lopez, Emily Mileham, Ashley Tucker, and Tom Whatley; the contracts and rights cadre of Tom Lloyd-Williams, Vanessa Kerr, and Emily Randle; the editorial assistance ensemble of Lota Erinne and Maudisa King; the administrative support alliance of Checkie Hamilton and Alex Osmond; and the leadership league of Kate Harvey, Lindsay Gordon, Lucia Watson, and Tracy Behar. It has been a joy and a privilege to collaborate with every one of you. Thank you.

ACKNOWLEDGMENTS

That's not even the whole team. Do-it-all editor Kassandra Barbaw has made this book so much better than I ever could have on my own. She dealt with my last-minute requests to review and improve what I wrote, researched examples, and fact-checked the many, many weird and wonderful facts contained herein. Cheers! And research assistant and PhD student Josephine Andreesen helped me improve the references at the beginning and end of the journey. Ekki Arbayu did a fantastic job with the illustrations.

Last but not least is my family. My father, Gary Fisher, did more than expose me to underage gambling—he read drafts of early chapters and helped me see what was interesting and important. And the rest of the clan, my children, Kaya and Miles (who also contributed an idea or two); my stepmother, Carole; and my siblings, Aaron and Brooke, have supported me and tolerated my yearslong chatter about the book.

But no one deserves more acknowledgment than my wife, Carola Emrich-Fisher. She was an invaluable test-reader and editor, not holding back when she was puzzled, bored, or annoyed by the earlier versions. And in the many moments when the book has taken over my life, she picked up the slack for the many things I didn't do. I couldn't have done this (or much else) without you!

NOTES

Introduction

xiii **"with $3,000 taped to his leg, a list of 200 endangered artists and intellectuals, and instructions to help them evacuate"**: "The True Story behind *Transatlantic* and the IRC," International Rescue Committee, last updated March 22, 2023, https://www.rescue.org/article/true-story-behind-transatlantic-and-irc.

xiii **the Emergency Rescue Committee (ERC)**: "The IRC's Impact at a Glance," International Rescue Committee, accessed November 1, 2024, https://www.rescue.org/uk/page/ircs-impact-glance.

xiii **"I had never done underground work before"**: Mordecai Paldiel, *Saving the Jews: Amazing Stories of Men and Women Who Defied the "Final Solution"* (Dallas, TX: Taylor Trade Publishing, 2000).

xiii **Fry couldn't do it alone**: "Varian Fry and the Emergency Rescue Committee," Rescue in the Holocaust, accessed November 1, 2024, https://www.holocaustrescue.org/varian-fry-and-erc.

xiv **praising "us" and blaming "them"**: Alexander P. Landry, Ram I. Orr, and Kayla Mere, "Dehumanization and Mass Violence: A Study of Mental State Language in Nazi Propaganda (1927–1945)," *PLOS One* 17, no. 11 (2022): e0274957, https://doi.org/10.1371/journal.pone.0274957.

xvi **six conditions you can use**: Most of these conditions were first documented by my mentor and collaborator J. Richard Hackman. But based on recent research and my experience trying to communicate what it takes to improve group dynamics, I've altered which six conditions to highlight and reframed some of the lessons of

Hackman's research. See J. Richard Hackman, *Leading Teams: Setting the Stage for Great Performances* (Boston: Harvard Business Review Press, 2002).

Chapter 1: The Myth of the Lone Genius: The Allure of Individualism in a Group-Based World

4   **According to Watson's memoir:** James D. Watson, *The Double Helix: A Personal Account of the Discovery of the Structure of DNA* (New York, NY: Atheneum, 1968; reprint, Hachette UK, 2012).

4   **As they told *Science News*:** Tina Hesman Saey, "What Was Rosalind Franklin's True Role in the Discovery of DNA's Double Helix?" *Science News* (blog), April 26, 2023, https://www.science news.org/article/rosalind-franklin-dna-structure-watson-crick.

6   **"the most unpleasant human being I had ever met":** Josh Gabbatiss, "James Watson: The Most Controversial Statements Made by the Father of DNA," *The Independent*, January 13, 2019, https://www.independent.co.uk/news/science/james -watson-racism-sexism-dna-race-intelligence-genetics-double -helix-a8725556.html.

6   **Nobel Prize committee overlooked her:** Burton Feldman, *The Nobel Prize: A History of Genius, Controversy, and Prestige* (New York, NY: Arcade Publishing, 2000), 58–59.

7   **"The Increasing Dominance of Teams in Production of Knowledge":** Stefan Wuchty, Benjamin F. Jones, and Brian Uzzi, "The Increasing Dominance of Teams in Production of Knowledge," *Science* 316, no. 5827 (2007): 1036–39, https://doi.org /10.1126/science.1136099.

7   **most papers receive fewer than ten:** Pedro Albarrán and Javier Ruiz-Castillo, "References Made and Citations Received by Scientific Articles," *Journal of the American Society for Information Science and Technology* 62, no. 1 (2011): 40–49, https://doi.org/10.1002 /asi.21448.

8   **science, education, and work are all getting more specialized:** Thomas W. Malone, Robert Laubacher, and Tammy Johns, "The Big Idea: The Age of Hyperspecialization," *Harvard Busi-*

ness Review (2011), 89, no. 7, pp. 56–67, https://hbr.org/2011/07 /the-big-idea-the-age-of-hyperspecialization.

9   **Edison was building on the work of many others:** Casey Cep, "The Real Nature of Thomas Edison's Genius," *The New Yorker,* October 21, 2019, https://www.newyorker.com/magazine/2019 /10/28/the-real-nature-of-thomas-edisons-genius.

9   **the "fundamental attribution error":** Lee Ross, "The Intuitive Psychologist and His Shortcomings: Distortions in the Attribution Process," in *Advances in Experimental Social Psychology,* ed. Leonard Berkowitz, vol. 10 (New York, NY: Academic Press, 1977), 173– 220, https://doi.org/10.1016/S0065-2601(08)60357-3.

9   **prone to "egocentric biases":** Michael Ross and Fiore Sicoly, "Egocentric Biases in Availability and Attribution," *Journal of Personality and Social Psychology* 37, no. 3 (1979): 322–36, https://doi .org/10.1037/0022-3514.37.3.322.

10   **famous example is The Lake Wobegon Effect:** Juliana Schro- eder, "Who's *Really* Doing the Work? The Impact of Group Size on Over-Claiming of Responsibility," *California Management Review* 60, no. 1 (2017): 88–101, https://doi.org/10.1177/0008125617727743.

10   **believe they have above-average intelligence:** Patrick R. Heck, Daniel J. Simons, and Christopher F. Chabris, "65% of Americans Believe They Are Above Average in Intelligence: Results of Two Nationally Representative Surveys," *PLOS One* 13, no. 7 (2018): e0200103, https://doi.org/10.1371/journal.pone.0200103.

10   **members' estimates added up to 235 percent:** Juliana Schro- eder, Eugene M. Caruso, and Nicholas Epley, "Many Hands Make Overlooked Work: Over-Claiming of Responsibility Increases with Group Size," *Journal of Experimental Psychology: Applied* 22, no. 2 (2016): 238.

10   **we can't credit or blame groups appropriately:** Vincent Y. Yzerbyt, Anouk Rogier, and Susan T. Fiske, "Group Entitativity and Social Attribution: On Translating Situational Constraints into Stereotypes," *Personality and Social Psychology Bulletin* 24, no. 10 (1998): 1089–103, https://doi.org/10.1177/01461672982410006.

12   **you need at least three people:** There's some disagreement

about whether a group of two is really a group or not. For our purposes, it doesn't really matter because we'll think of groupiness on a continuum. Dyads are a little less groupy than triads. See Richard L. Moreland, "Are Dyads Really Groups?" *Small Group Research* 41, no. 2 (2010): 251–67, https://doi.org/10.1177/1046496409358618.

12 **worst name in all social science: "group entitativity":** Anita L. Blanchard, Andrew G. McBride, and Brittany A. Ernst, "How Are We Similar? Group Level Entitativity in Work and Social Groups," *Small Group Research* 54, no. 3 (2023): 369–95, https://doi.org/10.1177/10464964221117483; Brian Lickel, David L. Hamilton, and Steven J. Sherman, "Elements of a Lay Theory of Groups: Types of Groups, Relational Styles, and the Perception of Group Entitativity," *Personality and Social Psychology Review* 5, no. 2 (2001): 129–40.

14 **classic definition of *team* was coined by:** You can read Richard's take on teams in his management classic *Leading Teams*. See J. Richard Hackman, *Leading Teams: Setting the Stage for Great Performances* (Boston: Harvard Business Review Press, 2002).

15 **un-teaming trend that was already occurring:** Amy C. Edmondson, *Teaming: How Organizations Learn, Innovate, and Compete in the Knowledge Economy* (San Francisco, CA: John Wiley & Sons, 2012).

16 **individualistic values have increased and collectivist values have declined:** Henri C. Santos, Michael E. W. Varnum, and Igor Grossmann, "Global Increases in Individualism," *Psychological Science* 28, no. 9 (2017): 1228–39, https://doi.org/10.1177/0956797617700622.

16 **We even speak with more individualistic language:** Igor Grossmann and Michael E. W. Varnum, "Social Structure, Infectious Diseases, Disasters, Secularism, and Cultural Change in America," *Psychological Science* 26, no. 3 (2015): 311–24, https://doi.org/10.1177/0956797614563765; Jean M. Twenge, W. Keith Campbell, and Brittany Gentile, "Increases in Individualistic Words and Phrases in American Books, 1960–2008," *PLOS One* 7, no. 7 (2012): e40181, https://doi.org/10.1371/journal.pone.0040181.

16 **we look to individuals as the cause of good and ill:** J. Richard Hackman and Ruth Wageman, "Asking the Right Questions About Leadership: Discussion and Conclusions," *American Psychologist* 62, no. 1 (2007): 43–47, https://doi.org/10.1037/0003-066X.62.1.43.

16 **People feel lonelier and more isolated:** Frank J. Infurna et al., "Loneliness in Midlife: Historical Increases and Elevated Levels in the United States Compared with Europe," *American Psychologist* (2024), https://doi.org/10.1037/amp0001322; Susan Jaffe, "US Surgeon General: Loneliness Is a Public Health Crisis," *The Lancet* 401, no. 10388 (2023): 1560, https://doi.org/10.1016/S0140-6736(23)00957-1.

16 **sociologist Robert Putnam observed decades ago:** Robert D. Putnam, *Bowling Alone: The Collapse and Revival of American Community* (New York, NY: Simon & Schuster, 2000).

17 **make "we" more important than "me":** Mark Van Vugt and Claire M. Hart, "Social Identity as Social Glue: The Origins of Group Loyalty," *Journal of Personality and Social Psychology* 86, no. 4 (2004): 585–98, https://doi.org/10.1037/0022-3514.86.4.585.

Chapter 2: The Alchemy of Synergy: When Groups Are More (or Less) than the Sum of Their Parts

20 **from Pink Floyd's Richard Wright to The Roots' Questlove:** "The 500 Greatest Albums of All Time," *Rolling Stone*, December 31, 2023, https://www.rollingstone.com/music/music-lists/best-albums-of-all-time-1062063.

20 **to British actress Dame Judi Dench:** Caleb J. Murphy, "On August 17, 1959, Miles Davis' 'Kind of Blue' Was Released," Soundfly, August 16, 2019, https://flypaper.soundfly.com/discover/on-august-17-1959-miles-davis-kind-of-blue-was-released.

20 **influenced countless musicians and artists since its release in 1959:** Martin Chilton, "Kind of Blue: The Jazz Album by Miles Davis That Transformed Music," *The Independent*, accessed June 19, 2024, https://www.independent.co.uk/arts-entertainment/music/features/miles-davis-kind-of-blue-jazz-album-a8799061.html.

20 **As comedian Martin Mull quipped:** "Writing About Music

Is Like Dancing About Architecture," Quote Investigator, last modified November 8, 2010, https://quoteinvestigator.com/2010/11/08/writing-about-music.

23 **That's only 76 percent of the sum of the parts:** Donelson R. Forsyth, *Group Dynamics*, 7th ed. (Belmont, CA: Wadsworth Cengage Learning, 2014). The numbers reported here are frequently cited, but Ringelmann's original research is a bit murkier because he isn't always clear about which parts of his studies the tables refer to. If you don't read French but want to get into the original data, check out David A. Kravitz and Barbara Martin, "Ringelmann Rediscovered: The Original Article," *Journal of Personality and Social Psychology* 50, no. 5 (1986): 936–41, https://doi.org/10.1037/0022-3514.50.5.936.

23 **waiting more than thirty years to publish:** Steven J. Karau and Aric J. Wilhau, "Chapter 1—Social Loafing and Motivation Gains in Groups: An Integrative Review," in *Individual Motivation Within Groups*, ed. Steven J. Karau (Cambridge, MA: Elsevier Academic Press, 2020), 3–51, https://doi.org/10.1016/B978-0-12-849867-5.00001-X.

23 **Bibb Latané and his colleagues conducted a clever experiment:** Bibb Latané, Kipling Williams, and Stephen Harkins, "Many Hands Make Light the Work: The Causes and Consequences of Social Loafing," *Journal of Personality and Social Psychology* 37, no. 6 (1979): 822–32, https://doi.org/10.1037/0022-3514.37.6.822.

25 **A meta-analysis of seventy-eight studies:** Steven J. Karau and Kipling D. Williams, "Social Loafing: A Meta-Analytic Review and Theoretical Integration," *Journal of Personality and Social Psychology* 65, no. 4 (1993): 681–706, https://doi.org/10.1037/0022-3514.65.4.681.

26 **It also occurs in mental tasks:** Steven J. Karau and Aric J. Wilhau, "Chapter 1—Social Loafing and Motivation Gains in Groups: An Integrative Review," in *Individual Motivation Within Groups*, ed. Steven J. Karau (Cambridge, MA: Elsevier Academic Press, 2020), 3–51, https://doi.org/10.1016/B978-0-12-849867-5.00001-X.

26 **"The actions of all are nothing more than the sum":** Donel-

son R. Forsyth, *Group Dynamics*, 7th ed. (Belmont, CA: Wadsworth Cengage Learning, 2014), 33.

26   **distilled his theory of cooperation to the equation:** Ivan D. Steiner, *Group Process and Productivity* (New York, NY: Academic Press, 1972).

27   **"when someone proves they exist":** I'm paraphrasing from a lecture Richard Hackman gave many years ago. I have dramatized the dialogue, but I'm confident it correctly reflects Richard's thinking.

28   **The researchers created puzzles of varying complexity:** Abdullah Almaatouq et al., "Task Complexity Moderates Group Synergy," *Proceedings of the National Academy of Sciences* 118, no. 36 (2021): e2101062118, https://doi.org/10.1073/pnas.2101062118.

30   **groups are open social systems:** Daniel Katz and Robert Louis Kahn, *The Social Psychology of Organizations* (New York, NY: John Wiley & Sons, 1978).

30   **Hackman called "conditions, rather than causes":** J. Richard Hackman, "From Causes to Conditions in Group Research," *Journal of Organizational Behavior* 33, no. 3 (2012): 428–44, https://doi.org/10.1002/job.1774.

Chapter 3: More than a One-Hit Wonder: How Groups Cooperate Effectively

31   **John, Paul, George, and Ringo avoided even being in the same room together:** Mikal Gilmore, "Why the Beatles Broke Up," *Rolling Stone* (blog), September 3, 2009, https://www.rollingstone.com/music/music-features/why-the-beatles-broke-up-113403.

31   **because of "internal dissent":** Doug Fieger, liner notes to *Retrospective* (media notes), 1992.

32   **"the best Rolling Stones album since 1978":** Will Hodgkinson, "I've Heard Hackney Diamonds. It's the Best Rolling Stones Album Since 1978," *The Times*, September 6, 2023, https://www.thetimes.co.uk/article/rolling-stones-hackney-diamonds-new-album-review-best-since-some-girls-1978-ftn2b3nvs.

32   **Effective cooperation has two dimensions:** Ruth Wageman,

Colin M. Fisher, and J. Richard Hackman, "Leading Teams When the Time Is Right: Finding the Best Moments to Act," *Organizational Dynamics* 38, no. 3 (2009): 192–203. These effectiveness criteria are slightly different from those that we use in this article, or that Hackman used. Hackman broke down socio-emotional performance into two components: member satisfaction and growth in the team's cooperative capacity. (The latter is often known as "viability.") However, these two components are highly correlated— members' satisfaction affects their willingness to continue working in that team. So I aggregated them here. But read the article for a different approach!

33   **As Keith Richards put it in 1974:** Steve Turner, "The Rolling Stones: A Career in Quotes," *The Guardian*, June 26, 2013, https:// www.theguardian.com/music/2013/jun/26/rolling-stones -in-quotes.

34   **staying together leads to better task performance:** Erik Gonzalez-Mulé et al., "Team Tenure and Team Performance: A Meta-Analysis and Process Model," *Personnel Psychology* 73, no. 1 (2020): 151–98, https://doi.org/10.1111/peps.12319.

34   **helping them avoid conflict:** Tom Kuypers, Hannes Guenter, and Hetty van Emmerik, "Team Turnover and Task Conflict: A Longitudinal Study on the Moderating Effects of Collective Experience," *Journal of Management* 44, no. 4 (2018): 1287–311, https:// doi.org/10.1177/0149206315607966.

35   **Mick Jagger and Keith Richards did?:** Jagger and Richards knew each other from school. But they lost touch and reconnected in a Dartford train station in 1961, leading them to form the band. See Colin McEvoy and Tim Ott, "How Childhood Friends Mick Jagger and Keith Richards Formed The Rolling Stones," Biography.com, October 20, 2023, https://www.biography .com/musicians/rolling-stones-origins.

35   **have studied for many years:** Teresa M. Amabile, Colin M. Fisher, and Julianna Pillemer, "IDEO's Culture of Helping," *Harvard Business Review* 92, no. 1/2 (2014): 54–61, https://hbr.org /2014/01/ideos-culture-of-helping.

35   **"the value of collaboration in business":** Rebecca Acker-

mann, "Design Thinking Was Supposed to Fix the World. Where Did It Go Wrong?" *MIT Technology Review*, February 9, 2023, https://www.technologyreview.com/2023/02/09/1067821/design-thinking-retrospective-what-went-wrong.

36   **they were on the oldest of old-school TV shows:** *The Deep Dive: One Company's Secret Weapon for Innovation*, Films Media Group, accessed October 22, 2024, http://films.com/title/9249.

36   **collaboration in terms of "multi-team systems":** Michael B. O'Leary, Mark Mortensen, and Anita Williams Woolley, "Multiple Team Membership: A Theoretical Model of Its Effects on Productivity and Learning for Individuals and Teams," *The Academy of Management Review* 36, no. 3 (2011): 461–78; Jonathan C. Ziegert et al., "Addressing Performance Tensions in Multiteam Systems: Balancing Informal Mechanisms of Coordination Within and Between Teams," *Academy of Management Journal* 65, no. 1 (2022): 158–85, https://doi.org/10.5465/amj.2019.1043.

36   **"cabals":** Valve, *Valve Handbook for New Employees*, accessed October 24, 2024, http://archive.org/details/valveemployeehandbook.

36   **or "teaming":** Amy C. Edmondson, *Teaming: How Organizations Learn, Innovate, and Compete in the Knowledge Economy* (San Francisco, CA: John Wiley & Sons, 2012).

37   **organizational psychologist Ruth Wageman and her colleagues:** Ruth Wageman et al., *Senior Leadership Teams: What It Takes to Make Them Great* (Boston: Harvard Business Review Press, 2008).

37   **autonomy, belonging, and competence:** Edward L. Deci, Anja H. Olafsen, and Richard M. Ryan, "Self-Determination Theory in Work Organizations: The State of a Science," *Annual Review of Organizational Psychology and Organizational Behavior* 4 (2017): 19–43.

38   **feelings of connection to other humans:** Geoffrey L. Cohen, *Belonging: The Science of Creating Connection and Bridging Divides* (New York, NY: W. W. Norton & Company, 2022).

38   **as toxic for our health as smoking or radiation:** Geoffrey L. Cohen, *Belonging: The Science of Creating Connection and Bridging Divides* (New York, NY: W. W. Norton & Company, 2022).

39 **characteristics of the task itself:** J. Richard Hackman and Greg R. Oldham, *Work Redesign* (Reading, MA: Addison-Wesley, 1980).

39 **covering 259 different studies including 219,625 actual human beings:** Stephen E. Humphrey, Jennifer D. Nahrgang, and Frederick P. Morgeson, "Integrating Motivational, Social, and Contextual Work Design Features: A Meta-Analytic Summary and Theoretical Extension of the Work Design Literature," *Journal of Applied Psychology* 92, no. 5 (2007): 1332–56, https://doi.org/10 .1037/0021-9010.92.5.1332.

39 **than smoking has on cancer risk:** Xiaochen Dai et al., "Health Effects Associated with Smoking: A Burden of Proof Study," *Nature Medicine* 28, no. 10 (2022): 2045–55, https://doi.org/10.1038/ s41591-022-01978-x.

39 **the influence of exercise on cardiovascular health:** Cristina Molina Hidalgo et al., "Effects of a Laboratory-Based Aerobic Exercise Intervention on Brain Volume and Cardiovascular Health Markers: Protocol for a Randomised Clinical Trial," *BMJ Open* 13, no. 11 (November 1, 2023): e077905, https://doi.org/10.1136 /bmjopen-2023-077905; Elaine M. Murtagh et al., "The Effect of Walking on Risk Factors for Cardiovascular Disease: An Updated Systematic Review and Meta-Analysis of Randomised Control Trials," *Preventive Medicine* 72 (March 1, 2015): 34–43, https://doi .org/10.1016/j.ypmed.2014.12.041.

40 **seeing your work help others:** Adam M. Grant, "The Significance of Task Significance: Job Performance Effects, Relational Mechanisms, and Boundary Conditions," *Journal of Applied Psychology* 93, no. 1 (2008): 108–24, https://doi.org/10.1037/0021-9010 .93.1.108.

41 **"leaked" an employee handbook:** Valve, *Valve Handbook for New Employees*, accessed October 24, 2024, http://archive.org/details /valveemployeehandbook.

41 **tried but abandoned a similar management model:** Andy Doyle, "Management and Organization at Medium," *The Medium Blog* (blog), March 4, 2016, https://blog.medium.com/manage ment-and-organization-at-medium-2228cc9d93e9.

41 **autonomy for *how* to achieve their goals, but cooperation requires agreement on *what* goals:** J. Richard Hackman, *Leading Teams: Setting the Stage for Great Performances* (Boston, MA: Harvard Business Review Press, 2002).

42 **Famed US Army General George Patton had it right:** George S. Patton, *War As I Knew It* (Boston, MA: Houghton Mifflin, 1947), "Reflections and Suggestions."

43 **conditions under which effective collaboration emerges:** J. Richard Hackman, "From Causes to Conditions in Group Research," *Journal of Organizational Behavior* 33, no. 3 (2012): 428–44, https://doi.org/10.1002/job.1774.

43 **Our tendency to cast ourselves as the main character:** Benjamin A. Rogers et al., "Seeing Your Life Story as a Hero's Journey Increases Meaning in Life," *Journal of Personality and Social Psychology* 125, no. 4 (2023): 752–78, https://doi.org/10.1037/pspa0000341.

Chapter 4: From Scream Team to Redeem Team: Launching Collaborations Beyond Team Building

45 **Except for 2004:** Nate Penn, "Dunk'd: An Oral History of the 2004 Dream Team," *GQ*, July 27, 2012, https://www.gq.com/story/2004-olympic-basketball-dream-team.

46 **"the worst 38 days of my life":** Wallace Matthews, "Stephon Marbury Calls 2004 Olympics Experience the 'Worst 38 Days of My Life,'" Complex, July 17, 2017, accessed December 20, 2023, https://www.complex.com/sports/a/wallace-matthews/stephon-marbury-calls-2004-olympics-experience-worst-38-days-of-my-life.

47 **"the Scream Team," as one ESPN headline put it:** "Scream Team: What Next?" ESPN.com, accessed October 7, 2024, https://www.espn.com/espn/page2/story?page=hoops/040816.

47 **lack of collective experience:** Eric Freeman, "New Details on What Went Wrong for USA Basketball in 2004," Yahoo Sports, August 3, 2016, https://sports.yahoo.com/news/new-details-on-what-went-wrong-for-usa-basketball-in-2004-000621369.html; *The Redeem Team*, Netflix, accessed October 24, 2024, https://www.netflix.com/title/81452996.

47   **"It's hard for Team USA":** Alvin Chang, "One Simple Reason the USA Men's Basketball Team Is Struggling," Vox, August 19, 2016, https://www.vox.com/rio-olympics-explainers/2016/8/19/12524532/team-usa-basketball-struggle.

48   **Lamar Odom was an amateur DJ and LeBron James a bookworm:** Nate Penn, "Dunk'd: An Oral History of the 2004 Dream Team," *GQ*, July 27, 2012, https://www.gq.com/story/2004-olympic-basketball-dream-team.

48   **There was talk about feelings:** "American Airlines Film Team Building by Tm Advertising," AdsSpot, accessed October 24, 2024, https://adsspot.me/media/tv-commercials/american-airlines-team-building-0369fd35cf9d.

49   **Tuckman came up with a model of group development:** Bruce W. Tuckman, "Developmental Sequence in Small Groups," *Psychological Bulletin* 63, no. 6 (1965): 384–99, https://doi.org/10.1037/h0022100.

49   **but subsequent research has found misleading:** Connie J. G. Gersick, "Time and Transition in Work Teams: Toward a New Model of Group Development," *The Academy of Management Journal* 31, no. 1 (1988): 9–41; Connie J. G. Gersick, "Marking Time: Predictable Transitions in Task Groups," *The Academy of Management Journal* 32, no. 2 (1989): 274–309.

50   **a study by University of California organizational psychologist:** Barry M. Staw, "Attribution of the 'Causes' of Performance: A General Alternative Interpretation of Cross-Sectional Research on Organizations," *Organizational Behavior and Human Performance* 13, no. 3 (1975): 414–32.

50   **has been replicated many times:** H. Kirk Downey, Thomas I. Chacko, and James C. McElroy, "Attribution of the 'Causes' of Performance: A Constructive, Quasi-Longitudinal Replication of the Staw (1975) Study," *Organizational Behavior and Human Performance* 24, no. 3 (1979): 287–99, https://doi.org/10.1016/0030-5073(79)90031-X.

52   **training intact groups in task-like environments:** Christina N. Lacerenza et al., "Team Development Interventions: Evidence-

Based Approaches for Improving Teamwork," *American Psychologist* 73, no. 4 (2018): 517–31.

52 **"The US continued to believe they could send their B-team and still win gold":** Alvin Chang, "One Simple Reason the USA Men's Basketball Team Is Struggling," Vox, August 19, 2016, https://www.vox.com/rio-olympics-explainers/2016/8/19/12524532/team-usa-basketball-struggle.

53 **teams can struggle when they have too much star power:** Roderick I. Swaab et al., "The Too-Much-Talent Effect: Team Interdependence Determines When More Talent Is Too Much or Not Enough," *Psychological Science* 25, no. 8 (2014): 1581–91.

54 **Deep-level diversity is about the actual differences:** Sarah Harvey, "A Different Perspective: The Multiple Effects of Deep Level Diversity on Group Creativity," *Journal of Experimental Social Psychology* 49, no. 5 (2013): 822–32, https://doi.org/10.1016/j.jesp.2013.04.004; Alana E. Jansen and Ben J. Searle, "Diverse Effects of Team Diversity: A Review and Framework of Surface and Deep-Level Diversity," *Personnel Review* 50, no. 9 (2021): 1838–53, https://doi.org/10.1108/PR-12-2019-0664; James R. Larson Jr., "Deep Diversity and Strong Synergy: Modeling the Impact of Variability in Members' Problem-Solving Strategies on Group Problem-Solving Performance," *Small Group Research* 38, no. 3 (2007): 413–36, https://doi.org/10.1177/1046496407301972.

54 **A meta-analysis of 146 studies of the diversity-performance relationship:** Hans van Dijk, Marloes L. van Engen, and Daan van Knippenberg, "Defying Conventional Wisdom: A Meta-Analytical Examination of the Differences between Demographic and Job-Related Diversity Relationships with Performance," *Organizational Behavior and Human Decision Processes* 119, no. 1 (2012): 38–53, https://doi.org/10.1016/j.obhdp.2012.06.003; Daan van Knippenberg and Julija N. Mell, "Past, Present, and Potential Future of Team Diversity Research: From Compositional Diversity to Emergent Diversity," *Organizational Behavior and Human Decision Processes* 136 (2016): 135–45, https://doi.org/10.1016/j.obhdp.2016.05.007.

55   **As famed biologist Edward O. Wilson put it:** Edward O. Wilson, in *Oxford Essential Quotations*, 4th ed., ed. Susan Ratcliffe (Oxford, UK: Oxford University Press, 2016), https://www.oxfordreference.com/display/10.1093/acref/9780191826719.001.0001/q-oro-ed4-00016553.

55   **demographically diverse groups initially tend to sort:** Allison M. Traylor et al., "It's About the Process, Not the Product: A Meta-Analytic Investigation of Team Demographic Diversity and Processes," *Organizational Psychology Review* 14, no. 3 (2024): 478–516, https://doi.org/10.1177/20413866241245312.

56   **surface-level diversity had no effect on performance:** Hans van Dijk, Marloes L. van Engen, and Daan van Knippenberg, "Defying Conventional Wisdom: A Meta-Analytical Examination of the Differences between Demographic and Job-Related Diversity Relationships with Performance," *Organizational Behavior and Human Decision Processes* 119, no. 1 (2012): 38–53, https://doi.org/10.1016/j.obhdp.2012.06.003.

57   **linked group composition to effectiveness:** John E. Mathieu et al., "A Review and Integration of Team Composition Models: Moving Toward a Dynamic and Temporal Framework," *Journal of Management* 40, no. 1 (2014): 130–60, https://doi.org/10.1177/0149206313503014.

57   **tools like the Myers-Briggs Type Indicator are unhelpful pseudoscience:** Adam M. Grant, "Goodbye to MBTI, the Fad That Won't Die," *Psychology Today*, September 18, 2013, https://www.psychologytoday.com/us/blog/give-and-take/201309/goodbye-to-mbti-the-fad-that-wont-die.

57   **only one emerged as a predictor of group effectiveness: social sensitivity:** Christoph Riedl et al., "Quantifying Collective Intelligence in Human Groups," *Proceedings of the National Academy of Sciences* 118, no. 21 (2021): e2005737118, https://doi.org/10.1073/pnas.2005737118.

58   **the "Reading the Mind in the Eyes Test":** Simon Baron-Cohen et al., "The 'Reading the Mind in the Eyes' Test Revised Version: A Study with Normal Adults, and Adults with Asperger Syndrome or High-Functioning Autism," *The Journal of Child Psychology and*

Psychiatry and Allied Disciplines 42, no. 2 (2001): 241–51, https://doi
.org/10.1017/S0021963001006643.

58   **besides their actual task-relevant knowledge and skills:**
Abdullah Almaatouq et al., "The Effects of Group Composition
and Dynamics on Collective Performance," *Topics in Cognitive Science*
16, no. 2 (2024): 302–21, https://doi.org/10.1111/tops.12706.

58   **women perform better than men on this test:** Rena Kirkland
et al., "Meta-Analysis Reveals Adult Female Superiority in 'Reading the Mind in the Eyes' Test," *North American Journal of Psychology*
15, no. 1 (March 2013): 449–58.

59   **On average, groups with three to seven members perform
best:** Nada Hashmi, G. Shankaranarayanan, and Thomas W.
Malone, "Is Bigger Better? A Study of the Effect of Group Size
on Collective Intelligence in Online Groups," *Decision Support Systems* 167 (April 2023): 113914, https://doi.org/10.1016/j.dss.2022
.113914; Ralph Kenna and Bertrand Berche, "Managing Research
Quality: Critical Mass and Optimal Academic Research Group
Size," *IMA Journal of Management Mathematics* 23, no. 2 (2012): 195–
207, https://doi.org/10.1093/imaman/dpr021; Patrick R. Laugh-
lin et al., "Groups Perform Better than the Best Individuals on
Letters-to-Numbers Problems: Effects of Group Size," *Journal of
Personality and Social Psychology* 90, no. 4 (2006): 644–51, https://doi
.org/10.1037/0022-3514.90.4.644; Susan A. Wheelan, "Group
Size, Group Development, and Group Productivity," *Small Group
Research* 40, no. 2 (2009): 247–62, https://doi.org/10.1177/10464
96408328703; Roger Guimerà et al., "Team Assembly Mechanisms Determine Collaboration Network Structure and Team
Performance," *Science* 308, no. 5722 (2005): 697–702, https://doi.org
/10.1126/science.1106340.

59   **team members' satisfaction peaks between four and five
members:** J. Richard Hackman and Neil Vidmar, "Effects of Size
and Task Type on Group Performance and Member Reactions,"
Sociometry 33, no. 1 (1970): 37–54, https://doi.org/10.2307/2786271.

60   **coined his famous Brooks's Law:** Frederick P. Brooks Jr., *The
Mythical Man-Month: Essays on Software Engineering* (London, UK:
Addison-Wesley Longman, 1995).

62   **"You can't blame the US players":** Nate Penn, "Dunk'd: An Oral History of the 2004 Dream Team," *GQ*, July 27, 2012, https://www.gq.com/story/2004-olympic-basketball-dream-team.

63   **"We all could be doing a whole bunch of things":** Mike Krzyzewski ("Coach K"), Coach K's Pre-Training Camp Speech, 2013, https://www.youtube.com/watch?v=dIGLhJx9LCI.

64   **clear, important goals are essential to launching an effective collaboration:** J. Richard Hackman, *Leading Teams: Setting the Stage for Great Performances* (Boston, MA: Harvard Business Review Press, 2002).

65   **Andrew Carton has studied the clarity-importance tension extensively:** Andrew M. Carton, "'I'm Not Mopping the Floors, I'm Putting a Man on the Moon': How NASA Leaders Enhanced the Meaningfulness of Work by Changing the Meaning of Work," *Administrative Science Quarterly* 63, no. 2 (2017): 323–69, https://doi.org/10.1177/0001839217713748; Andrew M. Carton and Brian J. Lucas, "How Can Leaders Overcome the Blurry Vision Bias? Identifying an Antidote to the Paradox of Vision Communication," *Academy of Management Journal* 61, no. 6 (2018): 2106–29, https://doi.org/10.5465/amj.2015.0375.

66   **discovered the depth of this principle:** Edwin A. Locke and Gary P. Latham, "Building a Practically Useful Theory of Goal Setting and Task Motivation: A 35-Year Odyssey," *American Psychologist* 57, no. 9 (2002): 705–17, https://doi.org/10.1037//0003-066X.57.9.705.

66   **Latham and his colleague James Baldes designed a study:** Gary P. Latham and James J. Baldes, "The 'Practical Significance' of Locke's Theory of Goal Setting," *Journal of Applied Psychology* 60, no. 1 (1975): 122–24, https://doi.org/10.1037/h0076354.

72   **Researchers call these "team charters":** John E. Mathieu and Tammy L. Rapp, "Laying the Foundation for Successful Team Performance Trajectories: The Roles of Team Charters and Performance Strategies," *Journal of Applied Psychology* 94, no. 1 (2009): 90–103, https://doi.org/10.1037/a0013257; William H. A. Johnson et al., "Do Team Charters Help Team-Based Projects? The Effects of Team Charters on Performance and Satisfaction in

Global Virtual Teams," *Academy of Management Learning & Education* 21, no. 2 (June 2022): 236–60, https://doi.org/10.5465/amle.2020 .0332.

73 **call this "job crafting":** Justin M. Berg, Jane E. Dutton, and Amy Wrzesniewski, "Job Crafting and Meaningful Work," in *Purpose and Meaning in the Workplace*, eds. Bryan J. Dik, Zinta S. Byrne, and Michael F. Steger (Washington, DC: American Psychological Association, 2013), 81–104, https://doi.org/10.1037/ 14183-005.

Chapter 5: Go Along to Get Along: The Influence of the Many on the Few

77 **but with a hint of derision that changed everything:** *The Redeem Team*, Netflix, accessed October 24, 2024, https://www.netflix .com/title/81452996.

78 **James Clear tells us about the British Cycling team that dominated the 2008 and 2012 Olympics:** James Clear, *Atomic Habits* (New York, NY: Avery, 2018).

78 **encourages us to mimic the behavior of those we identify with:** H. Peyton Young, "The Evolution of Social Norms," *Annual Review of Economics* 7, no. 1 (2015): 359–87, https://doi.org/10.1146 /annurev-economics-080614-115322; Michael Tomasello and Amrisha Vaish, "Origins of Human Cooperation and Morality," *Annual Review of Psychology* 64, no. 1 (2013): 231–55, https://doi.org/10 .1146/annurev-psych-113011-143812.

81 **"Social norms are among the least visible and most powerful forms":** Kenneth L. Bettenhausen and J. Keith Murnighan, "The Emergence of Norms in Competitive Decision-Making Groups," *Administrative Science Quarterly* 30, no. 3 (1985): 350–72, https://doi.org/10.2307/2392667.

84 **Alexander von Humboldt discovered "swinging stars":** Richard L. Gregory and Oliver L. Zangwill, "The Origin of the Autokinetic Effect," *Quarterly Journal of Experimental Psychology* 15, no 4 (1963): 252–61, https://doi.org/10.1080/17470216308416334.

85 **"As an adolescent with a great deal of curiosity about things":** Muzafer Sherif (1967), quoted in Ayfer Dost-Gozkan, *Norms, Groups,*

Conflict, and Social Change: Rediscovering Muzafer Sherif's Psychology (London, UK: Routledge, 2015).

85   **Two groups can see the same event but believe wildly different things about it:** Albert H. Hastorf and Hadley Cantril, "They Saw a Game: A Case Study," *The Journal of Abnormal and Social Psychology* 49, no. 1 (1954): 129–34, https://doi.org/10.1037/h0057880.

86   **with most people trusting the group rather than their own perceptions:** Dominic Abrams and John M. Levine, *The Formation of Social Norms: Revisiting Sherif's Autokinetic Illusion Study* (London, UK: Psychology Press, 2012), 29.

87   **We develop a shared reality:** Abdo Elnakouri et al., "In It Together: Shared Reality with Instrumental Others Is Linked to Goal Success," *Journal of Personality and Social Psychology* 125, no. 5 (2023): 1072–95, https://doi.org/10.1037/pspi0000427; E. Tory Higgins, Maya Rossignac-Milon, and Gerald Echterhoff, "Shared Reality: From Sharing-Is-Believing to Merging Minds," *Current Directions in Psychological Science* 30, no. 2 (2021): 103–10, https://doi.org/10.1177/0963721421992027.

87   **predict other group members' behavior, infer their intentions, and understand new events similarly:** Michael Tomasello and Amrisha Vaish, "Origins of Human Cooperation and Morality," *Annual Review of Psychology* 64, no. 1 (2013): 231–55, https://doi.org/10.1146/annurev-psych-113011-143812.

89   **But you'll also find Dvorak:** Benj Edwards, "iPhone Now Supports 86-Year-Old Dvorak Keyboard Layout Natively, Delighting Woz," *Ars Technica*, October 10, 2022, https://arstechnica.com/gadgets/2022/10/iphone-now-supports-86-year-old-dvorak-keyboard-layout-natively-delighting-woz.

89   **QWERTY configuration arose in response to telegraph operators' outdated Morse code habits:** Rupendra Brahambhatt, "QWERTY—History, Evolution, and Why Is It the Way It Is?," *Interesting Engineering*, June 22, 2021, https://interestingengineering.com/innovation/history-and-evolution-of-qwerty-keyboard.

90   **familiar, so much so that it has its own name: "status quo bias":** William Samuelson and Richard Zeckhauser, "Status Quo

Bias in Decision Making," *Journal of Risk and Uncertainty* 1, no. 1 (1988): 7–59, https://doi.org/10.1007/BF00055564.

91   **like Isaac Newton's first law of motion, groups tend to be inertial:** Connie J. G. Gersick and J. Richard Hackman, "Habitual Routines in Task-Performing Groups," *Organizational Behavior and Human Decision Processes* 47, no. 1 (1990): 65–97.

91   **largely through social norms toward prosociality:** Steven Pinker, *The Better Angels of Our Nature: A History of Violence and Humanity* (London, UK: Penguin UK, 2011); Brian Hare, "Survival of the Friendliest: *Homo sapiens* Evolved via Selection for Prosociality," *Annual Review of Psychology* 68, no. 1 (2017): 155–86, https://doi.org/10.1146/annurev-psych-010416-044201.

Chapter 6: You Will Be Assimilated: The Dark Side of Conformity Pressures

94   **more than all wild birds and mammals combined:** Patrick Schultheiss et al., "The Abundance, Biomass, and Distribution of Ants on Earth," *Proceedings of the National Academy of Sciences* 119, no. 40 (2022): e2201550119, https://doi.org/10.1073/pnas.2201550119.

94   **explain why the two species have outcompeted all others and become what he called "superorganisms":** Edward O. Wilson, *The Social Conquest of Earth* (New York, NY: Liveright, 2012).

95   **in favor of the collective:** Selin Kesebir, "The Superorganism Account of Human Sociality: How and When Human Groups Are Like Beehives," *Personality and Social Psychology Review* 16, no. 3 (2012): 233–61.

96   **not to test vision, but to test conformity:** Solomon E. Asch, "Effects of Group Pressure Upon the Modification and Distortion of Judgments," in *Groups, Leadership, and Men*, ed. Harold Guetzkow (Pittsburgh, PA: Carnegie Press, 1951), 177–90; Axel Franzen and Sebastian Mader, "The Power of Social Influence: A Replication and Extension of the Asch Experiment," *PLOS One* 18, no. 11 (2023): e0294325, https://doi.org/10.1371/journal.pone.0294325.

98   **It ordered the invasion of Cuba in hopes of triggering a popular uprising:** Morten T. Hansen, "How John F. Kennedy

Changed Decision Making for Us All," *Harvard Business Review,* November 22, 2013, https://hbr.org/2013/11/how-john-f-kennedy -changed-decision-making.

98   **conformity pressures allow seemingly smart, capable groups of people to make spectacularly bad decisions:** Irving L. Janis, *Groupthink* (Boston, MA: Houghton Mifflin, 1982).

99   **getting contradictory perspectives and information out there takes effort:** Colin M. Fisher, "An Ounce of Prevention or a Pound of Cure? Two Experiments on In-Process Interventions in Decision-Making Groups," *Organizational Behavior and Human Decision Processes* 138 (2017): 59–73, https://doi.org/10.1016/j.obhdp .2016.11.004; Felix C. Brodbeck et al., "Group Decision Making Under Conditions of Distributed Knowledge: The Information Asymmetries Model," *Academy of Management Review* 32, no. 2 (2007): 459–79, https://doi.org/10.5465/amr.2007.24351441; Carsten K. W. De Dreu, Bernard A. Nijstad, and Daan van Knippenberg, "Motivated Information Processing in Group Judgment and Decision Making," *Personality and Social Psychology Review* 12, no. 1 (2008): 22–49, https://doi.org/10.1177/1088868307304092.

101   **Robert Kennedy, the attorney general and John's brother, took Schlesinger aside:** Joshua Rosenbloom and Stephen Bates, *Kennedy and the Bay of Pigs* (Cambridge, MA: Harvard Kennedy School of Government, 1998).

101   **not one spoke against it:** Morten T. Hansen, "How John F. Kennedy Changed Decision Making for Us All," *Harvard Business Review,* November 22, 2013, https://hbr.org/2013/11/how-john-f -kennedy-changed-decision-making.

102   **crystallized into formal, repeatable group processes through socialization:** Songqi Liu et al., "Unpacking the Effects of Socialization Programs on Newcomer Retention: A Meta-Analytic Review of Field Experiments," *Psychological Bulletin* 150, no. 1 (2024): 1–26, https://doi.org/10.1037/bul0000422.

102   **According to media reports:** Sara Ganim and Chris Welch, "Parents: 'Criminal' Inaction by Penn State, Frat Members Led to Son's Death," CNN, May 15, 2017, https://www.cnn.com/2017/05/ 15/us/penn-state-fraternity-piazza-family-interview/index.html.

104 *Office Space*'s parody of corporate life influenced flair policies in the real world: Anthony D'Alessandro, "EMMYS: Mike Judge on How Viacom-Paramount Merger Influenced *Silicon Valley* & *Office Space*'s Impact on TGI Fridays," *Deadline* (blog), June 14, 2014, https://deadline.com/2014/06/mike-judge-silicon-valley-interview-making-of-787571.

106 only for symbolic purposes is an example of "coercive control": James R. Barker, "Tightening the Iron Cage: Concertive Control in Self-Managing Teams," *Administrative Science Quarterly* 38, no. 3 (1993): 408–37, https://doi.org/10.2307/2393374.

106 Bad is stronger than good in the brain: Roy F. Baumeister et al., "Bad Is Stronger Than Good," *Review of General Psychology* 5, no. 4 (2001): 323–70, https://doi.org/10.1037/1089-2680.5.4.323.

106 people feel worse losing one hundred dollars than they feel good finding one hundred dollars: Daniel Kahneman and Amos Tversky, "Chapter 6: Prospect Theory: An Analysis of Decision Under Risk," *Handbook of the Fundamentals of Financial Decision Making* (2013), 99–127, https://doi.org/10.1142/9789814417358_0006.

106 people who are working hard to avoid punishment: Andrew J. Elliot and Judith M. Harackiewicz, "Approach and Avoidance Achievement Goals and Intrinsic Motivation: A Mediational Analysis," *Journal of Personality and Social Psychology* 70, no. 3 (1996): 461–75, https://doi.org/10.1037/0022-3514.70.3.461.

106 avoiding punishment takes up so much of our mental energy: Kristin Byron, Shalini Khazanchi, and Deborah Nazarian, "The Relationship Between Stressors and Creativity: A Meta-Analysis Examining Competing Theoretical Models," *Journal of Applied Psychology* 95, no. 1 (2010): 201–12, https://doi.org/10.1037/a0017868.

107 Arendt's book *Eichmann in Jerusalem*: Hannah Arendt, *Eichmann in Jerusalem: A Report on the Banality of Evil*, 1st ed. (New York, NY: Penguin Classics, 2006).

Chapter 7: Red and Blue: How Groups Get Polarized

109 Twitter (now X) account for M&M's candy made an unusual announcement: M&M's (@MMsChocolate), "A message from

M&M's," X (formerly Twitter), January 23, 2023, https://x.com /mmschocolate/status/1617518785686274052.

110 **Infamous ex–Fox News commentator Tucker Carlson raged:** Acyn (@Acyn), "Tucker: M&M's will not be satisfied until every last cartoon character is deeply unappealing and totally androgynous. Until the moment you wouldn't want to have a drink with any one of them. . ." X (formerly Twitter), January 21, 2022, https://x.com/acyn/status/1484723825606479872.

110 **polarization is increasing in the Western world:** Diego Garzia, Frederico Ferreira da Silva, and Simon Maye, "Affective Polarization in Comparative and Longitudinal Perspective," *Public Opinion Quarterly* 87, no. 1 (2023), https://doi.org/10.1093/poq /nfad004.

111 **graduate student James Stoner stumbled upon group polarization accidentally:** James A. F. Stoner, "Risky and Cautious Shifts in Group Decisions: The Influence of Widely Held Values," *Journal of Experimental Social Psychology* 4, no. 4 (1968): 442–59, https://doi.org/10.1016/0022-1031(68)90069-3.

111 **Group interaction seemed to pull the collective toward the extremes:** Dean G. Pruitt and Allan I. Teger, "The Risky Shift in Group Betting," *Journal of Experimental Social Psychology* 5, no. 2 (1969): 115–26, https://doi.org/10.1016/0022-1031(69)90041-9.

112 **From an evolutionary perspective, it might even be useful:** Kiri Kuroda and Tatsuya Kameda, "You Watch My Back, I'll Watch Yours: Emergence of Collective Risk Monitoring Through Tacit Coordination in Human Social Foraging," *Evolution and Human Behavior* 40, no. 5 (2019): 427–35, https://doi.org/10.1016/j .evolhumbehav.2019.05.004.

113 **police found a nightmare in a house in Crestone:** Megan McCluskey, "The Bizarre True Story Behind HBO's *Love Has Won* Docuseries," *Time*, November 14, 2023, https://time.com/6333436 /love-has-won-true-story-hbo.

115 **the two most politically homogenous US cities in 2022:** https://bestneighborhood.org.

116 **85 percent of American married couples share a political party:** Shanto Iyengar et al., "The Origins and Consequences of

Affective Polarization in the United States," *Annual Review of Political Science* 22 (2019): 129–46, https://doi.org/10.1146/annurev-polisci -051117-073034; Shanto Iyengar, Gaurav Sood, and Yphtach Lelkes, "Affect, Not Ideology: A Social Identity Perspective on Polarization," *Public Opinion Quarterly* 76, no. 3 (2012): 405–31, https:// doi.org/10.1093/poq/nfs038.

116 **there's another force that explains polarization besides homophily:** Amit Goldenberg, "Extreme Views Are More Attractive than Moderate Ones," *Scientific American*, April 19, 2023, https:// www.scientificamerican.com/article/extreme-views -are-more-attractive-than-moderate-ones.

118 **nothing predicted shares and retweets better than outgroup hate:** Steve Rathje, Jay J. Van Bavel, and Sander van der Linden, "Out-Group Animosity Drives Engagement on Social Media," *Proceedings of the National Academy of Sciences* 118, no. 26 (2021): e2024292118, https://doi.org/10.1073/pnas.2024292118.

119 **"We have a harm-based moral mind":** Kurt Gray, *Outraged: Why We Fight About Morality and Politics and How to Find Common Ground* (New York, NY: Pantheon, 2025).

120 **But in the US now, there's a large divide for almost everything:** John Burn-Murdoch (@JBurnMurdoch), "It always blows my mind how much wider the partisan trust gap is for US media compared to the UK 👀 Most British media is trusted (or distrusted) about equally by supporters of both major parties. . ." X (formerly Twitter), January 9, 2024, https://x.com/jburnmurdoch/status /1744716508570550695.

120 **The group's shared reality becomes more idiosyncratic:** E. Tory Higgins, Maya Rossignac-Milon, and Gerald Echterhoff, "Shared Reality: From Sharing-Is-Believing to Merging Minds," *Current Directions in Psychological Science* 30, no. 2 (2021): 103–10, https://doi.org/10.1177/0963721421992027.

120 **Information that comes from outside can't penetrate this shared reality:** Eugen Dimant, "Hate Trumps Love: The Impact of Political Polarization on Social Preferences," *Management Science* 70, no. 1 (2024): 1–31, https://doi.org/10.1287/mnsc .2023.4701.

121 **those who have risen to power on our penchant for extremes:** Amit Goldenberg, "Extreme Views Are More Attractive Than Moderate Ones," *Scientific American*, April 19, 2023, https://www.scientificamerican.com/article/extreme-views-are-more-attractive-than-moderate-ones.

Chapter 8: The Idea Meritocracy: Winning the Battle Against the Dark Side of Conformity

123 **We grow complacent and forget to deploy our arsenal:** Daniel Kahneman, *Thinking, Fast and Slow* (London, UK: Penguin, 2011).

124 **prepare for the battle as thoroughly as Bridgewater Associates:** Eric Johnson, "Bridgewater Associates Founder Ray Dalio Has a 'Magical Formula' for Better Decision-Making," *Vox*, November 6, 2017, https://www.vox.com/2017/11/6/16610878/bridgewater-associates-ray-dalio-book-principles-life-work-decision-formula-kara-swisher-podcast.

125 **devil's advocacy is better than nothing:** Colin M. Fisher, "An Ounce of Prevention or a Pound of Cure? Two Experiments on In-Process Interventions in Decision-Making Groups," *Organizational Behavior and Human Decision Processes* 138 (2017): 59–73, https://doi.org/10.1016/j.obhdp.2016.11.004; Ulrich Klocke, "How to Improve Decision Making in Small Groups: Effects of Dissent and Training Interventions," *Small Group Research* 38, no. 3 (2007): 437–68, https://doi.org/10.1177/1046496407301974.

125 **as Adam Grant advises us, like scientists:** Adam Grant, *Think Again: The Power of Knowing What You Don't Know* (London, UK: W. H. Allen, 2021).

125 **agreement cascades, where we all pile on information and opinions in the same direction:** Michael Macy et al., "Opinion Cascades and the Unpredictability of Partisan Polarization," *Science Advances* 5, no. 8 (2019): eaax0754, https://doi.org/10.1126/sciadv.aax0754.

126 **The view of the US as liberators:** Karen Guttieri, Michael D. Wallace, and Peter Suedfeld, "The Integrative Complexity of American Decision Makers in the Cuban Missile Crisis," *Journal of*

Conflict Resolution 39, no. 4 (1995): 595–621, https://doi.org/10
.1177/0022002795039004001.

126 **groups make better decisions when leaders direct "how,"
not "what":** Randall S. Peterson, "A Directive Leadership Style
in Group Decision Making Can Be Both Virtue and Vice: Evidence from Elite and Experimental Groups," *Journal of Personality
and Social Psychology* 72, no. 5 (1997): 1107–21, https://doi.org/10
.1037/0022-3514.72.5.1107.

127 **most innovative and effective teams aren't solely focused on
the challenges they face internally:** Deborah Ancona, Henrik
Bresman, and David Caldwell, "The X-Factor: Six Steps to Leading High-Performing X-Teams," *Organizational Dynamics* 38, no. 3
(2009): 217–24, https://doi.org/10.1016/j.orgdyn.2009.04.003;
Deborah G. Ancona and David F. Caldwell, "Bridging the Boundary: External Activity and Performance in Organizational Teams,"
Administrative Science Quarterly 37, no. 4 (1992): 634–65, https://doi.
org/10.2307/2393475.

128 **Brokers offer what organizational sociologist Ronald Burt
calls a "vision advantage":** Ronald S. Burt, *Brokerage and Closure:
An Introduction to Social Capital* (Oxford, UK: Oxford University
Press, 2005).

128 **ability to take ideas from one project and apply them to totally different ones:** Andrew Hargadon and Robert I. Sutton,
"Technology Brokering and Innovation in a Product Development Firm," *Administrative Science Quarterly* 42, no. 4 (1997): 716–49,
https://doi.org/10.2307/2393655.

129 **Lincoln was determined to recruit the most capable candidates:** Doris Kearns Goodwin, *Team of Rivals: The Political Genius
of Abraham Lincoln* (New York, NY: Simon & Schuster, 2005).

129 **they adopt norms thoughtlessly:** Kenneth Bettenhausen and J.
Keith Murnighan, "The Emergence of Norms in Competitive
Decision-Making Groups," *Administrative Science Quarterly* 30, no. 3
(1985): 350–72, https://doi.org/10.2307/2392667; Kenneth Bet-
tenhausen and J. Keith Murnighan, "The Development of an
Intragroup Norm and the Effects of Interpersonal and Structural

Challenges," *Administrative Science Quarterly* 36, no. 1 (1991): 20–35, https://doi.org/10.2307/2393428.

129 **it's better than when we mindlessly proceed:** Connie J. G. Gersick and J. Richard Hackman, "Habitual Routines in Task-Performing Groups," *Organizational Behavior and Human Decision Processes* 47, no. 1 (1990): 65–97, https://doi.org/10.1016/0749-5978 (90)90047-D.

129 **they are great opportunities to learn:** Hoon-Seok Choi and John M. Levine, "Minority Influence in Work Teams: The Impact of Newcomers," *Journal of Experimental Social Psychology* 40, no. 2 (2004): 273–80, https://doi.org/10.1016/S0022-1031(03) 00101-X.

130 **Edmondson was studying nursing teams:** Amy Edmondson, "Psychological Safety and Learning Behavior in Work Teams," *Administrative Science Quarterly* 44, no. 2 (1999): 350–83, https://doi .org/10.2307/2666999.

132 **psychological safety—the shared sense that members can admit mistakes:** Amy C. Edmondson and Zhike Lei, "Psychological Safety: The History, Renaissance, and Future of an Interpersonal Construct," *Annual Review of Organizational Psychology and Organizational Behavior* 1, no. 1 (2014): 23–43, https://doi.org/10 .1146/annurev-orgpsych-031413-091305.

133 **groups with roughly equal speaking time perform better:** Christoph Riedl et al., "Quantifying Collective Intelligence in Human Groups," *Proceedings of the National Academy of Sciences* 118, no. 21 (2021): e2005737118, https://doi.org/10.1073/pnas.2005737118; Anita Woolley and Thomas W. Malone, "Defend Your Research: What Makes a Team Smarter? More Women," *Harvard Business Review* 89, no. 6 (2011): 32–33, https://hbr.org/2011/06/defend-your-research-what-makes-a-team-smarter-more-women.

135 **his masterpiece, *Exit, Voice, and Loyalty*:** Albert O. Hirschman, *Exit, Voice, and Loyalty: Responses to Decline in Firms, Organizations, and States* (Cambridge, MA: Harvard University Press, 1970).

135 **especially the less powerful:** Patricia Satterstrom, Michaela Kerrissey, and Julia DiBenigno, "The Voice Cultivation Process:

How Team Members Can Help Upward Voice Live on to Implementation," *Administrative Science Quarterly* 66, no. 2 (2021): 380–425, https://doi.org/10.1177/0001839220962795.

136 **real listening means the speaker feels understood:** Jeffrey Yip and Colin M. Fisher, "Listening in Organizations: A Synthesis and Future Agenda," *Academy of Management Annals* 16, no. 2 (2022): 657–79, https://doi.org/10.5465/annals.2020.0367.

136 **leading to an interesting phenomenon: the wisdom of crowds:** James Surowiecki, *The Wisdom of Crowds: Why the Many Are Smarter Than the Few* (London, UK: Abacus, 2005); Joshua Becker, Devon Brackbill, and Damon Centola, "Network Dynamics of Social Influence in the Wisdom of Crowds," *Proceedings of the National Academy of Sciences* 114, no. 26 (2017): E5070–E5076, https://doi.org/10.1073/pnas.1615978114; Zhi Da and Xing Huang, "Harnessing the Wisdom of Crowds," *Management Science* 66, no. 5 (2020): 1847–67, https://doi.org/10.1287/mnsc.2019.3294.

136–137 **often outperform even the most talented individual prognosticators:** Joaquin Navajas et al., "Aggregated Knowledge from a Small Number of Debates Outperforms the Wisdom of Large Crowds," *Nature Human Behaviour* 2, no. 2 (2018): 126–32, https://doi.org/10.1038/s41562-017-0273-4. There are a lot of caveats to the advantage of crowds over individuals. This study found that allowing small groups to interact and then averaging group estimates was better than directly averaging individual estimates. Other research has found that averaging expert estimates is better than averaging everyone. Zhi Da and Xing Huang, "Harnessing the Wisdom of Crowds," *Management Science* 66, no. 5 (2020): 1847–67, https://doi.org/10.1287/mnsc.2019.3294.

138 **Conformity pressures are too strong:** Serge Moscovici, Elisabeth Lage, and Martine Naffrechoux, "Influence of a Consistent Minority on the Responses of a Majority in a Color Perception Task," *Sociometry* 32, no. 4 (1969): 365–80, https://doi.org/10.2307/2786541; William D. Crano and Viviane Seyranian, "Majority and Minority Influence," *Social and Personality Psychology Compass* 1, no. 1 (2007): 572–89, https://doi.org/10.1111/j.1751-9004.2007.00028.x; Antonis Gardikiotis, "Minority Influence," *Social and*

Personality Psychology Compass 5, no. 9 (2011): 679–93, https://doi
.org/10.1111/j.1751-9004.2011.00377.x.

139 **Edwin Hollander calls "idiosyncrasy credits":** Edwin P. Hollander, "Conformity, Status, and Idiosyncrasy Credit," *Psychological Review* 65, no. 2 (1958): 117–27, https://doi.org/10.1037
/h0042501.

140 **Dan Forsyth calls a "tolerated deviant":** Dan W. Forsyth,
"Tolerated Deviance and Small Group Solidarity," *Ethos* 16, no. 4
(1988): 398–420, https://doi.org/10.1525/eth.1988.16.4.02a00030.

141 **groups that make good use of dissent are more creative and
do better:** Charlan J. Nemeth, *No!: The Power of Disagreement in a
World That Wants to Get Along* (London, UK: Atlantic Books, 2018);
Charlan J. Nemeth, "Differential Contributions of Majority and
Minority Influence," *Psychological Review* 93, no. 1 (1986): 23–32,
https://doi.org/10.1037/0033-295X.93.1.23.

142 **groundbreaking work on group development:** Connie J. G.
Gersick, "Time and Transition in Work Teams: Toward a New
Model of Group Development," *Academy of Management Journal* 31,
no. 1 (1988): 9–41, https://doi.org/10.5465/256496; Connie J. G.
Gersick, "Marking Time: Predictable Transitions in Task Groups,"
Academy of Management Journal 32, no. 2 (1989): 274–309, https://
doi.org/10.5465/256363.

142 **beginnings, midpoints, and endings:** J. Richard Hackman and
Ruth Wageman, "A Theory of Team Coaching," *Academy of Management Review* 30, no. 2 (2005): 269–87, https://doi.org/10.5465/
amr.2005.16387885; Ruth Wageman, Colin M. Fisher, and J.
Richard Hackman, "Leading Teams When the Time Is Right:
Finding the Best Moments to Act," *Organizational Dynamics* 38, no. 3
(2009): 192–203, https://doi.org/10.1016/j.orgdyn.2009.04.004.

143 **when they focus on stuff some people don't know:** Felix C.
Brodbeck et al., "Group Decision Making under Conditions of
Distributed Knowledge: The Information Asymmetries Model,"
Academy of Management Review 32, no. 2 (2007): 459–79, https://doi
.org/10.5465/amr.2007.24351441.

144 **best time to say this is just after interaction begins:** Colin
M. Fisher, "An Ounce of Prevention or a Pound of Cure? Two

Experiments on In-Process Interventions in Decision-Making Groups," *Organizational Behavior and Human Decision Processes* 138 (2017): 59–73, https://doi.org/10.1016/j.obhdp.2016.11.004.

144 **top five for easy fixes that most groups still don't do:** J. Richard Hackman, *Leading Teams: Setting the Stage for Great Performances* (Boston, MA: Harvard Business Review Press, 2002).

145 **Edmondson's voluminous work on this subject:** Amy C. Edmondson and Zhike Lei, "Psychological Safety: The History, Renaissance, and Future of an Interpersonal Construct," *Annual Review of Organizational Psychology and Organizational Behavior* 1, no. 1 (2014): 23–43, https://doi.org/10.1146/annurev-orgpsych-031413 -091305; Amy C. Edmondson, Richard Bohmer, and Gary Pisano, "Speeding Up Team Learning," *Harvard Business Review* 79, no. 9 (2001): 125–32, https://hbr.org/2001/10/speeding-up-team -learning; Amy C. Edmondson, "Strategies for Learning from Failure," *Harvard Business Review* 89, no. 4 (2011): 48–55, https:// hbr.org/2011/04/strategies-for-learning-from-failure; Amy C. Edmondson, *The Fearless Organization: Creating Psychological Safety in the Workplace for Learning, Innovation, and Growth* (Hoboken, NJ: Wiley, 2018).

147 **importance of a strong "developmental network":** Shoshana R. Dobrow et al., "A Review of Developmental Networks: Incorporating a Mutuality Perspective," *Journal of Management* 38, no. 1 (2012): 210–42, https://doi.org/10.1177/0149206311415858; Monica C. Higgins and Kathy E. Kram, "Reconceptualizing Mentoring at Work: A Developmental Network Perspective," *The Academy of Management Review* 26, no. 2 (2001): 264–88, https://doi.org/10 .2307/259122.

147 **simple dietary advice is to eat a variety of unprocessed foods:** Michael Pollan, "How to Eat," *Michael Pollan*, January 23, 2010, https://michaelpollan.com/reviews/how-to-eat.

Chapter 9: Always Competing: How Competition Shapes Us and Our Groups

152 **Competition with a rival helps group performance:** Brian E. Pike, Gavin J. Kilduff, and Adam D. Galinsky, "The Long Shadow

of Rivalry: Rivalry Motivates Performance Today and Tomorrow," *Psychological Science* 29, no. 5 (2018): 804–13, https://doi.org/10.1177/0956797617744796.

153   **Ethiopian runner Almaz Ayana:** Chris Chavez, "Ethiopia's Almaz Ayana Wins Gold with New Women's 10,000-Meter World Record," *Sports Illustrated*, August 12, 2018, https://www.si.com/olympics/2016/08/12/almaz-ayana-world-record-rio-2016-olympics-10000-meters-molly-huddle.

154   **we often have a physiological "challenge" response:** Kathleen V. Casto and David A. Edwards, "Testosterone, Cortisol, and Human Competition," *Hormones and Behavior* 82 (2016): 21–37, https://doi.org/10.1016/j.yhbeh.2016.04.004.

155   **Competition and performance have barely any detectable relationship:** Kou Murayama and Andrew J. Elliot, "The Competition–Performance Relation: A Meta-Analytic Review and Test of the Opposing Processes Model of Competition and Performance," *Psychological Bulletin* 138, no. 6 (2012): 1035–70, https://doi.org/10.1037/a0028324.

156   **amping up the heat will harm performance:** Robert B. Zajonc, "Social Facilitation: A Solution Is Suggested for an Old Unresolved Social Psychological Problem," *Science* 149, no. 3681 (1965): 269–74, https://doi.org/10.1126/science.149.3681.269.

156   **Social facilitation and inhibition allow us to predict when people will blossom or wilt:** Kristin Byron, Shalini Khazanchi, and Deborah Nazarian, "The Relationship between Stressors and Creativity: A Meta-Analysis Examining Competing Theoretical Models," *Journal of Applied Psychology* 95, no. 1 (2010): 201–12, https://doi.org/10.1037/a0017868.

157   **don't believe you have a chance to win, you don't get the "challenge" physiological response:** Alia J. Crum et al., "The Role of Stress Mindset in Shaping Cognitive, Emotional, and Physiological Responses to Challenging and Threatening Stress," *Anxiety, Stress, & Coping* 30, no. 4 (2017): 379–95, https://doi.org/10.1080/10615806.2016.1275585.

157   **had a one-hundred-forty-meter yacht called *Solaris* built for himself:** "Solaris: Roman Abramovich's Ultra-Luxurious Su-

peryacht," SuperYachtFan, accessed November 15, 2024, https://www.superyachtfan.com/yacht/solaris.

158 **"an anonymous Malaysian businessman" purchased an even more extravagant yacht:** "The Midas Touch: $4.8 Billion History Supreme Most Expensive Yacht Ever Sold," Atlantic Yacht and Ship, accessed September 12, 2024, https://atlanticyachtandship.com/the-midas-touch-4-8-billion-history-supreme-most-expensive-yacht-ever-sold.

158 **social psychologists have long known the explanation:** Michael J. Matthews and Thomas K. Kelemen, "To Compare Is Human: A Review of Social Comparison Theory in Organizational Settings," *Journal of Management*, August 26, 2024, https://doi.org/10.1177/01492063241266157.

158 **eternal competition in our minds is about something far more ephemeral—status:** Susan T. Fiske et al., "Status, Power, and Intergroup Relations: The Personal Is the Societal," *Current Opinion in Psychology* 11 (October 2016): 44–48, https://doi.org/10.1016/j.copsyc.2016.05.012; Cameron Anderson and Gavin J. Kilduff, "The Pursuit of Status in Social Groups," *Current Directions in Psychological Science* 18, no. 5 (2009): 295–98, https://doi.org/10.1111/j.1467-8721.2009.01655.x.

159 **Your place in these hierarchies doesn't just affect your psychology:** Bert Van Landeghem and Anneleen Vandeplas, "The Relationship Between Status and Happiness: Evidence from the Caste System in Rural India," *Journal of Behavioral and Experimental Economics* 77 (December 2018): 62–71, https://doi.org/10.1016/j.socec.2018.08.006.

159 **it also affects your physiology:** Modupe Akinola and Wendy Berry Mendes, "It's Good to Be the King: Neurobiological Benefits of Higher Social Standing," *Social Psychological and Personality Science* 5, no. 1 (2014): 43–51, https://doi.org/10.1177/1948550613485604; Andrew Baum, J. P. Garofalo, and Ann M. Yali, "Socioeconomic Status and Chronic Stress. Does Stress Account for SES Effects on Health?," *Annals of the New York Academy of Sciences* 896 (1999): 131–44, https://doi.org/10.1111/j.1749-6632.1999.tb08111.x; Franziska Reiss et al., "Socioeconomic Status, Stressful Life Situations and

Mental Health Problems in Children and Adolescents: Results of the German BELLA Cohort-Study," *PLOS One* 14, no. 3 (2019): e0213700, https://doi.org/10.1371/journal.pone.0213700.

159   **Olympic silver medalists were less satisfied than the bronze medalists they beat:** William M. Hedgcock, Andrea W. Luangrath, and Raelyn Webster, "Counterfactual Thinking and Facial Expressions Among Olympic Medalists: A Conceptual Replication of Medvec, Madey, and Gilovich's (1995) Findings," *Journal of Experimental Psychology: General* 150, no. 6 (2021): e13–e21, http://dx.doi.org/10.1037/xge0000992; Victoria Husted Medvec, Scott F. Madey, and Thomas Gilovich, "When Less Is More: Counterfactual Thinking and Satisfaction among Olympic Medalists," *Journal of Personality and Social Psychology* 69, no. 4 (1995), 603–10.

160   **tendencies as "envy up, scorn down":** Susan T. Fiske, "Envy Up, Scorn Down: How Comparison Divides Us," *American Psychologist* 65, no. 8 (2010): 698–706, https://doi.org/10.1037/0003-066X.65.8.698.

161   **To infer high status, we use small cues:** Susan T. Fiske et al., "Status, Power, and Intergroup Relations: The Personal Is the Societal," *Current Opinion in Psychology* 11 (October 2016): 44–48, https://doi.org/10.1016/j.copsyc.2016.05.012; Matteo Prato et al., "The Status of Status Research: A Review of the Types, Functions, Levels, and Audiences," *Journal of Management* 50, no. 6 (2024), 2266–308, https://doi.org/10.1177/01492063241226918.

161   **lowered eye gaze or a raised chin give us lightning-fast cues:** Hugo Toscano, Thomas W. Schubert, and Steffen R. Giessner, "Eye Gaze and Head Posture Jointly Influence Judgments of Dominance, Physical Strength, and Anger," *Journal of Nonverbal Behavior* 42, no. 3 (2018): 285–309, https://doi.org/10.1007/s10919-018-0276-5.

161   **we have two potential responses:** Larissa Z. Tiedens and Alison R. Fragale, "Power Moves: Complementarity in Dominant and Submissive Nonverbal Behavior," *Journal of Personality and Social Psychology* 84, no. 3 (2003): 558, https://doi.org/10.1037/0022-3514.84.3.558.

162   **still develop informal hierarchies:** Dacher Keltner et al., "Par-

adoxes of Power: Dynamics of the Acquisition, Experience, and Social Regulation of Social Power," in *The Social Psychology of Power*, ed. Ana Guinote and Theresa K. Vescio (New York, NY: Guilford Press, 2010), 177–208.

162   **Members disproportionately go to certain people for help and advice:** Teresa Amabile, Colin M. Fisher, and Julianna Pillemer, "IDEO's Culture of Helping," *Harvard Business Review* 92, no. 1/2 (2014): 54–61, https://hbr.org/2014/01/ideos-culture-of -helping.

162   **hierarchy is good for something:** Heidi K. Gardner, "Performance Pressure as a Double-Edged Sword: Enhancing Team Motivation but Undermining the Use of Team Knowledge," *Administrative Science Quarterly* 57, no. 1 (2012): 1–46, https://doi.org/10 .1177/0001839212446454.

162   **trait that actually matters:** Felicia Pratto et al., "Social Dominance Orientation: A Personality Variable Predicting Social and Political Attitudes," *Journal of Personality and Social Psychology* 67, no. 4 (1994): 741–63, https://doi.org/10.1037/0022-3514.67.4.741.

163   **believe their position is precarious fail to get the health and happiness benefits of status:** Gary D. Sherman and Pranjal H. Mehta, "Stress, Cortisol, and Social Hierarchy," *Current Opinion in Psychology* 33 (2020): 227–32, https://doi.org/10.1016/j.copsyc.2019 .09.013.

164   **too much hierarchy is bad for group effectiveness:** Lindred L. Greer et al., "Why and When Hierarchy Impacts Team Effectiveness: A Meta-Analytic Integration," *Journal of Applied Psychology* 103, no. 6 (2018): 591–613, https://doi.org/10.1037/apl0000291.

164   **when the heat is on, groups tend to look to the person at the top:** Heidi K. Gardner, "Performance Pressure as a Double-Edged Sword: Enhancing Team Motivation but Undermining the Use of Team Knowledge," *Administrative Science Quarterly* 57, no. 1 (2012): 1–46, https://doi.org/10.1177/0001839212446454.

164   **Flexible hierarchies have their own problems:** Catarina R. Fernandes et al., "What Is Your Status Portfolio? Higher Status Variance Across Groups Increases Interpersonal Helping but Decreases Intrapersonal Well-Being," *Organizational Behavior and Hu-*

man Decision Processes 165 (July 2021): 56–75, https://doi.org/10 .1016/j.obhdp.2021.04.002; Erik L. Knight and Pranjal H. Mehta, "Hierarchy Stability Moderates the Effect of Status on Stress and Performance in Humans," *Proceedings of the National Academy of Sciences* 114, no. 1 (2017): 78–83, https://doi.org/10.1073/pnas.1609 811114.

164 **causes people to become temporarily less capable:** Anandi Mani et al., "Poverty Impedes Cognitive Function," *Science* 341, no. 6149 (2013): 976–80, https://doi.org/10.1126/science.1238041.

165 **One reason it corrupts is psychological distance:** Yaacov Trope and Nira Liberman, "Construal-Level Theory of Psychological Distance," *Psychological Review* 117, no. 2 (2010): 440–63, https://doi.org/10.1037/a0018963.

165 **69 percent of study participants said it was more acceptable to sacrifice the life of one person experiencing homelessness:** Mina Cikara et al., "On the Wrong Side of the Trolley Track: Neural Correlates of Relative Social Valuation," *Social Cognitive and Affective Neuroscience* 5, no. 4 (2010): 404–13, https://doi .org/10.1093/scan/nsq011.

166 **how far he could push obedience to authority:** Stanley Milgram, "Behavioral Study of Obedience," *The Journal of Abnormal and Social Psychology* 67, no. 4 (1963): 371–78, https://doi.org/10 .1037/h0040525.

166 **identify with the broader cause in order to obey:** S. Alexander Haslam, Stephen D. Reicher, and Megan E. Birney, "Questioning Authority: New Perspectives on Milgram's 'Obedience' Research and Its Implications for Intergroup Relations," *Current Opinion in Psychology* 11 (October 2016): 6–9, https://doi.org /10.1016/j.copsyc.2016.03.007.

166 **"reluctance that even technically fully obedient participants need to overcome":** David Kaposi, "The Second Wave of Critical Engagement with Stanley Milgram's 'Obedience to Authority' Experiments: What Did We Learn?" *Social and Personality Psychology Compass* 16, no. 6 (2022): e12667, https://doi.org /10.1111/spc3.12667.

Chapter 10: The Escalator to Hell: The Conflict Within "Us" and Between "Us" and "Them"

169 **the most popular thinkers were the Sophists:** George Briscoe Kerferd, "Sophist," *Encyclopaedia Britannica*, last modified April 5, 2025, https://www.britannica.com/topic/sophist-philosophy.

170 **We call this productive side of conflict "task conflict":** Carsten K. W. De Dreu and Laurie R. Weingart, "Task Versus Relationship Conflict, Team Performance, and Team Member Satisfaction: A Meta-Analysis," *Journal of Applied Psychology* 88, no. 4 (2003): 741–49, https://doi.org/10.1037/0021-9010.88.4.741.

171 **that's unabashedly bad for group effectiveness:** Frank R. C. de Wit, Lindred L. Greer, and Karen A. Jehn, "The Paradox of Intragroup Conflict: A Meta-Analysis," *Journal of Applied Psychology* 97, no. 2 (2012): 360–90, https://doi.org/10.1037/a0024844.

171 **one of the strongest predictors of divorce is contempt:** John Mordechai Gottman, *What Predicts Divorce? The Relationship Between Marital Processes and Marital Outcomes* (New York, NY: Psychology Press, 2014), https://doi.org/10.4324/9781315806808.

173 **The Hatfield-McCoy feud:** "Hatfields and McCoys," *Encyclopaedia Britannica*, last modified March 1, 2025, https://www.britannica.com/topic/hatfields-and-mccoys.

174 **unfortunate tendency to escalate:** Randall Collins, "C-Escalation and D-Escalation: A Theory of the Time-Dynamics of Conflict," *American Sociological Review* 77, no. 1 (2012): 1–20, https://doi.org/10.1177/0003122411428221.

174 **"War Against the Americans to Save the Nation":** Ronald H. Specter, "Vietnam War," *Encyclopaedia Britannica*, last modified March 30, 2025, https://www.britannica.com/event/vietnam-war.

175 **two main ways in which conflict is sustained:** Dustin J. Sleesman et al., "Putting Escalation of Commitment in Context: A Multilevel Review and Analysis," *Academy of Management Annals* 12, no. 1 (2018): 178–207, https://doi.org/10.5465/annals.2016.0046.

175 **Popularized by economist Martin Shubik in 1971:** Martin Shubik, "The Dollar Auction Game: A Paradox in Noncoopera-

tive Behavior and Escalation," *Journal of Conflict Resolution* 15, no. 1 (1971): 109–11, https://doi.org/10.1177/002200277101500111.

176 **the best story I've ever heard about running a dollar auction:** J. Keith Murnighan, "A Very Extreme Case of the Dollar Auction," *Journal of Management Education* 26, no. 1 (2002): 56, https://doi.org/10.1177/105256290202600105.

178 **known as the "sunk-cost fallacy":** Daniel Friedman et al., "Searching for the Sunk Cost Fallacy," *Experimental Economics* 10, no. 1 (2007): 79–104, https://doi.org/10.1007/s10683-006-9134-0; Barry M. Staw, "Knee-Deep in the Big Muddy: A Study of Escalating Commitment to a Chosen Course of Action," *Organizational Behavior and Human Performance* 16, no. 1 (1976): 27–44, https://doi .org/10.1016/0030-5073(76)90005-2.

180 **people who are overconfident are seen as more competent by their peers:** Cameron Anderson et al., "A Status-Enhancement Account of Overconfidence," *Journal of Personality and Social Psychology* 103, no. 4 (2012): 718–35, https://doi.org/10.1037/a0029395.

180 **called it an "arrant act of hypocrisy":** Alvin S. Felzenberg, "William F. Buckley, Jr. and His Presidents," The Russell Kirk Center, December 24, 2017, https://kirkcenter.org/reviews/wil liam-f-buckley-jr-and-his-presidents.

180 **people don't like leaders who experiment with different courses of action:** Barry M. Staw and Jerry Ross, "Commitment in an Experimenting Society: A Study of the Attribution of Leadership from Administrative Scenarios," *Journal of Applied Psychology* 65, no. 3 (1980): 249–60, https://doi.org/10.1037/0021-9010.65 .3.249.

183 **take revenge when they perceive four qualities in a transgression:** This whole section on revenge owes a lot to Joshua Conrad Jackson, Virginia K. Choi, and Michele J. Gelfand, "Revenge: A Multilevel Review and Synthesis," *Annual Review of Psychology* 70, no. 1 (2019): 319–45, https://doi.org/10.1146/annurev-psych-010 418-103305. Thanks y'all!

183 **Anger is an aggressive, approach-oriented emotion:** Wesley G. Moons, Naomi I. Eisenberger, and Shelley E. Taylor, "Anger and Fear Responses to Stress Have Different Biological Profiles,"

Brain, Behavior, and Immunity 24, no. 2 (2010): 215–19, https://doi .org/10.1016/j.bbi.2009.08.009.

185 **Israeli president Isaac Herzog said:** Sanjana Karanth, "Israel Defense Minister Announces Siege on Gaza to Fight 'Human Animals,'" HuffPost UK, accessed November 8, 2024, https://www .huffingtonpost.co.uk/entry/israel-defense-minister-human -animals-gaza-palestine_n_6524220ae4b09f4b8d412e0a.

Chapter 11: Of Pigs and Potatoes: What We Can Do About Competition and Conflict

187 **because of yet another nineteenth-century pig:** Sarah Laskow, "In 1859, the United States and Britain Almost Went to War over a Pig," Atlas Obscura, September 13, 2017, http://www.atlasobscura .com/articles/pig-war-british-american-border-dispute-san -juan-island; Michael D. Haydock, "The San Juan Island's 'Pig War,'" HistoryNet, August 19, 2001, https://www.historynet.com /the-san-juan-islands-pig-war-february-01-american-history-feature.

190 **they were less likely than individuals to end up with extreme outcomes:** Andrea Morone, Simone Nuzzo, and Rocco Caferra, "The Dollar Auction Game: A Laboratory Comparison Between Individuals and Groups," *Group Decision and Negotiation* 28, no. 1 (2019): 79–98, https://doi.org/10.1007/s10726-018-9595-5.

191 **reasons groups in conflict de-escalate are nuanced and based on context:** Randall Collins, "C-Escalation and D-Escalation: A Theory of the Time-Dynamics of Conflict," *American Sociological Review* 77, no. 1 (2012): 1–20, https://doi.org/10 .1177/0003122411428221.

191 **national solidarity after terrorist attacks like September 11 lasts for about six months:** Randall Collins, "Rituals of Solidarity and Security in the Wake of Terrorist Attack," *Sociological Theory* 22 (2004): 53–87, https://doi.org/10.1111/j.1467-9558.2004 .00204.x.

192 **Robbers Cave and Middle Grove:** Gina Perry, *The Lost Boys: Inside Muzafer Sherif's Robbers Cave Experiment* (London, UK: Scribe UK, 2018); David Shariatmadari, "A Real-Life Lord of the Flies: The Troubling Legacy of the Robbers Cave Experiment," *The*

Guardian, April 16, 2018, https://www.theguardian.com/science /2018/apr/16/a-real-life-lord-of-the-flies-the-troubling -legacy-of-the-robbers-cave-experiment; Dominic Abrams and John Levine, "The Formation of Social Norms: Revisiting Sherif's Autokinetic Illusion Study," in *Handbook of Social Psychology*, ed. Susan T. Fiske, Daniel T. Gilbert, and Gardner Lindzey (New York, NY: Wiley, 2010), 29–50; Ayfer Dost-Gözkan, *Norms, Groups, Conflict, and Social Change: Rediscovering Muzafer Sherif's Psychology* (London, UK: Routledge, 2015); Aysel Kayaoğlu, Sertan Batur, and Ersin Aslıtürk, "The Unknown Muzafer Sherif," The British Psychological Society, accessed January 19, 2024, https://www.bps. org.uk/psychologist/unknown-muzafer-sherif; Muzafer Sherif, *The Robbers Cave Experiment: Intergroup Conflict and Cooperation* (Middletown, CT: Wesleyan University Press, 1988), originally published as *Intergroup Conflict and Group Relations*.

194 **formalized in the 1950s by Harvard psychologist Gordon Allport:** John F. Dovidio, Peter Glick, and Laurie A. Rudman, *On the Nature of Prejudice: Fifty Years After Allport* (Hoboken, NJ: John Wiley & Sons, 2008).

194 **has had, at best, mixed success:** Nikhil K. Sengupta et al., "Does Intergroup Contact Foster Solidarity with the Disadvantaged? A Longitudinal Analysis Across 7 Years," *American Psychologist* 78, no. 6 (2023), https://doi.org/10.1037/amp0001079.

194 **friends of friends from other groups can change people's attitudes:** Jasper Van Assche et al., "Intergroup Contact Is Reliably Associated with Reduced Prejudice, Even in the Face of Group Threat and Discrimination," *American Psychologist* 78, no. 6 (2023), https://doi.org/10.1037/amp0001144.

195 **doesn't always translate into less discrimination:** Markus Brauer, "Stuck on Intergroup Attitudes: The Need to Shift Gears to Change Intergroup Behaviors," *Perspectives on Psychological Science* 19, no. 1 (2023), https://doi.org/10.1177/17456916231185775.

195 **more contact didn't reduce prejudice:** Nikhil K. Sengupta et al., "Does Intergroup Contact Foster Solidarity with the Disadvantaged? A Longitudinal Analysis Across 7 Years," *American Psychologist* 78, no. 6 (2023), https://doi.org/10.1037/amp0001079.

195 **same thing when examining the prejudice of white Brits against foreigners:** Gordon Hodson and Rose Meleady, "Replicating and Extending Sengupta et al. (2023): Contact Predicts No Within-Person Longitudinal Outgroup-Bias Change," *American Psychologist* 79, no. 3 (2024): 451–62, https://doi.org/10.1037/amp 0001210.

197 **Sherif called "superordinate goals":** Bettina Höchli, Adrian Brügger, and Claude Messner, "How Focusing on Superordinate Goals Motivates Broad, Long-Term Goal Pursuit: A Theoretical Perspective," *Frontiers in Psychology* 9 (2018): 1879, https://doi.org/10 .3389/fpsyg.2018.01879.

198 **the US and the UK had several shared goals and interdependencies:** Howard Jones and Donald A. Rakestraw, *Prologue to Manifest Destiny: Anglo-American Relations in the 1840s* (Wilmington, DE: Scholarly Resources, 1997).

199 **"coopetition":** Ricarda B. Bouncken et al., "Coopetition: A Systematic Review, Synthesis, and Future Research Directions," *Review of Managerial Science* 9, no. 3 (2015): 577–601, https://doi.org /10.1007/s11846-015-0168-6; Paul Chiambaretto, Anne-Sophie Fernandez, and Frédéric Le Roy, "What Coopetition Is and What It Is Not: Defining the 'Hard Core' and the 'Protective Belt' of Coopetition," *Strategic Management Review* 6, no. 1 (2025).

200 **Rivals British Airways and Virgin Atlantic put aside their longtime, heated rivalry:** Martyn Gregory, *Dirty Tricks: British Airways' Secret War Against Richard Branson's Virgin Atlantic* (London, UK: Little, Brown, 1994), http://archive.org/details/dirtytricksin sid0000greg; Gwyn Topham, "BA and Virgin Atlantic Put Aside Rivalry for Return of Leisure Flights to US," *The Guardian*, November 8, 2021, https://www.theguardian.com/business/2021 /nov/08/ba-and-virgin-atlantic-put-aside-rivalry-for-return -of-leisure-flights-to-us-covid.

200 **known as Middle Grove:** David Shariatmadari, "A Real-Life Lord of the Flies: The Troubling Legacy of the Robbers Cave Experiment," *The Guardian*, April 16, 2018, https://www.theguard-ian.com/science/2018/apr/16/a-real-life-lord-of-the-flies-the -troubling-legacy-of-the-robbers-cave-experiment; Gina Perry, *The*

Lost Boys: Inside Muzafer Sherif's Robbers Cave Experiment (London, UK: Scribe UK, 2018).

202 **Competing against yourself:** Katy Milkman, *How to Change: The Science of Getting from Where You Are to Where You Want to Be* (London, UK: Vermilion, 2021); Coren L. Apicella, Elif E. Demiral, and Johanna Mollerstrom, "Compete with Others? No, Thanks. With Myself? Yes, Please!," *Economics Letters* 187 (February 2020): 108878, https://doi.org/10.1016/j.econlet.2019.108878.

205 **There are references in the endnotes:** Roger M. Schwarz, *The Skilled Facilitator: A Comprehensive Resource for Consultants, Facilitators, Coaches, and Trainers*, 3rd ed. (Hoboken, NJ: John Wiley & Sons, 2016); Roger Fisher and William Ury, *Getting to Yes: Negotiating an Agreement Without Giving In* (Houston, TX: Cornerstone Digital, 2012); Michael Wheeler, *The Art of Negotiation: How to Improvise Agreement in a Chaotic World* (Riverside, NJ: Simon & Schuster, 2013).

Chapter 12: The House Always Wins: When to Structure and When to Coach Your Groups

210 **even technicians were sometimes befuddled:** Julian E. Orr, *Talking About Machines: An Ethnography of a Modern Job* (Ithaca, NY: Cornell University Press, 2016).

210 **Xerox worked with organizational psychologist Ruth Wageman:** Ruth Wageman, "How Leaders Foster Self-Managing Team Effectiveness: Design Choices Versus Hands-On Coaching," *Organization Science* 12, no. 5 (2001): 559–77, https://doi.org/10.1287/orsc.12.5.559.10094.

212 **online slot game called *Ocean Magic*:** Eric Raskin, "One Week, One Million Dollars: New Jersey Advantage Players Fighting for Their Online Casino Winnings," NJ Online Gambling, February 26, 2019.

214 **accounted for 43 percent of ups and downs in team performance and member satisfaction:** Stephen E. Humphrey, Jennifer D. Nahrgang, and Frederick. P. Morgeson, "Integrating Motivational, Social, and Contextual Work Design Features: A Meta-Analytic Summary and Theoretical Extension of the Work

Design Literature," *Journal of Applied Psychology* 92, no. 5 (2007): 1332–56, https://doi.org/10.1037/0021-9010.92.5.1332.

219 **the 60:30:10 rule:** Ruth Wageman and Krister Lowe, "Designing, Launching, and Coaching Teams: The 60–30–10 Rule and Its Implications for Team Coaching," in *The Practitioner's Handbook of Team Coaching*, ed. David Clutterbuck et al. (New York, NY: Routledge, 2019), 121–37.

219 ***when* leaders should intervene:** Ruth Wageman, Colin M. Fisher, and J. Richard Hackman, "Leading Teams When the Time Is Right: Finding the Best Moments to Act," *Organizational Dynamics* 38, no. 3 (2009): 192–203, https://doi.org/10.1016/j.org dyn.2009.04.004.

Chapter 13: The *L* Word: When and Why Leadership Matters

222 **I could come up with 'Leadership Lessons from Turtles':** I actually presented leadership lessons from turtles as a joke in the introduction to what I hope were some deeper lessons about leadership from jazz. See Colin M. Fisher, "Leadership Lessons from Jazz Ensembles," in Ruth Wageman (Chair), *Leadership Lessons from Unusual Places*, symposium presented at the meeting of the Academy of Management, Philadelphia, PA, August 2007.

223 **even medieval musicians knew better:** "Conductor," *Encyclopaedia Britannica*, last modified March 29, 2024, https://www.bri tannica.com/art/conductor-music; Cristina Simón, "What Does an Orchestra Conductor Really Do?" The Conversation, November 2, 2023, http://theconversation.com/what-does-an-orchestra -conductor-really-do-216685.

223 **there still weren't specialized conductors:** "Conductor," *Encyclopaedia Britannica*, last modified March 29, 2024, https:// www.britannica.com/art/conductor-music.

223 **called them "a necessary evil":** Cristina Simón, "What Does an Orchestra Conductor Really Do?" The Conversation, November 2, 2023, http://theconversation.com/what-does-an -orchestra-conductor-really-do-216685.

224 **32 percent of orchestral musicians felt they had autonomy**

in their jobs: Mika Kivimäki and Miia Jokinen, "Job Perceptions and Well-Being Among Symphony Orchestra Musicians: A Comparison with Other Occupational Groups," *Medical Problems of Performing Artists* 9, no. 3 (1994): 73–76, https://www.jstor.org /stable/45440495. A more recent article gets similar results: In Norway, orchestral musicians report less control and acknowledgment than other kinds of musicians and are less satisfied than the general workforce. See Anna Détári et al., "Psychosocial Work Environment Among Musicians and in the General Workforce in Norway," *Frontiers in Psychology* 11 (2020): 1315, https://doi.org/10 .3389/fpsyg.2020.01315.

225   **professional string quartets came in first:** Jutta Allmendinger, J. Richard Hackman, and Erin V. Lehman, "Life and Work in Symphony Orchestras," *The Musical Quarterly* 80, no. 2 (1996): 194–219, https://doi.org/10.1093/mq/80.2.194.

226   **a pushy boss who tries to micromanage:** Colin M. Fisher, Teresa M. Amabile, and Julianna Pillemer, "How to Help (Without Micromanaging)," *Harvard Business Review* 99 (January/February 2021), https://hbr.org/2021/01/how-to-help-without-microman aging.

226   **shared leadership improves group effectiveness:** Lauren D'Innocenzo, John E. Mathieu, and Michael R. Kukenberger, "A Meta-Analysis of Different Forms of Shared Leadership–Team Performance Relations," *Journal of Management* 42, no. 7 (2016): 1964–91, https://doi.org/10.1177/0149206314525205; Vias C. Nicolaides et al., "The Shared Leadership of Teams: A Meta-Analysis of Proximal, Distal, and Moderating Relationships," *The Leadership Quarterly* 25, no. 5 (2014): 923–42, https://doi.org/10 .1016/j.leaqua.2014.06.006; Danni Wang, David A. Waldman, and Zhen Zhang, "A Meta-Analysis of Shared Leadership and Team Effectiveness," *Journal of Applied Psychology* 99, no. 2 (2014): 181–98, https://doi.org/10.1037/a0034531.

226   **the average tenure of an EPL manager:** Louis Hobbs, "Game Over: The Winners and Losers of the Managerial Merry-Go-Round," SportsBoom, accessed November 17, 2024, https://www. sportsboom.com/football/premier-league-manger-sacking-data

-analysis; Steve Madeley and Will Jeanes, "How Premier League Manager Exits and Tenures Compare to NFL, NBA, NHL and MLB," *The New York Times*, accessed November 17, 2024, https:// www.nytimes.com/athletic/5509303/2024/05/23/premier -league-manager-sackings-nfl-nba.

226 **it's the leader who takes the fall:** J. Richard Hackman and Ruth Wageman, "Asking the Right Questions About Leadership: Discussion and Conclusions," *American Psychologist* 62, no. 1 (2007): 43–47, https://doi.org/10.1037/0003-066X.62.1.43.

227 **even more blame when there was a large decrease:** James R. Meindl, Sanford B. Ehrlich, and Janet M. Dukerich, "The Romance of Leadership," *Administrative Science Quarterly* 30, no. 1 (1985): 78–102, https://doi.org/10.2307/2392813.

228 **A detailed study of Polish soccer managers:** Łukasz Radzimiński et al., "The Effect of Mid-Season Coach Turnover on Running Match Performance and Match Outcome in Professional Soccer Players," *Scientific Reports* 12, no. 1 (2022): 10680, https://doi.org/10.1038/s41598-022-14996-z.

228 **whether teams benefited from firing their leaders:** Jan Ketil Arnulf, John Erik Mathisen, and Thorvald Hærem, "Heroic Leadership Illusions in Football Teams: Rationality, Decision Making and Noise-Signal Ratio in the Firing of Football Managers," *Leadership* 8, no. 2 (2012): 169–85, https://doi.org/10.1177/17427 15011420315.

228 **consistent with other research on sports-leader turnover:** Jan Ketil Arnulf, John Erik Mathisen, and Thorvald Hærem, "Heroic Leadership Illusions in Football Teams: Rationality, Decision Making and Noise-Signal Ratio in the Firing of Football Managers," *Leadership* 8, no. 2 (2012), 169–185, https://doi.org/10 .1177/1742715011420315; Allard Bruinshoofd and Bas ter Weel, "Manager to Go? Performance Dips Reconsidered with Evidence from Dutch Football," *European Journal of Operational Research*, Sport and Computers, 148, no. 2 (2003): 233–46, https://doi.org/10 .1016/S0377-2217(02)00680-X; Gerd Muehlheusser, Sandra Schneemann, and Dirk Sliwka, "The Impact of Managerial Change on Performance: The Role of Team Heterogeneity," *Eco-*

nomic Inquiry 54, no. 2 (2016): 1128–49, https://doi.org/10.1111/ecin.12285; Jon Aarum Andersen, "A New Sports Manager Does Not Make a Better Team," *International Journal of Sports Science & Coaching* 6, no. 1 (2011): 167–78, https://doi.org/10.1260/1747-9541.6.1.167; Alex Bryson, Babatunde Buraimo, Alex Farnell, and Rob Simmons, "Special Ones? The Effect of Head Coaches on Football Team Performance," *Scottish Journal of Political Economy* 71, no. 3 (2024): 295–322, https://doi.org/10.1111/sjpe.12369.

229 **people pin more blame for poor performance on individuals:** Charles E. Naquin and Renee O. Tynan, "The Team Halo Effect: Why Teams Are Not Blamed for Their Failures," *Journal of Applied Psychology* 88, no. 2 (2003): 332–40, https://doi.org/10.1037/0021-9010.88.2.332.

229 **think about group leadership as "functional":** Frederick P. Morgeson, D. Scott DeRue, and Elizabeth P. Karam, "Leadership in Teams: A Functional Approach to Understanding Leadership Structures and Processes," *Journal of Management* 36, no. 1 (2010): 5–39, https://doi.org/10.1177/0149206309347376; J. Richard Hackman and Richard E. Walton, "Leading Groups in Organizations," in *Designing Effective Work Groups*, ed. Paul S. Goodman (San Francisco, CA: Jossey-Bass, 1986), 72–119.

230 **Group leadership is *shared*:** Jay B. Carson, Paul E. Tesluk, and Jennifer A. Marrone, "Shared Leadership in Teams: An Investigation of Antecedent Conditions and Performance," *Academy of Management Journal* 50, no. 5 (2007): 1217–34, https://doi.org/10.5465/amj.2007.20159921; Lauren D'Innocenzo, John E. Mathieu, and Michael R. Kukenberger, "A Meta-Analysis of Different Forms of Shared Leadership–Team Performance Relations," *Journal of Management* 42, no. 7 (2016): 1964–91, https://doi.org/10.1177/0149206314525205; Vias C. Nicolaides et al., "The Shared Leadership of Teams: A Meta-Analysis of Proximal, Distal, and Moderating Relationships," *The Leadership Quarterly* 25, no. 5 (2014): 923–42, https://doi.org/10.1016/j.leaqua.2014.06.006; Danni Wang, David A. Waldman, and Zhen Zhang, "A Meta-Analysis of Shared Leadership and Team Effectiveness," *Journal of Applied Psychology* 99, no. 2 (2014): 181–98, https://doi.org/10.1037/a0034531.

232 **designed a clever experiment:** Michael D. Johnson et al., "Functional Versus Dysfunctional Team Change: Problem Diagnosis and Structural Feedback for Self-Managed Teams," *Organizational Behavior and Human Decision Processes* 122, no. 1 (2013): 1–11, https://doi .org/10.1016/j.obhdp.2013.03.006.

232 **is an opportunity for change:** Hengchen Dai, Katherine L. Milkman, and Jason Riis, "The Fresh Start Effect: Temporal Landmarks Motivate Aspirational Behavior," *Management Science* 60, no. 10 (2014): 2563–82, https://doi.org/10.1287/mnsc.2014 .1901; Katy Milkman, *How to Change: The Science of Getting from Where You Are to Where You Want to Be* (New York, NY: Penguin, 2021).

Chapter 14: Groups of the Future: Or Our Future with Groups

237 **groups were retaining less information when meeting virtually:** Lisa Handke, Patrícia Costa, and Thomas A. O'Neill, "Virtual Teams: Taking Stock and Moving Forward," *Small Group Research* 55, no. 5 (2024): 671–79, https://doi.org/10.1177/104649 64241274129; Margaret M. Luciano et al., "Improving Virtual Team Collaboration Paradox Management: A Field Experiment," *Organization Science*, June 25, 2024, https://doi.org/10.1287/orsc .2023.17952.

237 **ravager of our life satisfaction—long commutes:** Jonas De Vos, Tim Schwanen, Veronique Van Acker, and Frank Witlox, "Travel and Subjective Well-Being: A Focus on Findings, Methods and Future Research Needs," *Transport Reviews* 33, no. 4 (2013): 421–42, https://doi.org/10.1080/01441647.2013.815665.

237 **establish communication norms:** Kristen M. Shockley et al., "Remote Worker Communication during COVID-19: The Role of Quantity, Quality, and Supervisor Expectation-Setting," *Journal of Applied Psychology* 106, no. 10 (2021): 1466–82, https://doi.org /10.1037/apl0000970.

237 **switching communication media makes collaboration harder:** Kathryn L. Fonner and Michael E. Roloff, "Testing the Connectivity Paradox: Linking Teleworkers' Communication Media Use to Social Presence, Stress from Interruptions, and Organi-

zational Identification," *Communication Monographs* 79, no. 2 (2012): 205–31, https://doi.org/10.1080/03637751.2012.673000.

238–239 **recovery times were drastically reduced from months to days:** Zhi Xian Ong et al., "Comparison of the Safety and Efficacy between Minimally Invasive Cardiac Surgery and Median Sternotomy in a Low-Risk Mixed Asian Population in Singapore," *Singapore Medical Journal* 63, no. 11 (2022): 641–48, https://doi.org /10.11622/smedj.2021136.

239 **patients were in significantly less pain:** Lars G. Svensson et al., "Minimally Invasive Versus Conventional Mitral Valve Surgery: A Propensity-Matched Comparison," *The Journal of Thoracic and Cardiovascular Surgery* 139, no. 4 (2010): 926-32.e1-2, https://doi .org/10.1016/j.jtcvs.2009.09.038.

239 **bristled at the new technology:** Amy C. Edmondson, Richard M. J. Bohmer, and Gary P. Pisano, "Speeding Up Team Learning," *Harvard Business Review* 79, no. 9 (2001): 125–32, https://hbr .org/2001/10/speeding-up-team-learning; Amy C. Edmondson, Richard M. Bohmer, and Gary P. Pisano, "Disrupted Routines: Team Learning and New Technology Implementation in Hospitals," *Administrative Science Quarterly* 46, no. 4 (2001): 685–716, https://doi.org/10.2307/3094828.

239 **"a Fad or the Future?":** Jason M. Ali and Yasir Abu-Omar, "Minimally Invasive Cardiac Surgery—a Fad or the Future?" *Journal of Thoracic Disease* 13, no. 3 (2021), https://doi.org/10.21037 /jtd-2020-mics-12.

239 **Amy Edmondson (of psychological safety fame) and her colleagues studied:** Amy C. Edmondson, Richard M. J. Bohmer, and Gary P. Pisano, "Disrupted Routines: Team Learning and New Technology Implementation in Hospitals," *Administrative Science Quarterly* 46, no. 4 (2001), 685–716, https://doi.org/10.2307/3094828.

240 **this was an opportunity for learning:** Amy C. Edmondson, Richard M. J. Bohmer, and Gary P. Pisano, "Speeding Up Team Learning," *Harvard Business Review* 79, no. 9 (2001): 125–32, https:// hbr.org/2001/10/speeding-up-team-learning.

241 **your goal isn't just about the technology:** Amy C. Edmondson, "Strategies for Learning from Failure," *Harvard Business Review* 89, no 4 (2011): 48–55, https://hbr.org/2011/04/strategies-for-learning-from-failure.

242 **failing to adopt a new technology comes from Polaroid:** Mary Tripsas and Giovanni Gavetti, "Capabilities, Cognition, and Inertia: Evidence from Digital Imaging," in *The SMS Blackwell Handbook of Organizational Capabilities* (Hoboken, NJ: John Wiley & Sons, 2017), 393–412, https://doi.org/10.1002/9781405164054.ch23.

243 **the "innovator's dilemma":** Clayton M. Christensen, *The Innovator's Dilemma: When New Technologies Cause Great Firms to Fail* (Boston, MA: Harvard Business Review Press, 2015).

244 **David A. Kolb's famous model of learning:** David A. Kolb, "Management and the Learning Process," *California Management Review* 18, no. 3 (1976): 21–31, https://doi.org/10.2307/41164649.

245 **the problems of today are scarier than the problems of yesterday:** Graham Farrell and Toby Davies, "Most Crime Has Fallen by 90% in 30 Years—So Why Does the Public Think It's Increased?" The Conversation, May 13, 2024, http://theconversation.com/most-crime-has-fallen-by-90-in-30-years-so-why-does-the-public-think-its-increased-228797; Steven Pinker, *The Better Angels of Our Nature: A History of Violence and Humanity* (London, UK: Penguin UK, 2011).

247 **In 1942, the ERC:** "How the Emergency Rescue Committee Became the International Rescue Committee and Where We Are Today," International Rescue Committee UK, accessed November 8, 2024, https://www.rescue.org/uk/page/history-international-rescue-committee.

247 **the organization helped nearly thirty-three million people in 2022 alone:** "The IRC's Impact at a Glance," International Rescue Committee UK, accessed November 8, 2024, https://www.rescue.org/uk/page/ircs-impact-glance.

247 **"advertise as still being performed by Amy":** Christopher Moyer, "From 'Mother God' to Mummified Corpse: Inside the

Fringe Spiritual Sect 'Love Has Won,'" *Rolling Stone*, November 26, 2021, https://www.rollingstone.com/culture/culture-features /love-has-won-amy-carlson-mother-god-1254916.

250 **Margaret Mead supposedly said:** "Never Doubt That a Small Group of Thoughtful, Committed Citizens Can Change the World; Indeed, It's the Only Thing That Ever Has," Quote Investigator, November 12, 2017, https://quoteinvestigator.com/2017/11/12 /change-world; Donald Keys, *Earth at Omega: Passage to Planetization* (Wellesley, MA: Branden Books, 1982).

252 **In his Nobel Prize acceptance speech, novelist William Faulkner said:** William Faulkner, "Nobel Prize acceptance speech, 1950," *Nobel Lectures, Literature, 1901–1967* (World Scientific Publishing Company, 1999), 439–47.

INDEX

ABOUT THE AUTHOR

Since his days as a professional jazz trumpet player, Dr. Colin M. Fisher has been fascinated by group dynamics. Originally inspired by the profound influence others had on his experience as a professional jazz musician when improvising, he has been studying group dynamics, creativity, and improvisation for almost twenty years. As associate professor of organisations and innovation at University College London's School of Management, he teaches students how to lead and work creatively in groups and organizations.

Colin's academic research has uncovered the hidden processes of helping groups and teams in situations requiring creativity, improvisation, and complex decision-making. He has written about group dynamics for both popular science and management audiences, such as his work in The Conversation UK, *Harvard Business Review*, and many other outlets, and his work has been profiled in prominent media outlets such as the BBC, *Forbes*, NPR, and *The Times*. He has also provided lectures and workshops to organizations around the world that are hoping to improve their creativity and collaboration.

His discoveries have been published in leading scholarly journals, including *Academy of Management Annals, Academy of Management Discoveries, Academy of Management Journal, Academy of Management Perspectives, Academy of Management Review, Journal of Applied Psychology, Negotiation Journal, Organizational Behavior and Human Decision Processes, Organizational Dynamics, Organization Science,* and *Small Group Research,* as well as in numerous book chapters and periodicals.

Colin received his PhD in organizational behavior from Harvard University and previously worked as an assistant professor of organizational behavior at Boston University's School of Management. Prior to his PhD he studied improvisation in the arts at New York University (MA) and jazz trumpet at New England Conservatory of Music (BMus). In his prior career as a jazz trumpet player, Colin was a longtime member of the Grammy-nominated Either/Orchestra, with whom he toured extensively and recorded several critically acclaimed albums.

Originally from Redmond, Washington, in the US, he now lives in northeast London with his wife and two children. He can sometimes be found performing at jazz jams throughout London.